NOT NICE

Stop People Pleasing, Staying Silent, & Feeling Guilty...
And Start Speaking Up, Saying No, Asking Boldly, And
Unapologetically Being Yourself

DR. AZIZ GAZIPURA

B. C. Allen Publishing & Tonic Books

Published by B. C. Allen Publishing and Tonic Books

1500 SE Hawthorne Blvd.
Portland, OR 97214
Now taking manuscript submissions and book ideas at any stage of the process
bcallenpublishing@gmail.com

Printed in the United States of America

First Printing, 2017

ISBN: 978-0-9889798-7-1

Neigther the publisher nor the author are engaged in rendering professional advice or services to the individual reader. The ideas, procedures, and suggestions contained in this book are not intended as a substitute for consulting with your physician or licensed mental health professional. All matters regarding your health require medical supervision. Neither the authors nor the publisher shall be liable or responsible for any loss or damage allegedly arising from any information or suggestion in this book.

While the author has made every effort to provide accurate Internet addresses at the time of publication, neither the publisher nor the author assume any responsibility for errors, or for changes that occur after publication.

Dr. Aziz Gazipura
The Center For Social Confidence

http://SocialConfidenceCenter.com

Thank you Elliot for teaching me new rules to live by.

Thank you Tony for showing me the power of massive, bold action.

*Thank you Christian for helping me get out of my head
and into my body.*

*Thank you Mom and Dad for your devotion
and unconditional support.*

*Thank you Zaim and Arman for showing me how
to love unconditionally.*

Thank you Al for seeing me bigger than I could ever see myself.

*Thank you Candace for bringing me profound joy and being
my half-side on this magical journey.*

*Thank you Great Spirit for this incredible gift of life. May I open fully,
hold nothing back, and give more than I receive.*

ALSO BY DR. AZIZ GAZIPURA

Books:
The Solution to Social Anxiety
The Art of Extraordinary Confidence

E-Books:
5 Steps To Unleash Your Inner Confidence
3 Ways To Enjoy Parties (Even If You're Shy)
How To Overcome Your Fear Of Public Speaking
7 Tips To Becoming A Conversation Master
Becoming Irresistible
Rejection-Proof: 5 Ways To Become Unfazed By Rejection

Confidence Training Programs:
The Confidence Unleashed System
The Confidence Code
30 Days to Dating Mastery
Confidence University

CONTENTS

PART 2: BOLD ASSERTION

NICE VERSUS NOT NICE – QUICK REFERENCE GUIDE

NICE	NOT NICE
You feel a strong need to be liked by everyone. Being disliked makes you very uncomfortable.	You don't feel a need to control other's perceptions to feel secure.
You typically put others first (self-sacrificing).	You take care of yourself first when needed, acting with healthy self-interest.
You feel overly responsible for everyone's feelings.	You support others when possible, while knowing each person is fully responsible for their own feelings.
You experience chronic guilt and fear of hurting others.	You honestly and lovingly express your true self, even though it sometimes leads to painful feelings.
You hide your opinions to avoid friction.	You freely speak your mind without the need to convince others or make them wrong.
You rarely express upset directly.	You share your grievances directly while taking ownership for your feelings instead of blaming.
You often don't say "no" to others, even when you want to.	You easily say no when you want to. And you say no when you need to, even though it's hard.
You avoid asking for what you want directly.	You vulnerably express your wishes and desires.
You hesitate to speak up until it's "the right thing" to share.	You jump in early, speak freely, and trust in yourself. You choose authentic over perfect.
You prefer to conform with others, even if you internally disagree.	You stand up for what you believe in, even when it creates friction.
You dismiss your own perception and experience as insignificant.	You highly value what you think, feel, and believe. It matters because you matter.
You value other's opinions of you more than your own.	You know yourself better than others and easily brush off negative comments.
You constantly worry if it was "good enough."	You contribute your gifts fully with unfettered boldness and fierce determination.
You seek safety in life.	You seek deep connection, authentic self-expression, love, growth, and meaningful contribution.
You live in fear.	You are the most powerful version of you.

INTRODUCTION:

DRIVEN BY FEAR, NOT VIRTUE

Nice is good, right?

It means you're caring, you don't hurt people, and you do the right thing. You put others first, avoid saying critical or mean things, and try to make others feel happy. Of course, this is all good, right?

Well, maybe…

After fourteen years of clinical experience, working with thousands of people from all different cultures, I began to question this assumption. In fact, I saw that clients who were trying the hardest to be nice people also felt the most anxious, guilty, and frustrated. They had difficulty standing up for themselves, felt obligated to please others, and worried about what people thought of them. They couldn't directly ask for what they wanted, freely say "no" when it was the right thing to do, or openly disagree with others' opinions, even though they had strong, well-developed beliefs. In short, they were trapped in a cage of niceness that prevented them from being their real selves.

That's when I started to realize that there was a problem with nice. That it was different than kindness, compassion, and love. It wasn't necessarily the same thing as being a good person. In fact, I started to question if being less nice actually allowed us to be *more* kind, generous, and loving people.

This idea was so opposed to what I grew up believing that, at first, I couldn't buy it. I thought it was important to put others first and prided myself on never showing that I was angry. I thought being considerate was a good thing, and the world didn't need more selfish people. But then I started to study nice, first in myself, and then in my clients, and I discovered something fascinating. **Being nice does not come out of goodness or high morals. It comes out of a fear of displeasing others and receiving their disapproval.** It's driven by fear, not virtue. In fact, I discovered that being nice can make us secretly less loving and more burnt out over time as we stray further and further from our authentic selves.

You may have noticed this pattern as well. In fact, if you're picking up a book called "Not Nice," then you must recognize that there is some flaw in our cultural assumption that nice is good, and more nice is better. Perhaps inside you too are feeling stressed out, overwhelmed, anxious, irritated, or guilty much of the time. Maybe being nice is blocking you from standing up for yourself, being honest with others, creating deeper relationships, or boldly expressing yourself in the world.

But, to be less nice, or even worse, not nice? How could you do such a thing? Isn't it wrong?

That's where I come in. As you'll see in the pages that follow, niceness and people-pleasing were my story, my cage, my curse. I know how hard it can be to break free from the tentacles of guilt and fear that keep us in niceness. I know how strong the commands of that inner voice can be. The one that tells us we're so bad for hurting someone's feelings or saying no. That others will be upset with us for speaking our minds, or leave us for being honest.

Despite what that voice of fear and doubt says, more is possible for you. It's possible to regain your freedom to express yourself, to say "no" and ask for what you want without guilt, and to unapologetically be yourself without all the worry about how others will react. As you do, life becomes better and better, and all your relationships thrive. You are able to find and create lasting love, form deep and fulfilling friendships, and become a powerful leader in your career.

Breaking out of the niceness cage, however, is not a simple brute force move. You don't just smash the side of the prison wall with a bulldozer and run free. Instead, finding your way out of niceness is more like maneuvering your way out of a straitjacket. You must wrestle with the old, long-standing beliefs that bound you with stories that it's bad to ask for what you want, or that you're selfish for saying no.

Part I of this book is dedicated to helping you see what nice *really* is and the toll that living this way is taking on you. As you see just how rooted in fear our nice patterns are, and how it's different from being a good and loving person, you'll naturally let go of the old beliefs that don't serve you. In these chapters you'll be wriggling around, pulling some Houdini moves to get out of your straitjacket.

In Part II, you will discover the five pillars of Not Nice: Have Boundaries, Own Your Shadow, Speak Up, Say No, and Be More Selfish. You will learn dozens of tools and strategies that you can use immediately to let go of guilt, fear, and hesitation. You'll discover exactly how to speak for yourself, say no, ask for what you want, and take care of yourself without guilt and anxiety. These chapters are a powerful force for liberation that will unlock a profound sense of freedom and joy.

Part III is about living life on your terms. As you shed nice patterns that don't serve you or others, you'll need to reclaim who you really are. You'll decide what is right for you, how you want to live, and determine your own rules. You will become the director of your life.

And Part IV, that's about action. Activities, games, and other fun exercises are strategically placed throughout the book to get you into action right away. This final section will give you a clear step-by-step framework to put everything you learned into practice. You'll also get to read some intriguing, funny, and sometimes painfully awkward stories from my own life about applying Not Nice as I wrote this book.

I am so glad you're here with me, and I'm so excited for you. Going from nice and restricted to bold and authentic can transform all aspects of your life. It unlocks power, freedom, and happiness. It reawakens the lightness and joy you had as a kid, and it allows you to truly enjoy deep, fulfilling relationships with friends, colleagues, and the love of your life.

I can't wait to see what the future has in store for you.

With Love and Gratitude,

Dr. Aziz
Portland, Oregon
2017

PART I:

WHAT'S WRONG WITH NICE?

CHAPTER 1:

WHAT IS NICE?

What is nice? It's a word we all know and use, but rarely stop to think about. Let's begin by seeing your initial responses to the word. I'm going to ask you a few questions. Take a moment to pause after each one to notice your immediate answer—the first thing that pops into your mind.

Are you a nice person?

Would other people describe you using that word?

What's your gut reaction to being nice? Is it positive? Something to aspire to? Or is it negative?

As you reflect on these questions, I would like to share something with you. Actually, it's a confession. Something that may not be popular or right in the eyes of the world.

My goal is to get you to stop being nice. Not only that, I want you to change how you see nice so it's no longer a good thing. No longer something you want to try to be anymore. My goal is for your internal reaction to change so that when you hear nice, instead of an inner "Ooh, that's good," you think, "Eww, no thank you."

Yes, I'm trying to influence you. To persuade you. Not for my sake, but for yours. Because as you'll discover in the pages to come, one of the biggest traps of niceness is the pressure to stay nice. It's the idea that being a nice person is the same thing as being a good person. And behind that is the fear that if you're less nice, or if you aren't nice all the time, then you are selfish, bad, wrong, and terrible. That you should feel guilty and ashamed of yourself. Eww. No thank you.

Now, I know that's a bold claim, and may be a tough sell. You probably have the same beliefs I did: nice is good. That it's the same as kindness, compassion, generosity, and being loving towards others. That's why we need to start with defining nice, showing what it really is, and how it's different from all these other positive virtues.

Let's get clear.

NICE DEFINED

Let's say you and I were heading to a dinner party together. You were my guest and you didn't know anyone else who was going to be there. As we were driving to the party, just as we pulled towards the house, imagine I turned to you and said, "Hey, when we get in there, be nice, OK?"

What would that mean to you? How would it change your behavior?

Perhaps you'd greet everyone with a smile, or try to be warm and enthusiastic. Maybe you'd appear to be interested in what people were saying, grin, and nod a lot. Maybe you'd laugh at the jokes and remarks people made, even if you didn't get them.

You might also avoid certain things. Perhaps you'd avoid interrupting, or speaking up before someone asked you a question. Maybe you'd restrain yourself and not make big gestures, speak up fully, or laugh loudly. If you were heeding my request, you most certainly would not bring up controversial topics, ask probing questions, or challenge others.

You'd be, you know, nice.

Does any of this sound familiar to you? Do you do any of these things on a regular basis, even if no one asks you to? It might be something you unconsciously tell yourself all the time.

And here's the really fascinating part. When you're at this party, trying to be nice, what are you focusing on? Are you in the moment, speaking freely, spontaneously asking what you're most curious about, and being fully engaged? Or are you observing yourself and others' reactions? Are you watching your language, and how others react to you, analyzing the situation? *Did they like that? Was it funny enough? Those two laughed, but she seems a little irritated by me. That guy by the drinks was completely disinterested in me. I wonder what I did that pissed him off?*

This is what being nice is. It's monitoring yourself to make sure you come across in a pleasing manner and don't offend anyone. It's making sure others like you and don't have any negative feelings. No upset, confusion, boredom, irritation, sadness, hurt, anger, or fear. No discomfort whatsoever. Just happy, positive, approving thoughts and feelings.

At its core, being nice is about being liked by others by making everything smooth. No waves, no friction. It's based on this (woefully inaccurate) theory: If I please others, give them everything they want, keep a low profile, and don't ruffle feathers or create any discomfort, then others will like me, love me, and shower me with approval and anything else I want (promotions, sales, friendships, dates, sex, attention).

This theory is bunk. It's an inaccurate map of human relationships. And like any inaccurate map, if you follow it, you will not get where you want to go. You will be lost.

That, my friend, is what nice really is.

Let's pause for a moment. Take a breath. What are you noticing in your mind and your body? Is this resonating with you? Are you having insights about yourself and how you show up in the world?

Are you noticing where you're holding yourself back to avoid disapproval or discomfort in yourself or others?

Are you skeptical? Is part of your mind saying "Yeah, but..."?

But isn't it good to be polite?

I'm not going to bring up something offensive.

Are you saying I should start being a jerk or an asshole?

No. Well, actually, yes. Because there's probably many things you would say and do when you are fully confident, authentic, expressive and free, that the inhibited part of you would judge as being "a jerk" or "bad."

That's just old fear-based nice conditioning. Don't worry, we'll get to that. But let's take a second to clarify this question about being nice versus being a jerk.

THE OPPOSITE OF NICE

The opposite of nice is not to be a jerk, or an asshole. It's not insulting others, saying bigoted or highly antagonizing things, bullying, or attacking people's characters. It's not telling others to "shut up," intimidating them, or pushing your little old grandma over in the kitchen.

The opposite of nice is being real. It's being direct, honest, and truthful. It's saying what you *really* think, expressing how you *really* feel, and sharing what's true for you in that moment. This authenticity allows others to see and know the real you, which allows you to really feel love and connection.

Not nice means speaking up and asserting yourself, your opinions, ideas, and desires. It's challenging others when you disagree, standing behind your convictions, and being willing to have difficult conversations. You do this because you want full contact with life and other humans instead of hiding who you are behind a polite wall of fear. When you do have conflict or disagreement, and you inevitably will if you're being not nice, then you are as vulnerable, skillful, and compassionate as you can be in your communications.

The opposite of nice is knowing who you are, what you believe in, and what you value. It's you being powerful and going after what you want because you are no longer held back by the fear of what others will think of you. It's you being fierce, determined, and courageous. It's you being your best self.

That means you are still kind, caring, attentive, generous, and loving. You still do things for other people, stretch yourself to give, even if it's hard, and be the kind of leader, mother, father, wife, husband, daughter, son, sister, brother, or friend that you want to be.

But you're not doing that to please others. You're not doing that so no one ever feels a hint of discomfort. You're not living in fear of what others will think, in self-doubt, in "Was that good enough?" and "Did everyone there like me?"

You come from a place of power. Of choice. Your inner mindset starts to sound like this:

I can choose to say yes, and I can choose to say no. I can hold back and keep quiet, or I can ask a tough question that challenges someone. If someone close to me is doing something that annoys me, I can bring it up and talk about it. When I really want something and the first response I get is a no, I ask questions and see if the other person is open to changing their mind. I'm completely free to choose exactly how I want to be in this moment, based on what feels right to me. I am the decider. I am the creator of my life.

I no longer avoid, walk on eggshells, tiptoe around, or do the dance.

I am me. The real me. And it feels good. I feel powerful. I feel free. I feel worthy.

This is the opposite of nice.

If you're still questioning how this all works, and how being "not nice" can actually be a good thing, you'll see exactly how soon. In fact, you'll discover that the more you let go of being nice, the more kind, generous, and truly loving you can be. Because fear, guilt, obligation, and distracting self-consciousness don't make you a more loving person; they create tension and resentment that limit your ability to truly give and love.

THE NICEST GUY YOU'LL EVER MEET

I understand the urge to be nice. I know how strong the invisible forces of guilt and fear can be. How difficult it can be to push through this to say what you really want, and express what you really think and feel. I also know how all-consuming the backlash of anxiety and guilt can be after you've been more direct, expressive, honest, or assertive.

Being the nice guy was part of my identity for a long time. In middle school, I started my quest to get everyone to like me. Not consciously, of course. I didn't wake up one morning and think to myself: *OK, Aziz. Remember! You must get everyone to like you today!*

Instead, I just began to worry about how I was viewed by others. *Do these people like me? Do they want to be my friend? Do girls think I'm cute? Are my shorts the right length? Are my socks the right height?*

I wanted to blend in. Be cool. Never be criticized, ridiculed, or rejected. Ever. And so, I began to sculpt my personality to avoid disapproval. If someone who I thought was cool or popular said something funny, I laughed. If people made fun of me for doing something, I stopped doing it. I wore the same clothes everyone else wore, changed the music I listened to, and talked just like everyone else. Boxers are cool and briefs (a.k.a. "tighty whities") are not? I got rid of them. Alternative music sucks and gangster rap is where it's at? I bought new CDs.

But even though I tried to change everything on the outside, I still had all kinds of uncool things in my house. I remember having my friends Tim and Mark come over to my house in seventh grade, and beforehand I would spend at least fifteen minutes scanning the entire house, hiding anything they could make fun of me for.

I made sure nothing could be used against me. No evidence of me being who I really was and what I really liked.

Now I understand that this story is typical; most people try to fit in with their peers during adolescence. But this seed of social anxiety and niceness continued to grow in my life. As I became interested in women and dating, I experienced an oppressive layer of fear that prevented me from approaching and chatting with the young women around me. I was so worried about their perception of me, that I avoided most interactions entirely. If I did engage, I felt nervous, silly, and ungrounded.

For years, women didn't seem attracted to me. My people-pleasing and excessive niceness repelled them, although I didn't know this at the time. I thought it was because I was not cool enough, strong enough, tall enough. Too ugly, too boring, too nerdy.

This negative identity didn't just exist in my dating life; I perceived myself as socially unskilled, awkward, and unworthy of a large circle of friends. Speaking up, standing out, and being a leader of any form was out of the question.

This continued year after year. I saw my future as confined and limited. I started to talk myself into being OK with settling. *I'm just not the kind of guy who's going to have a relationship, or much success in life.*

Then, one night, I reached a breaking point. I was a senior in college, finishing the time in my life that movies told me was supposed to be a crazy adventure of parties and hot dates. My life was no such thing. Instead, my world was safe, small: going to class, being with friends, and playing lots of video games.

To my credit, I had been slowly working up the courage to approach women I was attracted to. After three to five months mustering the nerve, I'd ask one woman out, confront rejection, and then wait again. I clung to the walls at parties, avoided meeting strangers and creating new connections, and never spoke up in a group of people.

After working up my courage to ask yet another woman out and receive another rejection, something inside me snapped. I'll never forget that night. I came home, totally discouraged, completely hopeless. I felt a heavy sadness, a deep pain of helplessness, resignation, frustration, and depression. This was my life, and I knew there was no way out because I'd tried to change and failed.

When I got home, the lights were off in the apartment. I assumed my roommate was out, which was unfortunate because I felt so down it would have been nice to hang out with him. Being with Chris always cheered me up. But it looked I was alone.

So, I made myself some noodles, poured a jar of Ragu spaghetti sauce on top, and headed to my room to do what I did best: play Warcraft III. I loved that game. It was a place where I could forget all my troubles, ignore my bleak, loveless future, and immerse myself in competition, strategy, and play.

I sat at my desk, blowing on my steaming noodles as the game booted up. Then the screen popped up that said: *Do you want to log in to Battlenet?* Battlenet was where you linked up to battle some dude across the country or world in all out warfare. I'd seen that screen ten thousand times.

I dragged my mouse towards the Log In button—and then froze.

I heard a muffled, high-pitch sound coming from somewhere in the apartment. At first, I was scared, but then my mind instantly identified the source: it was a woman laughing. Then I heard a second, deeper voice and realized my roommate was home. He was in his room with his girlfriend, sharing a sweet moment. Her laughter burst through the walls again, this time louder, more joyful.

I sat there, looking at the steam rising from my noodles, listening to her laugh as the Warcraft Orc on the Battlenet Login screen stared back at me. And in that moment, my life changed.

I could see and feel my future unfolding before me. The veil of denial had been lifted and I felt the pain of loneliness, longing, inadequacy, and settling that were in store for me if life continued this way. I knew I was not going to experience what I really wanted, that I would miss out on everything that mattered to me, and would die full of regret for a life not fully lived.

This was my rock bottom. Over the years I've seen that each client has their own threshold moment when they hit a similar point and they can't take it any more: they decide to change.

Sometimes that moment is provoked by dating, relationships, and love. They're unable to meet and date the people they want, they endure poor treatment from partners who are only moderately interested, or they watch their marriage go down in flames.

For others, it's their social life. They can't take another day of being uncomfortable in their own skin, feeling inauthentic, phony, or forced in their interactions. They're sick and tired of holding back their opinions, feeling guilty for never doing enough, and being so terrified of upsetting others that they're sick to their stomach with worry about it.

And for some, it's the moment they get passed over for another big promotion, not because they're not skilled, but because they're not "leadership material." They refuse to stay stuck at the same level as younger talent passes them by simply because others are outspoken and bold with their opinions.

I don't know what your moment was, but if you're reading this book, I have a strong hunch that you've had at least one of these moments that has led you here. In those moments, there is a tremendous amount of pain, but there is also something else.

That night there was another feeling awakening inside of me that was stronger than hopelessness. It was like a tidal wave building in force and size. It was a mixture of anger, resistance, and raw energy. It was a complete and total rejection of that bleak existence. It was power.

In that moment, I decided: *I'm willing to do whatever it takes.* I will study whatever I need to, practice whatever I need to, force myself to take action and do anything—no matter how scary or uncomfortable—again and again and again until I break out of this cage and create the life I want. I will not quit. I will not stop.

I didn't have a name for it then, but I know what it is now. I call it Unstoppable Energy. When I'm speaking to someone, I can tell if they have activated this energy. If they have, then I know success is inevitable; it's just a matter of time.

With that energy and determination, everything turned around. I made tremendous progress in my confidence and in being less nice. I began studying eBooks and online courses about how to meet women and be more confident. I discovered I could challenge the negative voice in my head and do the opposite of what it said. I made a practice of facing my fears. All of them. One by one.

With this courage and willingness, life began to open up all around me. I was able to approach a stranger of any age or gender, and start talking with them. I could speak up in groups, make jokes, and seek out public speaking. Women started going out with me. It was mind-blowing and changed the way I perceived reality.

Success, right? Absolutely. Massive success and massive progress. And yet, I soon realized an interesting fact of life. Once you overcome one challenge and break through to the next level, you're not done. There's another, higher quality problem waiting for you when you get there, challenging you to step up and grow again. It's a beautiful quality of life that requires us to continually grow, expand, and become the people we're meant to be.

For me, that next level challenge was the hardest thing I've ever faced.

THERE'S SOMETHING WRONG WITH ME

With all my online studies and practice, I learned to walk taller, look people in the eye, and approach others instead of avoiding them. I learned how to engage with women, flirt, create sexual tension and openly express my desire. I learned how to be more bold and confident... for a little while.

Soon I discovered that I could make a good first impression. I could appear fully confident. And maybe even go on several dates and sleep with a woman. I could speak my mind with friends and acquaintances. I could share my ideas in groups. But after doing these sorts of things, my nice guy impulses would come back with a vengeance. It was almost like I learned how to suppress it temporarily, but it had simply retreated to the shadows, waiting for its opportunity to pounce.

I'd be more bold and speak up, but then the next day I would replay the interaction and second guess myself. Or worse, just tear myself to shreds. *Why did you say all that? You talked way, way too much! You seemed so over-excitable and lame. Pathetic.*

Or I'd boldly initiate a conversation and be the smoothest, most charming guy you could imagine. We'd go on a date or two, and it would go incredibly well. But then my anxiety would surge back. Especially after we'd have sex for the first time. I would instantly feel responsible for all of her feelings. I would start scanning for all the ways I could reassure her and give her the impression that I loved her, that I was the man of her dreams, that I never liked any other woman as much as I liked her, and that all I wanted to do was spend all day, every day with her.

This may sound like a caring, considerate, and ideal way to enter into a relationship. In fact, with my wife, Candace, I frequently tell her how much she means to me, how grateful I am she's with me, and seek to reassure her when she's feeling insecure. That is just one of the many beautiful gifts of love.

But this was different. This was niceness to the max. Because I *didn't* really love these women yet. In fact, we didn't even know each other yet, and we weren't the right match. I was so skin-crawlingly uncomfortable with her experiencing any negative emotion, that I played a role. I took complete responsibility for every single one of her feelings, and I was held hostage by my own fear of guilt and self-loathing should she feel bad.

Sound extreme? It was! It also was very painful. This nice guy compulsion prevented me from saying no. Instead I pretended to have certain feelings, and avoided difficult conversations.

What if I was dating other people and wasn't sure yet who I wanted to be in a relationship with? And what if (gasp), it was not with her?

I could never say that!

What if I wanted to do my own thing on a Saturday night and I didn't feel like hanging out?

What?! How could I be so heartless!

And so, with all this fear and pretending and avoiding, my romantic relationships didn't last. I could only sustain this charade for a few weeks or months. At that point, I could no longer confine myself and I would hastily end the relationship, which was often a surprise to her because until then I was the best guy in the world and "everything was perfect."

A few times I tried to "white knuckle it" and push through my anxiety to stay in a relationship longer. I tried this with a sweet, intelligent, and beautiful woman from San Francisco. She was amazing and we got along so well that I told myself: *This is it! No more fleeing!*

I met her at a Whole Foods supermarket in the Bay Area. All my years of practicing bold action paid off, as I was able to simply walk up to her and start a conversation in the bulk foods aisle. She had sandy blond hair, a beautiful smile, and piercing blue eyes that were fully alive with energy and enthusiasm for life. We instantly connected about health and nutrition. I was infatuated.

Our first dates were fun, interesting, and exciting. We were both life-long learners and had studied different areas, so we were sharing back and forth like crazy. She was incredibly sexy and I was instantly drawn in. And then the pattern started all over again...

It really began in earnest after the first time we made love. That experience, like many of the times I first made love with a new partner, was awkward. At that time, I didn't have the confidence to talk about sex before, during, or after. I was too nice. I didn't want to make anyone uncomfortable, or say anything that might hurt or upset my partners.

I remember sitting at my kitchen table the next morning, eating breakfast, and feeling so uncomfortable. I wanted to say something, to talk about our experience. It wasn't terrible, but it just felt off. I didn't feel connected to her during sex and I had all kinds of questions about her experience. But she seemed relaxed and fine, so I thought: *This is all in my head. I'm too insecure. If I reveal anything she'll feel bad and I'll look like a loser.* So, I finished my oats, walked her to her car, and said nothing more of it. In fact, we never talked about sex in our entire time together. Not once.

Sure enough, at the two month mark I started to feel the urge to flee. I had anxiety before I'd go to her house and urges to hastily break up. I knew the pattern well, and this time I'd resolved to not act on it. I was going to push through, dammit!

But four months into our relationship, I started having panic attacks when I spent time with her. I remember one sunny summer day at a beautiful park in the city, relaxing on a blanket in a grassy field, catching some sun together. From the outside, this scenario seems perfect, but inside I was tense, uncomfortable, and down. I hid all this from her, of course, and put on my best happy face.

I needed to use the bathroom so I walked across the park and over a little hill to find one. Upon getting there, I was flushed with one of the most intense feelings of fear I've ever had. I got dizzy and had difficulty breathing. I felt an overwhelming sense of dread. My mind was racing with frenzied and incomplete thoughts: *I can't go back there. I just can't. I have to get out. I have to get away!*

I tried to breathe and calm myself down, to slow my thoughts, but it was no use. My mind was throwing images at me of literally running out of the park, getting back into my car, and driving away, leaving her in the park on that blanket, lying in the sun.

A few times I tried to start walking back towards her, and the dread became so intense, I turned back towards the bathroom. I paced back and forth in front of the bathroom for what felt like an eternity.

The experience was eerily similar to when I was a small child and had just woken up from sleepwalking. I would often awaken in a state of panic and fear in some random room in our house. I would be too scared to go back into my bedroom, and have an urge to go to my parents' room. But I was too terrified to do that as well. So, I would pace back and forth between the two, feeling increasing dread, as I got closer to each one.

After pacing and panicking for a good long while, I began to regain my composure. I looked up at the tops of the dark green pine trees against the bright blue sky. Focusing on nature helped. "OK. OK." I said to myself. "I'm OK."

I pulled myself together and began walking back to our blanket. I was probably gone for fifteen or twenty minutes—a slightly unusual amount of time to go pee. When I returned she was just lying there in the sun. The silky white skin of her stomach lay exposed and her arms flopped lazily over her head.

"Hey," she said as she squinted up at me.

"Hey," I replied.

She didn't seem to notice that I'd been gone too long. Or that I looked a little disheveled. She was lost in reverie on a beautiful, sunny summer day. I kept my fear, doubts, and utter insanity to myself.

As this pattern of getting close and then fleeing continued, relationship after relationship, I began to develop a terrible belief about myself. I kept asking myself: *Why can't I have a relationship? Why do I freak out?*

And then my mind came up with an answer, as it always does when you ask it a question. Unfortunately, if you ask a bad question, you get a bad answer. The answer to my question was this:

Because there's something wrong with me. I'm not capable of close connection, an intimate relationship. There's something fundamentally flawed or broken inside of me. That's why.

Uplifting, huh?

But guess what? I have good news for you. As your score increases, your life gets better. Way better. You feel completely different, your relationships transform, and your level of power, influence, and success skyrocket. You start living on your terms.

That might sound like a dramatic claim. But after experiencing it myself, and then guiding so many people through the liberation process, I have no doubt about what's possible for you. What if you woke up each morning and could focus on whatever you wanted? Your health, meditation or exercise, or your family. What if you felt excited, happy, and energized about your day, instead of worried about what might happen, dreading potentially uncomfortable conversations?

What if you woke up next to the love of your life? Your relationship was solid because you can talk about anything and you know there's nothing that you can't work through together. You feel deeply seen, known, and loved for who you are, and you have an incredible, stable source of love that allows you to step out more boldly into the world.

What if you were a leader in your field that people sought out for advice, guidance, and your wise perspective? What if you could freely speak up, have direct conversations, and be the kind of person who said what needed to be said?

And most importantly, what if you just felt comfortable to be yourself around anyone, in any situation, without fear of whether they were going to like you or not? Without worrying about how they were taking everything you said, and if you were upsetting or offending anyone. Life without all the overanalyzing, guilt, and discomfort. Can you imagine it?

How amazing would that feel? What a relief it would be.

My question for you is: are you ready to make that happen?

Regardless of what your Nice Score was, you can do this. No matter how uncomfortable you feel about disagreeing, being honest, or interrupting someone, you can do this. No matter how long you've been stuck in the cage of the nice person, you can break free.

CHAPTER 2:

PLEASE LIKE ME

"I am realizing that when we try to be nice, and try to be liked, we end up being repulsive across all areas of life."
- K.B.

At its root, being nice is about being liked, which in itself is not a bad thing. It's actually the most natural desire in the world. Let's say your friend was about to introduce you to someone at a party, and you could choose between these two options:

Option A: That new person likes you.
Option B: That new person doesn't like you.

Which one would you pick?
Exactly.
But the problem with nice is that it takes a normal human desire and turns it into an absolute necessity. It turns a preference into a serious attachment that we obsess over, as if somehow we won't be OK if this person is upset with us, or bored by us, or in any way not super excited about us.

For many people, their Good Person list includes being agreeable, saying yes, giving to others, being quiet, being humble, and other versions of polite, obedient, and non-offensive. It also can include succeeding, winning, getting things on their first try, never failing, and other demands for rapid and total achievement in all things they try. For some it demands they always feel happy, upbeat, positive, and have a "good attitude."

The Bad Boy/Bad Girl list usually includes being outspoken, saying no to others, being aggressive, being selfish, challenging people, saying what you want, being honest, and even being authentic, vulnerable, or real. For many, failing, not being the best, and feelings such as sadness, anger, and fear are all unacceptable.

What are you noticing about your lists? What are you discovering about yourself? What memories does this exercise bring up?

I'd suggest you let yourself reflect on this over the next day or two. If memories that you haven't thought of in a while come up, don't ignore them. Instead, pay attention to the messages being conveyed in those memories. How were you being conditioned? The more you see that being nice is just a pattern you learned to get love and avoid pain, the more quickly you can recondition yourself and break free.

At this point, you may have questions about how you could possibly receive love from others if you didn't live up to the Good List and sometimes did things on the Bad List. As you'll see in the pages to come, the love and connection you deeply crave doesn't come from pleasing others and hiding all your perceived flaws. It actually comes from boldly being yourself, saying what you actually think and feel, and sharing yourself with the world.

You may also want to reflect on the questions above while focusing on your other parent. How did you need to be for him or her? Who could you never be?

This kind of reflection can produce powerful insights into what has been driving your thoughts, feelings, and actions for many years.

It's also part of the process of liberating yourself so you can become all of who you are, which leads to being more powerful, alive, vibrant, attractive, and successful.

THE APPROVAL SEEKER

Regardless of the origins, it appears everyone has an internal Approval Seeker. This is the part of us that wants people to like us, hates conflict, disconnection, and discord. This is the part that wants everything to be smooth, for everyone to get along, and everyone to love us.

While this desire for harmony and connection is completely natural, it can become problematic. When we are being nice, we are usually identified with the Approval Seeker inside of us. Instead of it being just another part that's influencing our feelings and behaviors, it becomes the only part. It's driving the bus, determining where you go, what you say, and what you do. It begins to run your life.

When this happens, our primary goal in life becomes getting approval from others. Or, more specifically, avoiding disapproval from others. Because our Approval Seeker really has two missions it's trying to carry out: a prime directive and a secondary objective, if you will. While achieving *both* objectives is ideal, it is most important to achieve the prime directive before worrying about the secondary one. Here are the Approval Seeker's objectives:

1. Avoid judgment, criticism, dislike, and disapproval at any cost.
2. Earn positive perceptions, feelings, and approval from others.

Objective number one definitely outweighs number two. So, if you're with a group of people you don't know that well, you will do things to avoid disapproval first. This might include speaking when spoken to, smiling and nodding, being polite and agreeable.

Perhaps loudly telling that funny story about your cousin getting sick on his fortieth birthday would be seen as hilarious and get you tons of approval from this new group. But maybe it wouldn't. Maybe it would be awkward-city with tons of confused and offended looks. Not worth the risk. Just stick with the prime directive.

Speaking of the prime directive, our Approval Seeker is looking to complete this mission with complete and resounding success. Total domination. When it says it doesn't want *any* disapproval, it means absolutely, positively, no disapproval.

Here is the Approval Seeker's typical list of success criteria for avoiding disapproval:

1. **No one has a negative thought or judgment about me.** This includes my appearance, my attire, my job and income, the way I speak or move, my actions or choices, or any other qualities about me.

2. **No one feels any negative or uncomfortable emotions in my presence due to me.** No fear, discomfort, uncertainty, aversion, irritation, upset, confusion, or dislike.

3. **No one demonstrates any non-verbal signs of disapproval.** No one furrows their brow, curls their lip, or has any other physical sign of judging or disliking me. Only positive or neutral facial expressions must come my way.

A perfectly reasonable set of goals here... Until our next interaction with a human being. With this unconscious criteria, and our Approval Seeker driving the bus, we're screwed.

How do you think this strong need to avoid all negative thoughts and feelings from others impacts you? Does it make you more relaxed or less relaxed? More confident or less confident? More powerful or less powerful? More yourself or less yourself?

That's right, it's going to make you a self-conscious, neurotic mess. Trust me, I know this first hand, having let my Approval Seeker run the show for more than fifteen years of my life. It will make you run all your nice person habits double and triple time. And don't get me started if the person you're talking to is beautiful, handsome, confident, powerful, or successful. Then it becomes even worse. Their disapproval is even more important to avoid because their perception means more than yours does. I mean, after all, they are a better person because they're skinny, or muscular, or rich, right?

Speaking of which, how does your Approval Seeker show up? What specifically do you do to avoid disapproval? Also, what do you do to try to win the approval of others?

This usually arises as an urge to impress others. Perhaps you try to appear very intelligent or highly knowledgeable about a particular subject. Maybe you play up experiences you've had, exaggerating a bit so others see you as exciting or cool. Maybe you name drop, or tell a certain story again and again because it makes you look important. These are just a few examples of the many subtle ways we try to earn the approval of others.

One pattern I recently observed in myself was to earn approval through achievement. I noticed a hard-driving part of me that I call Double More (because it always wants me to do double and more of what I'm doing) pushing me to achieve more quickly. It was impatient to get to the next level and dissatisfied with my current rate of progress. When I explored why I needed to achieve more and faster, I found the urge came from a desire to impress others. Specifically my dad and one of my mentors.

Pay attention in yourself over the next few days to see how you might try to earn approval from others. While these behaviors are not highly problematic, they do pull you away from your authentic self, and subtly reinforce the idea that you are not worthy of love and approval right now, as you are.

YOUR APPROVAL SEEKER

Let's explore how your Approval Seeker shows up in your life. What things do you do to make sure people like you? What things do you avoid, so others won't be upset?

Take a moment to reflect on this now. The more self-aware you can become, the more power you have to transform yourself and your results. Be sure to think about each of the core areas in your life—your work and career, dating and romantic life, friends and family.

15 Common Signs of Approval Seeking

1. Avoiding No

You avoid saying no to others. You fear they will become upset or think you're a bad person, so you usually say yes, even if it adds more stress to your life.

2. Hesitation

You often wait for the "right thing" to say (and thus speak way less than you normally do).

3. Nervous Laughter

You're quick to laugh at whatever another person says, even if it's not that funny. Your laugh might come too quickly, too often, or at inappropriate times.

4. Difficulty with Endings

You have difficulty ending things, from conversations to friendships to romantic relationships. As a result, you may drag things out longer than you really want to.

5. Overly Agreeable

You smile, nod, and are very agreeable with others (regardless of your actual opinions on the subject).

6. Avoiding Disagreement

You avoid disagreeing with others, challenging others, or stating alternative perspectives.

7. Fear of Judgment

You're afraid of the judgments of others (which can lead to nervousness, hesitation, over-thinking, and social anxiety).

8. Fear of Upset

You're often afraid that others are secretly angry or critical of you, even though they seem to like you when you're together. This can lead to a constant background unease that you may have "done something wrong" that someone is upset about.

9. Pressure to Entertain

You feel pressure to have something great to share, such as a funny or highly engaging story about an adventure you've had.

10. Second Guessing & Conversational Replays

During an interaction, you experience self-consciousness and doubt about how you are coming across. You imagine you should be someone "better" than you are. Afterwards, you replay the interaction in your mind and find all the things you did wrong, ways you may have upset the other person, and things you should have said.

11. Habitual Apologies

You're quick to apologize out of habit, even for minor transgressions, like starting to speak at the same time as someone else.

12. Submissive Body Language

You demonstrate submissive body language, such as looking away frequently or keeping your eyes down.

13. Putting Others First

You have a strong habit of putting others' needs ahead of your own, thinking it is selfish to do otherwise.

14. Not Stating Desires

You rarely state what you want directly. Instead, you may suggest or imply something and hope the other person detects it. You often question your desires and think they might be either too much or not worth asking for.

15. Attempting to Fit In & Impress

You try to fit in to groups by pretending to be interested in things you are not, or exaggerating about your experiences, wealth, or achievements. All submission to peer pressure is approval seeking.

The Cost of Approval Seeking

How many of the fifteen signs on that list do you notice in yourself? Over the years, I've seen this pattern with clients: The more you try to avoid disapproval and earn approval, the more you suffer. This is because each of these behaviors is pulling you away from yourself, and draining you of social power.

Small things like submissive body language, habitual apologies, and nervous laughter can have a big effect on your life. They can reduce your romantic options, make people want to talk with you less, and even determine the difference between being hired or being passed over during a job interview.

Bigger patterns like being overly agreeable, feeling anxious about entertaining others, and avoiding conflict, can all create limited, tense experiences. You become limited to a box of your own making.

When you combine that with a deep fear of upsetting others and a belief that they're making harsh judgments that condemn your character and worth, then you're in big trouble.

And trouble is the right word for it. With a strong need for approval, it can feel like you're walking through life like a student who is wandering the halls without a hall-pass. At any time, someone might jump out and chastise you for doing something wrong, and they'd be justified. This creates a chronic unease and fear that makes it very hard to relax, let go, enjoy your relationships, feel love, and be in the moment. It undermines your self-esteem because you value others' opinions more than your own; it sucks the joy out of life.

Approval Seeker Activate!

For some people, the Approval Seeker is driving the bus in almost all of their interactions. When I was struggling with social anxiety, I felt the need for approval whenever I spoke with strangers, in the classroom, with colleagues at work, women I was interested in, men who seemed confident... the list went on and on.

The only time I was not seeking approval, was when I was with my family or close friends. In those situations, I perceived I already had their approval, so I could relax and be myself.

How frequently does your Approval Seeker show up? For most people, this pattern is not fully conscious. They aren't walking into a meeting thinking: *I sure hope everyone in there approves of me. I will make sure I hesitate, only say witty and intelligent things, and agree with everything so I avoid their disapproval.*

Instead, you just might feel anxious before the meeting. You are hoping it "goes well" and you get whatever outcome it is you want: to be hired, to get the sale, to have your ideas heard and accepted, and so on. You might feel nervous about speaking up, or compare yourself to someone else during the meeting, and feel inferior. Afterwards you might replay certain moments, criticizing yourself for missing opportunities to speak up and say things better than you did.

All of that is based on approval seeking. You wanted people in that meeting to like you, and to accept you and your ideas. That's what creates the nervousness, the comparisons, and the attachment to being seen in a certain way.

So how frequently does your Approval Seeker show up? It might not be in every interaction, like it was for me. It may only be in certain situations at work, when you have to deal with people you find intimidating or powerful. It might show up in your dating life when you meet someone you think is beautiful or handsome. It might show up in your romantic relationship as concerns over your body and appearance, as wondering if your partner still finds you attractive.

Pay attention over the next few weeks to when your Approval Seeker activates. You want to become better and better at spotting it as it's happening. This gives you great power to become conscious of the old patterns that used to run you, and to choose something different for yourself.

For example, just last month I noticed my Approval Seeker coming on strong when I had an opportunity to interact with someone whom I admire who is highly successful in my field. He is a highly respected and famous author and teacher. Leading up to the interview I was nervous, and during our conversation I was more enthusiastic and agreeable than I normally would be. Afterwards, I started to second-guess myself and replay our conversation, searching for verbal missteps. While it was uncomfortable, I was excited to identify this behavior because now I knew what I needed to work on in order to grow my confidence. I decided that one of my primary social goals was not to be intimidated by anyone, no matter how successful.

The goal here is not to completely eliminate this desire for approval from your life. That's an extreme demand, and probably impossible to do. Instead, notice where the urge for approval is strongest. And, as best as you can, do so with curiosity, compassion, and love.

You're not on a witch-hunt here. You're not looking to find that wretched monster and slay it. In fact, **this part of you that so desperately wants others' love and approval needs your love and approval more than anything else.** In the second and third parts of this book, you'll learn how to heal this longing and release the never-ending quest for approval. But first, you need to become aware. If this habit of approval seeking is unconscious and you aren't aware of when you're doing it, then it will be difficult to break free.

The Approval Seeker Versus The Powerful You

In this chapter, we're exploring the part of you that wants approval from others. But there is another part of you that is already whole, complete, secure, and capable. This is The Powerful You. Throughout the course of this book, you're going to activate and strengthen this part more and more, until eventually being powerful is just how you show up in the world, wherever you go.

To distinguish between the two, here is a list of some of the differences between these two parts of you:

• The Approval Seeker wants to be liked by everyone.
• The Powerful You doesn't need to control anyone's perception. You focus on showing up as 100% yourself, knowing that you only need to find your people, not everyone.

• The Approval Seeker sees others as better and their opinions as mattering more.
• The Powerful You knows that you matter. Your thoughts, feelings, and opinions are worth sharing, simply because they come from you. You know that looks, wealth, or any other external marker does not increase someone's inherent worth as a human.

• The Approval Seeker needs something from others in every interaction.

how to connect with others starting with our first relationships, which is usually a mother, father, and siblings. In these early relationships, we learn how to connect and attach emotionally to other humans, in the deepest ways possible. This has been studied extensively, and led to a branch of psychology called Attachment Theory.[2]

For our purposes, I am going to summarize the theory. Basically, when it comes to attaching emotionally to others, we can feel safe and secure in that attachment, or we can feel unsafe and insecure. If we are secure, we feel held, supported, and loved. We trust the other person will be there for us. We trust that if they leave to go to the store, or out with friends, that they will return to us. We feel worthy of love. We trust that we will receive that love, even if we make a mistake, fail at something, are in a bad mood, or otherwise "mess up."

However, if our attachment is insecure, we feel anxious and unsafe. We fear that others will leave us at any time. If we say something wrong, do something wrong, or are in a bad mood, they're gone. We deal with this fear by either trying to please and be perfect so no one will leave us, or by being aloof and distant. The old, "I don't need anyone" Clint Eastwood cowboy routine. I am a rock. I am an island.

So underneath the people-pleasing patterns of the nice person is insecurity. Of not being strongly and deeply connected with others. This is why I felt unlovable for many years; I wasn't strongly connected to anyone.

This kind of attachment makes us see relationships as a tightrope. There is a very narrow path—the width of a single rope—that we must walk across to stay in the relationship. We must move slowly, carefully, methodically. We must plan our every step to keep our balance, lest we fall. And the fall from a tightrope is not a small misstep that we can easily recover from. No, if we fall from a tightrope, we fall long and hard–into a net if we're lucky, onto the pavement if we're not.

---

2. For a condensed and highly accessible review of how Attachment Theory works

This is how the young, emotional part of our brain sees relating to others. One false move and I'm plummeting to my death. Hence the strong sense of threat. The fear, anxiety, worry, rumination, and avoidance at all costs. Hence the strange phenomenon where you want to do something different, such as speak up, be more direct, or say no, and yet you find yourself doing the opposite: holding back, people-pleasing, and saying yes!

This frustrating pattern occurs because the emotional centers in your brain have more control of your behavior than your intellect. In the face of perceived threat, they hit the override switch, and you end up doing something different. Just as if you decided one morning, "I'm going to walk out into the freeway today and see what happens." Your self-preservation system would almost certainly kick in and prevent you from carrying that out.

As you read this book and apply what you learn, and take the small risks that I suggest throughout, you will retrain this part of your brain. You'll begin to experience a more secure sense of connection with those close to you, including your family, friends, dates, colleagues, clients, and even strangers.

You'll start to see that there is no threat in the disapproval of others, which allows you to relax in a deep and powerful way. You'll also see that being in healthy relationships with others is not at all like walking on a tightrope. It's actually more like a five-lane freeway. You can veer left, right, and all over the place, and still stay connected. **There is so much more space than you realized to be you and share who you are.** In fact, people are secretly begging for it.

---

and impacts adult relationships, I recommend Amir Levine and Rachel Heller's book, *Attached: The New Science of Adult Attachment and How It Can Help You Find — and Keep — Love*. To go deeper, you can look up articles by John Bowlby, who is the psychologist who pioneered the field of Attachment Theory.

CHAPTER 3:

GUILT BUBBLE

Niceness and guilt. These two go together like peanut butter and jelly. In fact, if you told me about a friend of yours who is "extremely nice," so nice they are "the nicest person you'll ever meet," I would bet a large amount of money at high odds that this person experiences the following three things:

1. Lots of guilt. They frequently feel guilty about letting people down, hurting people's feelings, putting themselves first, and so forth.

2. Tons of resentment. They will be angry with others, their partner, their parents, their friends, their boss, their neighbors, and their colleagues. Of course, they would be unaware of most of this because to be angry and resentful is not nice; it's not allowed. Hence, it's stuffed down. Which brings me to the third prediction.

3. Physical Pain. This friend most likely has some recurring pain in the form of headaches, migraines, neck pain, back pain, knee pain, ankle pain, foot pain, or stomach pain. They may have several diagnoses, had surgeries, be on medications, go to chiropractors and physical therapists, yet never remain pain-free for long (more on this fascinating phenomenon in chapter 5.)

I know this because I experienced all three of them for years, and have seen many nice clients suffering similarly. I also know this because there are certain fundamental patterns that all humans follow. For example, stifling feelings leads to resentment. This is like a math or physics formula; it happens every time, predictably and repeatedly.

When I was living life as the ultra-nice guy, my approach to you, and any other human, would follow this little algorithm.

1. Avoid doing anything to lose your approval.
2. Do not do anything to hurt your feelings.
3. Do not display anger or irritation or do anything that might make you upset.

You know, "be nice," right?

We looked at number one from this list in the last chapter. This chapter is all about the second one: never hurting others' feelings.

JUST BE NICE

"If you don't have anything nice to say, don't say anything at all."
- 900 million parents worldwide.

This second guideline seems to make sense, right? Don't do anything to hurt others' feelings.

Who could possibly argue with that rule? It seems like something any kind, loving, good person would live by, right?

Well... Maybe. And maybe not. What if someone wants to talk with you and you don't want to talk with them? What if someone is prattling on with their eighth story about their car engine upgrade and you aren't in the least bit interested? What if someone asks you to go out with you and you don't want to? What if a person you're dating really likes you and wants to become your girlfriend or boyfriend, but you're not excited about it? What if someone bothers, annoys, irritates, or pisses you off?

You stuff these impulses way down into your belly of course! You stop being so selfish and force yourself to be patient, to be flexible, to just go with the flow, and "be nice." So, you talk to that person. Or, better yet, you actively engage them and pretend to be really excited to see them. "Hey Arthur! How's it going?!"

You endure conversations that don't interest you; you do things you don't really want to do; and you end up dating someone weeks, months, or years longer than you should. Yes, years. I've talked with clients who have been wanting to end their relationships for a long time, and the only thing that's keeping them there is guilt. "But my partner will be crushed!" Guilt, and maybe a dash of fear. "If I leave, I'll never find anyone else. I'm scared of being alone."

Furthermore, what about annoyance, irritation, and anger? Those aren't nice, are they? Stuff those down in your belly too. And smile. Don't forget to smile.

Ugh. What makes us do this? Why are we so disconnected from ourselves? Why are we so afraid to be ourselves? The answer, my friend, is guilt. Good, old-fashioned, guilt.

HEALTHY GUILT VERSUS DESTRUCTIVE GUILT

Your mom or dad, or whoever told you to not hurt others' feelings had good intentions. They wanted you to be kind, compassionate, aware of others, and a good person. This is healthy. If someone is able to harm others without feeling discomfort, guilt, or remorse, that's part of the diagnostic criteria for being a sociopath.

So, there is such a thing as healthy guilt. Guilt is a feeling of regret or remorse for doing something that you would rather have not done. This happens to all of us. We are tired, or hungry or self-absorbed and we say or do something that we don't really mean.

Just two days ago, my second son Arman woke up around 5a. as he is known to do. He is a little guy, just ten months old. He is bright-eyed, quick to smile, and absolutely adorable. I love him so much it hurts. As he woke up, I took him out of the bedroom so my wife and other son could keep sleeping.

Unfortunately, in this moment, I had a strong need to pee. Experience has taught me that setting little Mani down in the bathroom is not ideal because he makes a hasty crawl-dash towards the toilet, where he attempts to dip his little pudgy hands into the mysterious contents within.

The alternative solution, which is holding him in one arm while peeing, has also become problematic. He's a gigantic and strong baby, and often attempts to launch himself out of my arms.

Therefore, I decide to set him down in the living room, right next to the bathroom, leaving the door open so he could see and hear me. As I walked into the bathroom to experience sweet relief, I heard his piercing cry. Not the kind of cry that's a slow BUILD, so I could quickly take care of business and then get him. No, this was the banshee wail that would wake up the house. Grrr. I walked back to the living room, feeling angry. I just wanted to pee for God's sake! As I reached down to pick him up, my teeth were gritted tight and I wrapped my hands around his body with more force than was needed. I hastily lifted him up, my body language screaming, "Ughhh, what do you want now?"

As soon as I had him in my arms, I noticed big tears streaming down his face and for some reason his left eye was puffy. When he felt my angry energy, he cried even harder. This instantly snapped me out of my self-absorbed state and I saw this sweet little guy in front of me. His small sad face and puffy left eye broke my heart. I felt so bad.

I hugged him tight, right against my heart as he calmed down. "I'm sorry buddy," I said as I swayed back and forth. "I love you. I'm sorry I picked you up like that." I felt his little heart against mine and he instantly calmed down and rested his body against mine as we shared a magic moment in the early morning light. I still had to pee, but that didn't matter anymore.

Even as I write this, my heart hurts a little and I cry. This is healthy guilt. This is the warning light that goes off when I'm out of alignment with my values, with who I want to be as a father. This guilt wakes me up and guides me back on track. This is very different from destructive guilt.

DESTRUCTIVE GUILT

Destructive guilt is the guilt that most people feel most of the time. It is a chronic sense of failing others, falling short, not doing something right, not being good enough, and otherwise being "bad."

Here are just a few examples of destructive guilt from my life and the lives of some of my clients.

Linda is asked out on a date by a man who is an avid bicyclist. He suggests they go for a bike ride on their date. Linda doesn't really like that idea for a first date, and doesn't even own a bike. Nevertheless, she feels guilty about telling him she'd rather do something else.

A friend asks Antoine if he can hang out on Saturday evening. Antoine doesn't really feel like going out, but he doesn't have specific plans. He tells his friend he won't be able to make it and feels strong guilt afterwards.

Chelsea is having an issue at work where one of her co-workers comes to talk with her many times per day. This interrupts her work-flow and she doesn't particularly enjoy the conversations. When she imagines telling her co-worker she's busy and can't talk right now, she experiences a crushing sense of guilt and feels bad.

Vihaan is in a committed relationship and he loves his partner. When he is out with his friends who are single, he feels guilty if he talks to other women. He also feels guilty for noticing women he finds attractive.

I walk into the house after work and my wife is having a rough moment, feeling overwhelmed and exhausted taking care of the two kids. I feel guilty for not having been there during the day to help her.

Whatever You Do, Don't Break the Rules

I could go on for days and days, listing clients' stories and my own. So much guilt, so much of the time. That's why I refer to it as a Guilt Bubble. It's like an energy field. It surrounds us everywhere we go. It distorts reality and turns neutral events into terrible, bad things we've done to hurt others and destroy the world.

When living in the Guilt Bubble, we're like the villain of our own movie. Always hurting people, letting them down, doing "bad" things. This is a life swallowed by destructive guilt.

What exactly is destructive guilt? As you read the examples above, what did you notice? Is there a trend? A common theme that makes them all the same? Take a moment to review them now, what exactly makes this destructive?

Some of the examples involve saying "no" to someone. Expressing what you want and don't want. This can stir up all kinds of guilt, especially if you imagine the other person wants something else.

Then there's poor Vihaan. I relate to his struggle, as it's something that caused me great pain in many of my relationships. I used to feel so guilty for noticing, talking to, or feeling attracted to other women. What is going on here?

Each of these scenarios involves breaking a rule. If we break certain rules, we feel guilt. Regardless of whether the rule makes sense, is realistic, or we're consciously aware of it.

What are the rules impacting the people in the scenarios above? Take a quick second to guess each one. This is an extremely valuable and life-changing skill to develop. If you can uncover the hidden rule behind your bad guilt, you can break free from it. Often, you'll see just how extreme and unrealistic these rules really are. You'll say to yourself, "I've been trying to live by *that*?"

Read those scenarios one more time and take a quick guess for each one. What is the underlying rule that they are breaking?

Once you've done that, continue reading.

Linda:

I should be flexible and go with the flow. If he's really excited about it and I shoot him down, he'll feel rejected and sad. It's not OK to make someone feel that way.

Antoine:

I should always say yes to my close friends' requests, unless I have specific plans that make me unavailable.

Chelsea:

I should listen politely to my co-worker whenever he wants to talk. If I send him away, he'll feel hurt, angry, and lonely. It's not OK to make someone feel that way.

Vihaan:

I shouldn't notice, talk to, or feel attracted to other women. Doing so will hurt my partner's feelings and that is unacceptable.

Aziz:

I should be there to help Candace whenever she needs it, so she never struggles alone with the kids.

Even as I write out my rule and make it more conscious, I start to be free of it. When I see it on paper, it's crazy. And it's treating Candace as if she's a fragile creature that can't handle demand, challenge, or discomfort.

In truth, I know that **demand, challenge, and discomfort are the forces that cause us to grow and become our fullest, most powerful selves.** In fact, they're the very signs that we are developing. They're essential, healthy, and necessary. Not to mention that Candace is incredibly strong and resilient. She works through challenging and uncomfortable feelings and lets them go more rapidly than anyone I've met.

These rules are not coming from our rational, adult minds. They're coming from deep within our emotional brain that recorded hundreds of lessons from our years of Nice Training. Lessons that your parents consciously taught you, and lessons that you learned just by being an observant, intelligent child. Mom gets mad when I resist her and say no; therefore, saying no is bad. Dad gets upset when I disagree with him; therefore, disagreeing with others is bad.

Many of these rules are not even things you would agree with if you slowed down and examined then consciously. They're just old programs you picked up long ago that continue to guide your feelings and behavior, regardless of whether you believe them.

In just a few chapters, we are going to have you come up with your own set of rules. Your own Bill of Rights that determines who you want to be in this world and how you want to show up. Not because someone else told you that you should, or out of fear of displeasing others, but from deep in your own core. You will decide from a place of power what is right for you.

But before you can do that, you have to flush out all the debris. You can't install a new program on top of a bunch of old, conflicting ones. You have to uninstall those, then install the one you want, the one that will serve you best, the one that is the real you finally coming out to play and enjoy your only life.

YOUR RULES

So, what are your rules?

You actually have hundreds or even thousands of rules in your head about all aspects of life. From what food you order at a restaurant, to how you respond to a solicitor, to what color your shoes should be based on your outfit. Don't worry, we don't need to uncover every single rule. That would be a long, exhausting, and unnecessary exercise (although perhaps interesting).

No, we're interested in only one set of rules—the ones that tell you how you "should" be. How you should be around others, what you should say and do, and what you should never say and do. These are the rules about what is acceptable and appropriate. What will make others like you, or reject you. They're also rules about how you should feel, and which feelings are OK to express and which ones are best kept hidden.

This is the set of rules you unconsciously use to determine whether you are "good" or "bad." Whether you are a worthy, lovable human being, or a guilty, bad, selfish, terrible, unlovable wretch.

Sound extreme? It's not an exaggeration. All of us have an inner critic that acts like a prosecutor and a judge. It's constantly evaluating what we do, think, and feel. It's inside our minds, so it's aware of our innermost world, including the stuff we prefer no one else know about.

If we have unrealistic rules that are impossible to follow, like "I should never feel sad," then we suffer. If we have faulty rules that tell us to do two conflicting things at the same time, like "be honest and speak your mind" and "never hurt others' feelings or cause upset," then we suffer. This suffering can take many forms.

For me, it created a perpetual sense of failing, falling short, and being inadequate. I felt anxious and afraid. I thought I was afraid of others and their judgments. Actually, I was afraid of my own inner critic, who would ruthlessly attack me if I broke even the smallest rule.

This created a deep and lasting sense of shame, as if there was something terribly wrong with me that I couldn't fix. Needless to say, I didn't have the best self-esteem as a result. And when our self-esteem is low, and we don't think much of ourselves, life is awesome, right? No! Life is hard. We don't reach out to people because we think we're not good enough for them. We don't offer our opinions because we think we're not smart enough. We don't hold relaxed eye contact for long because we fear others will see all the badness right beneath the surface.

This causes us to feel held back, stuck, and limited in many areas of life. It creates that frustrating and depressing feeling that we can't get what we really want, and never will. You know the one I'm talking about, right? It sometimes leads to anger, sometimes to despair, but at the end of the day, it's just pain. The pain of not living the life we want, of missing what matters most, and not truly enjoying this magical experience of being alive. Worst of all, we know on some level that what's holding us back is ourselves, but trying to just push through and "fake it until you make it" doesn't work.

Let's get cracking. Coming up with this list of rules will change your life. Because when you discover these rules, you are discovering the exact decisions that determine how you think, act, and feel. Uprooting the ones that are toxic and unhelpful can liberate you from decades of oppressive guilt. Changing one rule can transform relationships from confined obligation-fests into joyous experiences of sharing more love than you ever thought possible.

These statements are not hype. Changing your rules is that powerful. The majority of this book is about helping you do just that. In Part II and III, we are going to obliterate the toxic rules that oppress you. You're going to get a fresh, clear, and empowering perspective on how to relate to others, so you can be the most alive, unfettered, fearless, and free version of yourself.

If you're excited about that, then stick with me here. Because if we don't do the work in life, we never get the results we want. Moreover, this inner work is the most valuable thing you can do to transform your relationships, feelings, income, success and everything else. So, let's get to work.

THE LIST

Now you're going to create a list of the main rules that affect you on a daily basis. There is a very easy way to discover these rules because they all use the exact same word: should.

I will ask you prompting questions about each of the core areas of your life. For each one, write out a list of all the ways your mind tells you that you should or should not be.

For example: How should you be in conversations with others? What should you not do?

I should not interrupt someone when they're talking.
I shouldn't look away when someone is talking.
I shouldn't change the subject.
I should convey that I'm interested in them.
I should ask questions to show I'm interested.

Make sense? This is just a short sample of your potential rule list for conversations. Good God, this area is dominated by our rules! Every client I work with who struggles with conversation confidence has dozens of rules for how they should be in every interaction. On top of that, the rules are very serious and if you break them it's a big deal. It's horribly offensive, people hate you, you're an asshole, and you die a miserable lonely death in a basement apartment somewhere.

Enough of all this nonsense. Let's get free. Ready to make your list? I'll ask you some questions about different areas of your life, and then you come up with a list for each area. Some areas will have a short list of rules, and some areas will have a much longer list.

Below all these questions, I have an example of a list of my rules from about seven years ago, when I was doing a deep dive into this stuff. You can review that if you're unsure, or if you just want to see how messed up I am. I mean was. *Was*. I'm perfect now.

Relationships:

Are you in a romantic relationship right now? If not, think back to the last one. If you've never been in one, imagine being in one now. Think about daily life and how you relate to your girlfriend, boyfriend, spouse, or partner. What are some of the areas of conflict, frustration, or challenge that arise? Perhaps you have discussions or fights about these things. Or, perhaps you keep these things inside, and only you know about certain complaints, frustrations, or challenges. As you reflect on your relationship, ask yourself these questions:

How should I be in in my relationship?
What should I do?
What should I *never* do?
What's OK, and what's not OK for me to do, think, and feel?

Then write out a list of your shoulds in this area. Do that now.

If you are stuck or unsure, you can refer to my list below to get some ideas. If you are surprised by how many rules you found, that's a good thing. The more rules, and the more tough they are to follow, the more restricted your life is. Discovering them is a huge step toward breaking free.

Now, let's expand beyond romantic relationships. Take a moment to reflect on these questions, and then add more to your list of shoulds:

How should you be as a son or daughter?
If you have children, how should you be as a parent? (This list can be a doozy!)
How should you be around colleagues and co-workers?
How about strangers?

Take a few minutes to write out your shoulds about your relationships now.

Conversations:

It might seem strange to have a category just for conversations since we covered relationships. However, given my focus on social anxiety over the last fifteen years, I've found that most people have a ton of rules around exactly how they should be in conversations. These can make conversations confining, boring, draining, or oppressive experiences that leave us feeling anxious, dissatisfied, and dreading more. This is why it's important to uncover the exact rules you have in conversations as well; so, you can make the experience of talking and connecting with others easy, enjoyable, spontaneous, and fun.

Take a moment to think about all the different kinds of conversations you have–with friends, coworkers, acquaintances, business associates, and strangers.

How should you be in conversations with others?
What are you supposed to do?
What are you supposed to never do?

Write this list of shoulds now.

Work & Business:

Think of all the things you do during the day at work. The colleagues you interact with, the projects and tasks you focus on, and customers or clients you might deal with. As you imagine going through your workday, what do you notice about your rules?

How should you be at work?
What activities and tasks should you be doing?
How should you be doing things?
Are you doing enough?
What are things you shouldn't be doing?
Make your list of work rules now.

Sex:

This is another area with many hidden rules. When people refer to "sexual hang-ups," they are often referring to places we're uncomfortable because we have unconscious rules that tell us certain things are bad or unacceptable. These rules can create shame around our desires, and tension and inhibition during sex.

Think back to some of your sexual experiences, especially moments when you felt tense, uncomfortable, or ashamed. I know it's not pleasant, but this is powerfully healing because you are uncovering the rules that made you feel that way. What were you saying to yourself at the time?

How should you be during sex?
What should you be able to do?
What should happen?
What should never happen?
What's OK, and what's not OK?

Money:

Ahh, sex and money. What everyone wants more of, right? Yet, we have so many rules in both areas that create great amounts of suffering, regardless of how much we get. Take a few moments to think about your relationship with money. How do you feel when you think about the topic? Happy, excited, energized? Tense, anxious, or scared? Sad or down? Frustrated or dissatisfied? Ashamed? Whatever you feel is a clue to what your rules are.

How should you be with money?
What should you be doing more of?
What should you be doing less of?
How much should be earning?
What should you be able to do in this area?

Health:

Health, including our food choices, exercise habits, and appearance, is a hot button for rules. We have so many of them, and they are often all-or-nothing, extreme, conflicting, or distorted. This can lead to large amounts of shame, guilt, judgment, and fear about our bodies, our appearance, our diets, and everything else health related. Let's bring out all these rules into the light of your awareness.

How should you be with your health and self-care?
What should your body look like?
How much should you weigh?
How should you be eating?
What should you never do?

OK! That's enough. Whew, so many rules. So much inner policing and control going on. How exhausting.

Were you surprised by how many there are? When I do this exercise, I'm always shocked at how many rules I have for myself. No wonder I feel tense and confined in this situation. I am!

Here, as promised, is my list of rules from some years back. I've done this exercise numerous times. Each time it changes as I grow and evolve. This one is from seven years ago, before I'd met Candace or had my children.

Aziz's Rules (Circa 2010)

<u>Relationships</u>

I should never say or do anything that causes pain in another.

I should care for everyone who cares for me.

I should always feel loving towards my parents and want to spend lots of time with them.

I should always listen to and provide support to people who are in need.

I should be able to make every client (or other struggling person) feel substantially better.

I should assertively and confidently approach every beautiful woman I see (and win her approval).

I should always be direct, assertive, and honest with everyone.

I should be totally honest with everyone all the time.

I should assertively ask for my needs in all situations.

I should be more outgoing and spend more time with my housemates.

I should be outgoing and friendly with everyone at work.

I should be better with little kids.

I should never want people to notice me and view me as special or great.

I should be the perfect son, brother, friend, lover, therapist.

Conversations

I should be charming and witty and always know what to say.

I should never allow an awkward moment of silence in the conversation.

I should always find a way to be interested in what the other person is saying.

I should be affirming, positive, and encouraging when they're talking.

I should listen and reflect their viewpoints.

I shouldn't disagree with others.

I shouldn't debate with others.

I shouldn't dismiss their viewpoints.

I shouldn't change the subject abruptly.

I shouldn't look away while they're talking.

I shouldn't do anything that makes them feel like I'm not 100% fully interested and engaged.

Work Activities

I should never do things people could disapprove of.

I should be more ambitious, driven.

I should be creating a website and coaching business in my spare time.

I should keep track of every client and document at work.

I should be completely knowledgeable and competent.

I should never make a mistake.

Sexual Activities

I should be totally uninhibited to say and do whatever I want.

I should be more comfortable talking dirty.

I should be more masculine, direct, and assertive.

I should be the perfect lover.

I should always bring her to orgasm (before myself).

I should always get and maintain an erection.

I should always be able to orgasm.

Money and Finances

I should spend less money.

I should earn more money.

I should eat out less.

I should have better understanding of investments and finance.

I should understand my taxes better.

I should know what I'm spending and where and have a clear, precise budget.

Health & Self-Care

I should never use porn.

I should never smoke tobacco.

I should only use pot once every two weeks, tops.

I should have better posture.

I should stretch more.

I should never eat fast food or junk food.

I should eat more greens.

I should cook my own dinners.

I should be more fit and muscular.

What do we do with this fine list of inner laws? Burn it. Free yourself and live with no rules! No, I'm kidding. I have no idea what you wrote down. Perhaps you had: "I should never hit my child." That's a rule worth keeping. You may still agree with some of your rules, those that are actually in line with your values and how you want to be.

Other rules might seem oppressive and extreme. If you ask why you should follow that rule, and your mind says, *Because you should. To disobey would be bad and wrong.* That, as you'll see in Part III, is not sufficient reason to keep a rule. It has to fit with who you are and come from your values, not some old programming unconsciously passed down from your parents, who got it from their parents, and so on.

For now, you're just going to do one more thing with this list. Go through and mark the rules that really reflect your core values. Ones that affirm who you are and how you want to be. Mark those with a star or a smiley face.

Then, go through and look for the rules that are crushing you. The ones that keep you feeling confined, inadequate, guilty, and stuck. The ones that are life restricting and preventing you from being your full, free, alive self. Mark those suckers with an unhappy face. We'll get back to them soon.

So now, you have the core distinction between healthy guilt and destructive guilt. Healthy guilt comes from your true values and keeps you on track. Destructive guilt comes from faulty rules that you don't really agree with, but accepted when you were young. Making this list helps you determine which rules are which.

Destructive guilt can also occur when you break one of your values. Instead of healthy guilt kicking in to steer you in the right direction, destructive guilt swoops down and smashes you, telling you what a rotten person you are. In this case, the reason the guilt turned sour is because of its intensity, duration, and global assessment of you as a terrible father, or mother, or friend, or boss. This intense self-attack doesn't help you reaffirm your values and course-correct, it diminishes your self-esteem and makes you less likely to make lasting positive changes.

As you read the second part of this book, you will strengthen your own viewpoints, beliefs, and self-esteem. This will allow you to combat this guilt and not fall victim to it so easily. You will also discover dozens of new rules that will liberate you and help you create healthy, satisfying relationships. Then, in Part III, you will further define your own rules and release old ones that don't serve you.

But before we leave this discussion of guilt, there is one important thing to talk about. This is a pattern that causes endless guilt, makes it insanely difficult to say no, ask for what you want, speak up for yourself, or do much of anything without feeling like a bad person. It's the pattern of taking too much responsibility for other people's feelings.

OVER-RESPONSIBILITY

"Baby, are you OK?" my wife asked me in the darkness.

I was lying in our sprawling family bed, which manages to hold my wife, our two small children, and me. Usually feeling their warm little bodies next to mine and listening to them breath brings me a great sense of joy and deep peace. Not tonight. Tonight, I was feeling tense, agitated, and miserable. It was late on Thursday and I had just completed my coaching, teaching, and training calls for the week. Instead of feeling satisfied, fulfilled, and proud, I felt scared and uneasy.

"I feel so guilty," I replied. "Like everyone wants something from me and I'm letting everyone down."

"Oh... Like who?" she asked in a whisper.

"I feel like everyone in my mastermind program wants more of my time and attention during the group calls, and the coaches on my team want more supervision and training calls." No one had stated this. In fact, people were often expressing gratitude about their wins and progress. I knew what I was saying was distorted and inaccurate, but I was completely lost in the story.

"And I feel like I'm letting you and Zaim and Arman down. You guys want more time with me and I'm letting you down too. My kids are growing up and I'm missing it," I added, on a dramatic note.

"You're awfully involved for a dad who's missing it," my wife replied. Funny and sweet. Just two of the two hundred reasons why I love her.

Now that I'd gotten the stories out, I was able to feel my feelings more. We talked late into the night, enjoying a rare opportunity for uninterrupted adult conversation, even if it meant less sleep.

During our conversation, I realized how much of my stress and guilt was coming from taking too much responsibility for everyone in my life. It was my job to make sure everyone felt completely comfortable at all times. No missing, no wanting, no frustration. In fact, I needed to anticipate their desires and preemptively satisfy them before they became upset. Because if someone was upset with me for any reason, it was my fault and I was a bad guy who needed to fix it instantly.

This is Over-Responsibility, one of the many curses of the nice person. I'm no stranger to this one, and I have actively worked to let go of a vast majority of my care taking of others. Yet, as evidenced by the story above, it's still there. Especially when I take on more, step outside of my comfort zone, and reach a new level of impact and influence. The more people I interact with, the more opportunities there are for that nice guy programming to pop up and start running amok.

Over-Responsibility is another pattern we learned in childhood. As young children, we would see Mom or Dad get angry, anxious, or sad, and instantly assume it was our fault. When we are very young, we are unable to understand that others are separate people, with their own experiences, feelings, and desires. This capacity doesn't come online until we're older, but by then we may have already made some strong decisions. We figure out the best way to respond when we "make Dad angry" or "make Mom anxious." We might decide to hide, approach, console, hug, act out, try to be funny, or become completely quiet and still.

Flash forward twenty, or thirty, or fifty years, and we may be doing the same thing. You walk into your office on Monday morning of the successful business you own. Rock star. You're navigating all the challenges of your industry, making tough decisions, and have steadily grown your business for five years in a row. Yet, when you walk through those doors and the first employee you interact with seems tense, irritable, and short, your mind starts to spin.

What's going on with him? Is he pissed at me because I was out of the office on Thursday and Friday last week? Was it too much work and he didn't like it?

Beneath these worried thoughts is anxiety. There's fear, tension, and discomfort in your body. A sense of threat. All is not well. *I must figure this out and solve it in order to be safe, to be at peace.*

That's exactly what Over-Responsibility does to us. It makes us feel completely responsible for everyone else's feelings, with a strong compulsion to make sure everyone feels happy, relaxed, content, and generally good in all scenarios. This might sound impossible and problematic. It is. It becomes even more so as you interact with more and more people, whether it be in business, your love life, or socially.

This tendency to take too much responsibility for others' feelings creates large amounts of anxiety and guilt (as well as hidden resentment). In fact, the rules from your list that are causing you the most guilt are likely ones that demand you don't "cause" any negative feelings in others. The nicer someone is, the more guilt they feel about this.

TAKING CARE VERSUS CARE-TAKING

It's amazing what language can do. I've discovered over years of doing clinical psychology work and then coaching that sometimes a single word change can make the difference between strong fear, and mild anxiety. Or a "big fight" and a "simple discussion."

For example, the Semantic Technique I learned while training with Dr. David Burns at Stanford University, is simple yet powerful, and only changes one word. With all those toxic rules, you simply replace the word "should" with "prefer."

"I should get 100% of the questions right" becomes, "I'd prefer to get 100% of the questions right."

"I should have said something different" becomes, "I'd prefer to have said something different."

This one is powerful. Feel free to begin using it now with the rules you uncovered that don't serve you. We will do much more in Part II to dismantle those; this is just a simple technique you can use immediately.

Another simple word shift is between "taking care" of others versus "care-taking" others. What's the difference? Taking care of others means being aware of other people and their needs, and considering these in your decisions. It comes from respecting others, and wanting to support them and maintain good relations.

Care-taking is a different story. In Merriam-Webster dictionary, it's defined as:

1. The act of taking care of land or buildings while the owner is not there.
2. To give physical or emotional care to someone (such as a child, or old person, or someone who is sick).

Obviously, the second definition is more relevant in our discussion, but the first one also reveals something interesting. I'm taking care of someone's land or buildings, and they're not even there. Therefore, in that situation, I am entirely responsible. If their shit burns down while they're gone, that's 100% on me.

Similarly, in the second definition, notice the examples of people one might care-take. Children, the elderly, and the infirm. These people need certain kinds of help because they cannot do it themselves. Your grandmother might need someone to help lift her out of her wheelchair and into the bed because her legs are not strong enough to do so herself. My kids need me to help them understand and regulate their emotions because they don't know how to yet. In these instances, care-taking is great. It's needed.

However, when we're living in a world where we're entirely responsible for the feelings of everyone around us, we become constant care-takers. We are subconsciously assuming and treating others as if they are young children who cannot manage their own feelings. This misconception creates stress, burnout and an endless supply of bad guilt. It sets up unrealistic demands of how responsive you should be, and causes you to give more than you want to, and say "no" much less than you need to.

This urge to care-take can exist in all relationships, but it tends to be strongest in our dating and intimate relationships. This is because we like, love, or care about another person deeply, and what we say and do does affect them emotionally. This makes it next to impossible to be direct and honest if we have a strong habit of care-taking. We just couldn't possibly hurt their feelings in any way.

"I couldn't possibly tell him that I don't want to keep seeing him. He's so sweet and loving."

"I just can't break up with her. It's going to break her heart, and I can't do that to her. She can't handle it."

When clients in my groups say things like this, I often highlight the care-taking by exaggerating it. "You're right. They probably can't handle that. How could you do that to them? The only reasonable and honorable thing to do is to stay with her. Eventually you should marry her and have children."

This often makes them laugh and smile, and breaks the care-taker trance. But our work is far from done. Even if they see it's absurd, and that it's in their best interest to break up, they feel oppressive amounts of guilt and waves of I'm-a-bad-person-ness.

I know this feeling well, and I know how overpowering it can feel. Once the guilt switch flips, it can feel like no matter what we say to ourselves, nothing can stop the onslaught. I remember one instance when I agreed to help Candace move. This was when we first began dating, and she was in the early stage of the divorce process. She was moving out of the home she shared with her ex-husband and into her own place.

Being the "good boyfriend," I said I would help her move. When I got there, however, I was overwhelmed with a strong urge to leave. It was too much, too soon. Too much involvement in her relationship with her ex-husband, and I didn't like it.

For the vast majority of my life, I would have felt this discomfort and stuffed it down. I would have followed my inner set of shoulds and been the nice guy. In this case: you should help your girlfriend move.

Fortunately, I'd been doing some of the work you're doing right now. I was in a men's group that was helping me see that noticing my inner reactions and taking care of myself are good things. They actually allow me to be supportive and loving in the long term.

In fact, I'll never forget what one group member told me. His name was Allen and he was a former divorce attorney in his late sixties. He said, "Aziz, every time I saw a case where the wife had a new boyfriend, and he showed up to all our meetings, and was the real knight-in-shining-armor type, their relationship was over in a few months."

Snap. His words struck me as true and I could see from the outside exactly why this would be the case. Too involved. Too pleasing. Too nice.

And so that sunny summer afternoon I told Candace, "I'm sorry, baby. I don't think I can help you do this. It feels too involved. I think I'm going to leave and let you and your friends take care of it."

She understood. Two of her friends looked at me as I shared this, and one said, "Oh..." Candace later told me this was because her friends liked me and were disappointed I wouldn't be hanging out that afternoon. I, of course, didn't interpret it that way. Here's what my mind did:

"Oh..." = "Wow, what a selfish asshole you are. Your poor girl-friend is going through so much, leaving her home of ten years, and all she needs is some support and someone to help her pack up, but you are just going to leave because you feel uncomfortable. What a bad, selfish, bad, bad person you are. I look down upon you, sir."

And that's exactly how I felt driving away. Like a bad, bad person. Disrespectful and unworthy of love. At least that's what my mind was telling me. But, at the same time, I knew something was different. Even though I was feeling badly, part of me knew this was good. I knew I was taking a step towards shedding the nice guy programming that had been controlling my life for decades. I knew I was onto something.

Here's the thing. You are not responsible for other people's feelings. They're not incompetent children. They're adults who can handle their own feelings. They can work through disappointment, hurt, anger, sadness, and upset. In fact, doing so will make them stronger and healthier in the long run. You cannot stop others from feeling all discomfort, or all pain. It is an impossible task, a fool's errand.

You'll learn exactly how to turn this new philosophy into a reality in the second part of this book. For now, watch your tendency and urge to care-give during the next few days and weeks. Pay attention to your discomfort around being honest or direct. Notice when you're uncomfortable with someone having unpleasant feelings. And notice how much you avoid saying or doing things to make sure no one ever feels upset. Notice how much you manage, control, and construct what you say to preserve everyone's feelings. You just might be surprised at how often and intensely this happens. The more you notice, the better, because awareness will set you free (combined with action of course).

But What About Jesus?

One major source of guilt for many people is due to their religious and spiritual beliefs. In an attempt to guide us to being more generous, kind, loving, and godly people, we are taught how to be and how not to be. This can provide the foundation of a powerful moral compass and a deep sense of integrity. It can also create unobtainable standards that lead to a continual spring of inadequacy and guilt.

I was raised as a Muslim and went to Christian schools. Even though my family was not very religious, I was exposed to the teachings of the Old Testament, Jesus, and the prophet Mohammad (peace be upon him). The guidance in these teachings can be helpful, soothing, and healing.

However, it all depends on how it is taught and how we understand it. Just the other morning, I was listening to a preacher's sermon. I enjoy reading and listening to teachings of all faiths and cultures, from Christian to Taoism to Lakota. In this sermon, the preacher was encouraging people to "be like Jesus."

"In your lives, you must think and act like Jesus. Test every thought to make sure it's obedient with Christ." He went on to say, "Jesus is our standard. Ask yourself, 'Would Jesus think this way. Would Jesus act this way? Would Jesus feel this way?'"

He then gave a description of what Jesus was like, "Jesus is love, joy, peace, patience, kindness, gentleness, meekness, and self-control. He is not envious or greedy, and does not harbor selfish ambition."

So far so good, right? This seems to be guiding us towards being more loving, better humans. Except, what if you feel impatient? What if you binge on the chips and soda and don't have self-control at the super bowl party? What if you feel bitter or secretly "harbor selfish ambition"?

While some people may be good at seeing these things in themselves, and then meeting them with love, compassion, and God's forgiveness, that's not what I've seen in most. Most people feel bad and guilty for having these flaws, weaknesses and imperfections. They harbor deep self-loathing and feel guilty on a daily basis for continually falling short.

The unconscious logic goes something like this: *If I think, feel, or act in a wicked way, then I should be punished. I will criticize myself brutally, which will make me feel unlovable and worthless, which will motivate me to "try harder" and "do better."*

While it may seem effective at first glance, and indeed may be how you were raised as a child, this doesn't lead to the best results. Increased self-criticism and self-hatred leads to more shame, which actually leads to more behavior that is negative. Because when you feel terrible inside, how loving are you with others? When you feel terrible inside, how much self-control do you have to eat better and take care of yourself?

My goal here is not to challenge your faith or religious convictions. My goal here is to help you out of guilt, into forgiveness and ease with yourself. If you're a Christian, or a Muslim, or Jew, or anything else, my goal is to make you a happier, more loving, better one. The key is to release this oppressive layer of guilt. It's not making you a better person; it's not bringing you closer to God or your brothers and sisters on this planet. It's isolating and destroying you. And it's time for a change in how you treat yourself.

CHAPTER 4:

DON'T BE MAD

"Hello?" I said as I picked up my phone.

"Hi, is this Aziz?" said a man's voice.

"Yes," I replied.

"Hi, this is Brandon from Elite Phlebotomy. You're scheduled for a blood draw at 6 a.m. One of my employees called in sick, something to do with her kid. I don't have anyone who can come out there. Can we reschedule?"

This blood draw required a fast. Which meant I woke up, went to the gym and worked out without eating anything. It sucked and my workout was hard. I had a mild headache. I was pissed.

"So, here's the thing. I've already collected my urine sample, and that needs to go out today. I also fasted this morning and went to the gym, which was difficult. Now I'm heading home early to make it to this appointment in ten minutes, so rescheduling at this point is not cool."

That's right, not cool. I said it. My voice was calm and firm. I didn't sound angry or aggressive, I sounded firm and a little irritated, which I was.

"Oh, OK. Let's see," said Brandon. "I have another draw now, but I can come by around 7 a.m. today. Would that work?"

"That could work," I replied. "You'll be here at 7a.m.?" I confirmed.

"Yes," he said.

Sound simple?

The truth is I never would have done something like this years ago. I would have been much more agreeable, accommodating, and flexible. I also would not have let any irritation or dislike of the situation show in my voice, because showing any form of anger was bad. Years ago, I was trapped in a cage of niceness and terrified of my own anger, other's anger, disagreement, and conflict.

In this chapter, we are going to uncover that pattern of conflict avoidance so you can see how this operates inside of you. This will give you insight, and perhaps profound relief. Living in constant fear of anger and conflict creates chronic tension and persistent anxiety. You might not even realize just how much unease it is currently creating in your life.

Do you remember the example about over-responsibility from the previous chapter in which I was up at night, worried about letting everyone down? While it was showing up as guilt and anxiety, guess what was really underneath? If I let people down, they'll be upset with me, angry. This fear of someone being upset is often lurking behind our anxiety and guilt.

Once you know how to handle confrontation, and that it's not that bad, you naturally begin to feel more solid, safe, strong, and confident in the world. That is exactly what you'll learn how to do in the next part of this book. But first, you must transform the way you think about anger, conflict, and upset in general.

Let's start with this question: is anger good or bad?

What do you think? What's your initial gut reaction? For most nice people, anger is an unacceptable, undesirable, and generally bad emotion. If one is nice, one shouldn't feel angry, irritated, or upset with others.

These are the stories I lived by for decades. I would get anxious or depressed, but never angry. Sure, once in a while I'd feel enraged at another driver on the road, but these instances were internal and hidden.

I used to be so uncomfortable with anger that not only would I stuff it down, I would secretly judge others for not doing the same. If my friend was driving us somewhere, and he was pissed off at another driver, I'd think: *Man, he really needs to calm down. He gets way too worked up.* If I heard someone sound irritable or raise their voice in a conversation, I'd judge them as not patient enough, or otherwise emotionally weak and out of control.

Do you have similar views of anger? Is it a sign of weakness? Of not being patient, flexible, assertive, evolved, or spiritual enough? Is it a problem and a bad sign for relationships if someone gets angry? How many times per week do you get angry?

ANGER-PHOBIA

My discomfort and judgment came from a deep fear of anger—in myself and in others. This came from being a sensitive kid who felt things deeply, both my own emotions and those of people around me. Growing up, I had two models of anger, as did most of us. Mom and Dad.

My dad is like many men of his generation. He was taught to be tough, not too "soft," to man up and get things done. Don't think too much, and certainly don't sit around feeling your feelings. This leads to a limited capacity to identify and express emotion, especially tender or vulnerable feelings. As a result, fear, inferiority, hurt, resentment, and other emotions stay inside until the pressure reaches a critical level and the valve breaks, and out pours anger. Hot, loud, and intense.

My dad's loud, booming voice scared me as a kid. Whether he was yelling at me or my mom or brother, I felt a terrible, scared, sick feeling in my stomach. This taught me that anger is no good. It hurts people, it's out of control, it's unproductive, it's bad.

My mom tended to be more passive. She absorbed anger and didn't fight back. She was very patient with us and only occasionally

In a recent session, I was exploring the challenges a client was facing at work. She had a boss who interrupted her, shot her ideas down, and generally made it difficult for her to speak up confidently in meetings and other group discussions. She felt demoralized and insecure about her performance. She also felt anxious before meetings, and generally became quiet.

As we discussed the situation and I heard examples of what her boss would say to her, I said, "Wow, that sounds really annoying. I would be pissed if someone talked to me that way." I made sure I sounded pissed as I said that sentence. This subtly gave her permission to feel angry, which I could see she was not allowing. She was just aware of feeling anxious and inferior.

"Yeah," she replied, laughing.

I find when I speak to clients' anger directly, they often laugh. I think it's the laugh of relief. *It's OK to feel angry here, whew.*

"Do you feel angry about being interrupted and shot down?" I asked.

"I do." She said quickly. "I hate it. And I get so angry at her for doing it. Inside I want to scream and tell her to shut up. But I could never do anything like that, obviously. In fact, I can't say anything critical to her at all. She's so sensitive."

Notice what just happened there. My client acknowledged her anger, which is actually a great step forward out of the nice cage into the more authentic, powerful version of herself. But she limited her ability to feel it. She started to move towards it, then immediately jumped to, "but I could never say anything about it."

There is a big difference between feeling and doing. We can feel whatever we want. In fact, I believe it's optimal and extremely healthy to feel everything inside ourselves. This includes all emotions, especially the ones that are uncomfortable that we call "negative," including anger, sadness, fear, hurt, loneliness, emptiness, rage, and many others. The more we can give ourselves complete permission to feel anything, and know that it doesn't mean anything about us, the freer we become. In addition, it doesn't mean we necessarily have to *do* anything either. We're just feeling.

So, in the example with this client, it would be beneficial for her to feel her anger towards her boss. I mean *really* feel it. In fact, later in that session we did a role-play where she expressed all her anger towards her boss, as if she were speaking directly to her. The more she got into it, the more expressive and heated it became.

This is good. This is huge. When you stop suppressing anger and let yourself feel it, knowing it won't automatically make you do something, you become much more confident and powerful. My client is not going to go say all these things to her boss. That would be ineffective. But she needs to feel her anger in order to release it. By doing so she not only feels relief, she also reconnects to her power and her sense of agency. She is back in the driver's seat of her life; she is a creator rather than a victim.

Now we can discuss how to communicate assertively with her boss and others at work. She can use her anger as fuel to speak up. The anger is like a hot fire that releases energy and heat. It is raw, wild, and intense. But we can run this energy through an internal machine that refines it and turns it into something productive—assertiveness. You'll learn much more about how to use this energy and speak up for yourself consistently and powerfully in Part II of this book.

CONFLICT AVOIDANCE

If you learned that anger is bad, it hurts others, and shows you are weak or unlovable, guess what happens? Avoidance, of course. If something is scary, uncomfortable, threatening and only leads to pain and problems in relationships, and it makes you a "bad person," then why on earth would you *not* try to avoid it?

So, we become masters of conflict avoidance. The nicer we are, the better we become at this. And it's not just conflict. We become skilled at avoiding all forms of argument, disagreement, tension, differing opinions, or upset. Instead of bending over backwards to accommodate people, we become like ultra-flexible yogis who can contort their bodies into strange shapes.

You may be aware that you're doing this conflict avoidance dance, and you may not be. I became so skilled at this that it was like a program that was running in the background of a computer. I didn't even consciously do it most of the time. It came across in every aspect of my behavior: the way I greeted people, what I would say, the questions I would ask, what I would share versus hold back, how I looked at people, and so much more.

Are you a master of conflict avoidance and great at smoothing things over? Do you instantly pick up what mood someone is in and start to accommodate it? If they seem tense or upset, do you try to cheer them up? Or do you steer clear, tiptoe around, and walk on eggshells so as to not disturb them?

Let's uncover two of the major ways you might be consistently avoiding conflict, disagreement, or friction. Going into this topic directly can be a little uncomfortable, especially if you've been avoiding it for years. Worse still, part of you knows that uncovering these patterns will eventually lead to you having more conflict, disagreement, and friction in your life. Yikes!

However, here's why it's a good thing. While conflict and disagreement don't *feel* good, they're part of having direct contact with your fellow humans. Direct contact means you show up fully, are present with others, look them in the eye, listen to them, share what you think and feel, and have a real connection. It's the opposite of staying small, avoiding eye contact, and displaying just a small fraction of yourself that you hope will receive their approval.

This is an important point, and amounts to a fundamental shift in how you move through the world. I spent many years afraid of direct contact. I wanted love and connection, just like every human does, but I didn't want tension, differing opinions, anger, or any of that scary stuff. I just wanted nice, pleasant inter-actions amongst nice, pleasant people.

Unfortunately, partial contact creates partial connection and only partial fulfillment. It's cowardly. It's being too scared to put myself out there in the world. It's trying to get the good feelings without any risk. It's trying to fill my heart up while still keeping it guarded and defended. And it doesn't work.

If you want to experience a rich, fulfilling, meaningful and significant life, direct contact is required. You must step up and claim your right to be here: *Here I am. I am here. I have a right to be here. I belong here. I am me, and I matter. Not because I'm the smartest, or the best, or perfect. Just because. Permission was granted by my birth.*

In other words, to have the life you want—love, relationships, suc-cess, confidence, power, freedom—you must be all in. You must be willing to feel the full spectrum of human emotion, and experience the full spectrum of human contact. This includes laughter, shared joy, and sweet harmony. Those moments where you feel in harmony, madly in love, and like your life is magnified a thousand-fold by having someone so amazing to share it with. But it also involves dis-agreement, having hard conversations, and navigating conflict and hurt feelings. Believe it or not, conflict is your doorway to having the life you really want.

> *"The cave you fear to enter holds the treasure you seek."*
> - Joseph Campbell

THE SUBMISSIVE STANCE

The most common form of conflict avoidance is simply to adopt a submissive stance in our relationships. This tried and true strategy has been used throughout time, and is one that I used for years. It harkens back to our days as pack animals with a clearly defined social hierarchy. Think wolves, or chimpanzees.

In that pack, you have the leaders, or the ones that are vying for "alpha" status. You also have the members of your tier two crew, who are not gunning for the top, but they're sure to hang on to their position in the pack. Then you have your omega-types. These ones are down at the bottom of the hierarchy, afraid of others, passive, submissive.

A number of years back I watched a documentary about this status hierarchy in wolves, lions, and other animal packs. It was fascinating. I remember watching the alpha wolf chasing off the omega from a caribou carcass. The alpha wolf had already eaten, and the tier two wolves were surrounding the fallen beast, eating as much as they could. The poor omega wolf tried to get close and he was chased off, for no reason, other than to communicate: *Not yet. You don't eat until I say you can eat. Got it?*

The segment on adolescent lions was even more intense. There was a pack of seven male lions who banded together to hunt, until they grew up enough to meet some lionesses and make stuff happen. At one point, they killed a zebra and were in a tight circle around the animal as they ate. There was just enough space for six of the seven lions. Everyone but the omega. The only place he could get access was the zebra's head. He sat there timidly licking the hairy scalp, ready to dash off should the alpha, or any other lion in the pack, decide to chase him. As I watched this disturbing display, the narrator said in a calm Australian accent, "in these types of packs, the omega does not often get enough food to eat, and does not survive. Even if he does, he is not a desirable male and will never find a mate." Harsh.

While these examples might seem extreme and irrelevant to us highly evolved humans, you may be surprised by how much we operate in similar ways. Have you ever been nervous to make eye contact with someone? Have you ever made eye contact and then instantly looked away, without consciously doing it? It was as if some deep instinctual programming forced you to look down, even though you were intending to meet their gaze head on. Guess what? Deep instinctual programming made you do that.

We are primates and we are pack animals. In any given social situation, we're assessing where we fall in the pack hierarchy and behaving accordingly. Based upon appearance, wealth, position in an organization, authority, knowledge, clothing, skill level, and many other criteria, we are determining if we are above or below this person. This happens mostly unconsciously, but is happening nonetheless.

When we're afraid of conflict, confrontation, or friction of any kind, we automatically adopt the most submissive stance we can. To imagine what that might be, think back to our chimpanzee or wolf friends. The omega wolf does not look at the alpha directly, he keeps his head down, his movements are fast and appear nervous, and his eyes dart from left to right. If another wolf passes him, he steps back, out of his way. If they move towards him directly—if they confront him—what does he do? He rolls onto his side or back and lifts his paws up to expose his belly. The universal gesture of supplication and submission. "Please don't hurt me."

Chimpanzees will do very similar things. They will also produce a large smile to indicate they mean no harm. "Please, do not hurt me; I am no threat to you."

Do you see any subtle forms of these behaviors in how you interact with others? Do you often avoid eye contact, tending to look away or look down often? If someone speaks their mind firmly and strongly, do you tend to step aside and let them take the floor? Do you hesitate and avoid speaking up in groups? Are you nervous or hesitant in settings where there are authorities, bosses, or the "executive team"? Do you avoid directly approaching women or men that you find attractive?

Perhaps you do the primate smile thing. That one was my bread and butter. I'd smile so much while talking with people. I'd also be quick to laugh at anything they said. And my laugh would be a bit too hard, too much, too forced. We often smile and laugh to send the social signal: *I like you. Please like me.*

Another submissive stance favorite that seems to be unique to humans is the heavy use of apologies. We can say "I'm sorry" so frequently, and for so many different things, it just becomes a habit. We end up apologizing hastily if we bump shoulders on the train, both grab the door handle at the same time, start to speak up at the same time, and so many other instances that don't actually warrant an apology. We may consider it "politeness," but it is actually rooted in submissiveness and conflict avoidance. Don't worry, I have a fun game in store for you in Chapter 12 that will help you end over-apologizing.

For now, can you see how you're moving through life, adopting a submissive stance everywhere you go? Or for you it might not be everywhere, just in certain situations at work or in your romantic life. When I really got just how much I was doing this, how much it pervaded every social interaction I had, I was shocked. And I decided I needed to do something about it fast.

The good news is changing your stance towards others is relatively easy. It does require awareness, effort, and leaning into the edge of your comfort zone. That's exactly what you're here to learn how to do. Sure, it can be uncomfortable at first, but compared to our wolf and lion friends, we have it easy. I don't think the omegas in those packs could simply choose to show up differently. Their pack structure is in large part based on physical strength. If that omega wolf decided one day that he wasn't going to take it, and approached the alpha directly, he'd be beat down hard.

However, our hierarchies are much more abstract and malleable. In fact, as soon as you stop buying into a given metric of status, you've broken free. For example, if you truly did not care about how much money someone had, you would walk into a room full of billionaires and interact freely and confidently. You could start conversations, make jokes, and just be yourself. If, on the other hand, you were locked into the cultural mindset that your net worth equals your human worth, then it would be a different story. You'd be nervous about entering that room, you'd be hesitant to approach people, join into groups, and engage others for fear of them looking down upon you.

In just a few short chapters, you'll be learning exactly how to end this insanity, so you can boldly be yourself around anyone, no matter how wealthy, accomplished, or beautiful. We'll also help you eliminate the submissive stance so you show up as your full, powerful self–the real you–not some inhibited, timid, limited version of yourself.

To clarify, I'm not saying that smiling, laughing, choosing not to share your opinion, or apologizing are weak things that only a "timid loser" would do. Each of these is an important part of connecting with others and necessary at times. The difference is when and how we do them. If they become habitual, excessive, and compulsive from a fear of conflict or a need for approval, then they backfire as social connectors. They reduce our confidence and push others way. We must change these habits.

Over-Accommodating

To accommodate means to "fit with the wishes or needs of." There-fore, accommodating another person may involve doing something that fits their wishes or needs. Sounds pretty good, right? Do things for others. Help them get what they want. Do what they want you to do. Then they'll be pleased, feel happy, and like being with you.

This is actually a recipe for a good relationship that is based on both people bringing value to the other person's life. It's the basis of friendship, business partnerships, customer/client relationships, and romantic relationships. And… it goes too far.

When our primary objectives are to avoid disapproval, disagree-ment, friction, or any sort of conflict, we tend to veer too far into what can be called over-accommodating. This means giving too much of yourself, doing too much of what other people want, and not paying attention to what you want and need.

Below I'm going to share the five major costs of nice that can wreak havoc in people's lives. I personally experienced all five for many years, and I know them inside and out. As I study them more and more, they become clear and obvious. They are surprisingly predictable and common.

However, many people do not understand them. I certainly didn't for many years. I would just think to myself: *Why do I feel so anxious? Why does my stomach hurt all the time? Why do I feel lonely, and why does my chest ache so much? Am I depressed? Is there something wrong with my brain chemistry? I've heard it runs in my family after all...*

When we're not aware of what's causing these symptoms, they can feel like mysterious problems that come out of nowhere. They disappear once in a while, only to reappear again, without warning. They scare us, hurt us, and cause us tremendous pain. They are like specters that haunt us, often in solitude because we're reluctant to share our pain with others.

As I write this section below, I realize that I have a choice. I have so much passion about this, so much energy and drive to liberate myself and everyone else who's open-minded and ready; I can get quite fired up. So, my choice is this: I can be mild, toned down, and not controversial to make sure no one objects or gets upset. You know, be nice. On the other hand, I can state exactly what I've seen to be true in myself and thousands of other people. I can passionately share the real and shocking costs of being too nice. Guess which one I'm going to choose?

In the words of the great Samuel L. Jackson as Arnold in the 1993 movie, *Jurassic Park:* "hang on to your butts."

THE 5 SPECTERS OF NICE

1. ANXIETY

As you've seen from the last few chapters, trying hard to be a nice person means attempting to please others, feeling bad for not living up to your rules or for hurting others' feelings, and avoiding anger and conflict. This creates anxiety. You are worried that others will not like you, about being a "bad person" and losing relationships because of it, and about getting upset or other people being upset. Life is full of fear.

Is this your experience? How much time do you spend worrying? Worrying about others' feelings, your performance, and whether so-and-so thinks you're such-and-such: good or bad, smart or stupid, hot or not. How about the fear of saying the wrong thing, losing face, or making a fool of yourself?

For many years, I had a terrible habit of replaying conversations in my head. Usually the ones I'd replay were the most awkward, strange, or embarrassing. Although sometimes I'd pick a seemingly ordinary one and replay that as well. As I replayed them, repeatedly, my mind would pick apart all the things I did wrong. All the ways I spoke too much (or too little), said the wrong thing, didn't do it quite right, or otherwise sucked. This is a kind of rumination, which is just another form of anxiety.

And don't get me started on the anxiety about other people's feelings. I experienced so much stress over making sure everyone felt OK. If I suggested the movie or the restaurant, I had a hard time enjoying myself because I was responsible for everyone's experience. If I invited several people to do something and they didn't know each other, I had to make sure everyone liked each other and had a great time. If I said or did anything that could offend, bother, hurt, or annoy someone, my anxiety would skyrocket (and guilt would soon follow). Can you relate?

I can go on and on, but I think you get my point. Anxiety takes a toll on your mind and body. It keeps you in a fight, flight, or freeze state with your nervous system all wound up, shooting cortisol, adrenaline, and norepinephrine through your system. It can mess with your sleep, digestion, libido, sexual functioning, and your mood, to name just a few. It's not pretty, and I'm afraid it gets worse…

2. RESENTMENT & RAGE

Anxiety is already unpleasant, especially if it's frequent and strong. But in the fight-flight-freeze response that is built into our nervous system, flight (which is anxiety) is only one of them. We also have a fight response somewhere down in there because we humans are strong, proud, spirited animals. We're not easily broken. Even when oppressed for a long time, we have a way of eventually fighting back and breaking free. This is true inside of you as well.

While you may only be aware of the fear, inferiority, desire to please, pressure to perform, and other anxiety, that doesn't mean that's all that's happening inside of you. There is also an inner response of anger occurring as well. This one took me quite some time to see and believe in myself, because I was a flexible, relaxed, nice guy who loved everybody, right? Let me use an example to highlight the process.

Let's say Jim has a boss who is the worst. He demands long hours out of all his employees, berates them if they don't get everything done just the way he wants, and threatens to demote or fire people if they displease him.

Jim really needs this job; it pays well and he has two small children at home and a mortgage on a new house. How do you imagine Jim feels in this situation? That's right, stressed. He feels his time is scarce, as if there's more to do than he has time for. He feels nervous before meetings, and worried that he might be the one to receive his boss' wrath that day. He adopts a pleasing attitude towards his boss and other seniors, hoping to get on their good side as he keeps his head down and does the best job he can.

What else is Jim feeling? Pissed. He's angry because there is a part of him that does not like to be treated that way. That part hates all the demands and the stress. That part certainly does not like the berating and threats from his boss. That part is mad as hell and wants to tell his boss to shove it (and maybe much more). Now Jim might be aware of this, or he may not. It really depends on how fused he is with his nice-guy mask. If he's aware of it, he may talk himself down and say, "I know, it's terrible. But hey, we gotta pay the bills. Just stick with it for one more year, then you can move to a different company that's better." This allows him to push the anger down just a little, so he doesn't spew it out in his next business meeting. This is called suppression, and it's something we do all the time.

If Jim is not that aware of his anger, he may just feel stressed. He may be irritable with his wife and kids because it's safer to be angry at home than with his boss at work. This is called displacement. A lot of his anger might be repressed, which means it's pushed down and hidden. His nice guy persona is so effective; it heads all this anger stuff off at the pass, long before it reaches his conscious mind. Because Jim is a nice guy. He doesn't want to hit his boss in the face with a baseball bat. How outrageous and absurd. (Although I bet if I made a joke about hitting his boss with a baseball bat that Jim would laugh and love it.)

As you read about Jim, what are you seeing about the ways you build up anger and resentment in your own life? This example is extreme, but resentment is a subtler form of anger that is happening all the time in all of us. Moreover, the nicer you are, the more resentment you have. Because we hate to be mistreated. We get secretly angry and enraged when someone threatens us or berates us, like Jim's boss. And when we're walking around the world as ultra-nice people, we are treating everyone around us as if they're Jim's boss.

Think about that for a moment because it will blow your mind. If you're anxious about pleasing others, and you're worried about what others think, and you're afraid they will reject you for your looks, for the way you talk, for how smart you are, for being not good enough… what are you imagining others are like? Harsh, judgmental, critical, quick to reject, intolerant, and dismissive. This makes you super anxious because their opinion means a lot, often more

With each injury, once it occurred, I ceased that activity forever. My life became more and more restricted. My perception of myself as having a weak body that was defective and destined for injury became more and more entrenched. Little did I know that it was all due to being too damn nice.

What? How on earth could being too nice cause stomach pain, irritable bowel, TMJ, back pain, wrist pain, or plantar fasciitis? Those are physical conditions, aren't they? Well, yes, and no. They are definitely physical conditions, and are extremely painful. There's no denying that. However, the part that is misunderstood by many people is that they are not caused by a structural problem in your body, but an emotional problem.

HOW NICE CREATES PAIN

Remember Jim's anger in the last section? Well it turns out that part of Jim really doesn't want him to become aware of that anger. The same is true for us. We all have what are called "defense mechanisms." These are ways that our mind attempts to minimize our emotional pain and discomfort.

For example, one classic defense mechanism is denial. If something painful is happening, you simply declare it is not happening. If things are going downhill fast in his marriage, a man might tell his friends, and truly believe, "My wife loves me. She thinks I'm the greatest guy in the world." If someone smokes cigarettes, they are generally in a state of denial about what impact this is having on their body and what the consequences will be down the line.

These defenses exist to minimize the experience of uncomfortable or painful feelings, such as anger, hurt, fear, terror, sadness, and grief. They often operate below our conscious awareness. Hence, we rarely think: *Hmm, I'm starting to feel some terror about knowing life is impermanent and I'm going to die. I'm also feeling deep grief about my brother being ill. Now, to defend myself against these feelings, I'm going to maximize my stress about work and focus on my upcoming project as if it's life or death.* Instead, we just feel stressed about this damn project at work, check our email forty-seven times per day, and worry about what will happen if we don't pull it off perfectly.

When we were trained to be nice growing up, we learned that certain feelings are acceptable, such as happiness, gladness, gratitude and excitement. Other feelings, like sadness and fear are less acceptable and should be kept to a minimum. Other feelings, like anger and aggression are in their own category and never OK. Especially anger at family, loved ones, people who've done things for us, and so on.

When an unacceptable feeling starts to form in our mind and body, our defenses kick in to keep it out of awareness. It's tagged as "not OK," and labeled as a threat. This can make us feel anxious simply about acknowledging and feeling an emotion.

Anger and rage at our boss, spouses, kids, neighbors, friends, or anyone else can be seen as highly threatening to our identity and sense of self. *I am a good person. A loving person. A nice person. I don't feel those terrible things.* But what if these feelings start to build up to the point where we may notice them? Enter the ultimate defense: physical pain.

This is the perfect defense because it's absorbing and distracting. Have you ever woken up with a neck so painfully sore that you could barely turn your head? How much do you think about that during the day? Heck, how much do you think about that per minute?

Ow, yep. It's still hurting when I turn it that way. Man, this is bad. Is my pillow too soft? Was it from sitting too long at the computer yesterday? Then I went to the gym and did those pull-ups. It was all those pull-ups. I'm doing those wrong. I wonder what I'll do tomorrow for my workout. I may have to cut those out. Why does this keep happening to me? This is so annoying. I bet I have a rib out. I should set up an appointment with my chiropractor...

The pain is completely absorbing and provides the ultimate distraction from our underlying threatening feelings. Now we're stressed, afraid, and self-pitying. These feelings are miles away from the threatening rage or sadness underneath.

3. Go to the TMS Wiki. It is an amazing resource with endless stories of how people healed and eliminated a wide range of physical problems using the methods from Dr. Sarno's books: http://www.tmswiki.org/

4. Watch this short clip on YouTube of a 20/20 segment where they interview Dr. Sarno: https://www.youtube.com/watch?v=vsR-4wydiIBI

(Clips are sometimes removed from YouTube, so if this one is no longer there, simply go to YouTube and do a search for: "John Sarno 20/20")

I wish you all the best on your journey, and would absolutely love to hear our story of breaking free from physical pain and limitation. You can email it to me at: DrAziz@SocialConfidenceCenter.com.

4. POWERLESSNESS

Another specter than haunts you when you're nice is a feeling of powerlessness. This makes sense, because you are. At least as long as you're living by the self-imposed rules of the nice person.

Living by these rules, you must put others first, be extremely accommodating, only do what others want, only express the parts of you that others will like, avoid speaking your mind, and be quiet and polite. These rules are robbing you of your power and force.

As a result, you don't feel like you have much impact or influence in the world. Other people are promoted ahead of you, other people are chosen for opportunities, and other people get dates and find love. You are waiting on the sidelines, being nice, and playing by the rules.

As we do this, we have the unspoken expectation that goes something like this. If I'm nice and play by all these rules, then life will bring me good things. People will like me, respect me, hire me, promote me, date me, love me, and be my friend.

The problem is this plan doesn't work. It doesn't bring you the things you really want. The nice stance is inherently a passive one. It's the path of avoidance of discomfort and hoping that life will magically turn out the way we want it to. It's a life of fear with a thin rationalization: *I'm choosing to live this way because it makes me a "good person."*

To challenge those rules and change how you are in the world can stir up anxiety and guilt. I can't become "one of those people." Those selfish jerks and assholes who just take what they want from others and from life. And so we decide to stick to the same game, but just play it harder. Be nicer, more pleasing, more accommodating, more giving, and more polite. Eventually, this will all pay off. Eventually my time will come.

This disconnection from our power removes our personal agency, our sense of "I can make things happen." When this is gone, we fall into a victim stance towards life. As I talk about in my book, *The Art of Extraordinary Confidence*, the victim stance severely limits our capacity in life and destroys our confidence. It leads to a phenomenon called learned helplessness, where we train ourselves to see things as out of reach or impossible, so we don't even try.

I want closer friends, I want a girlfriend, I want a husband, I want a better job, I want to start my own business, I want to feel more comfortable around others, and I want to date more easily. All of these desires are things we wish for and hope for, but don't actually make a reality. Because we've bought into the excuses and stories that tell us it's too hard, too scary, too uncomfortable. We tell ourselves self-defeating stories, such as: *I just can't do that, I'm not good enough at talking with people*, or my personal favorite, the vague, *there's something wrong with me.*

All of this is nonsense. They are excuses and stories we generate to keep us from having to face our fears and take action. The nicer we are, the more powerless we feel, and the more trapped we become in this land of hesitation, self-doubt, and inaction.

In what areas of your life do you feel powerless? Where are you wishing things would be different, but you don't really believe they can be?

5. ISOLATION

The final specter of niceness is particularly sad and ironic. We do all this nice stuff, put others first and sacrifice what we want, and try so hard, all because we want to be liked, to be loved. We try to be nice to others so they feel good around us and want to spend more time with us, whether it's friends, colleagues, or a new lover. We show up as our best selves, hold back our judgments and criticisms, focus on other people, and are attentive, kind, generous, and caring. We do the right thing. We are good people.

We hope this will give us a deep sense of love and connection. A feeling of closeness, intimacy, and the joy that can come from those sweet experiences. Yet, this feeling is elusive, and hard to come by. Even if we talk with colleagues, spend time with friends, or go on a date, we still feel lonely. We don't feel deeply connected to others, and we don't really trust that they absolutely love and adore us. We can't rest easy in knowing we're loved and held. Instead, there can be a chronic underlying feeling of loneliness and anxiety.

This sense of isolation is another direct result of niceness. Because when we're being nice and people respond well, something is a little off. They might like you, or even love you, but they don't really *know* you. They know a part of you; they know your mask or persona. And while this might give you some connection in the form of people to hang out with and talk to, it doesn't give you the connection you really seek.

This only comes when we share more of ourselves with others. When we are able to remove the mask and share what's really going on–how we really feel and think, including our fears, desires, challenges, and dreams. This also includes expressing ourselves. If you're silly, or like to do funny voices, or passionately sing classic rock songs with your eyes closed, this needs to come out as well. It's not just what you share that makes you. It's also how you share it, how you show up, how life moves through you.

And nice is a big stop sign on all of that. On the sharing, the vulnerability, the authenticity, and the self-expression. It is a controlled, managed, and rigid way of being in the world, which keeps the real you trapped.

Whew, what a list. What did you notice about yourself as you read about these specters? Which ones tend to haunt you the most?

Do you want to live the rest of your life dealing with these same challenges? Do you want to feel perpetually anxious about people's approval, guilty about not doing enough for others, and scared of them being upset? How many more years of anxiety, resentment, physical pain, powerlessness, and isolation do you want to live with?

These are important questions to ask yourself, because they will activate dissatisfaction with the way things are right now. That is a good thing. Because that discomfort can create a powerful force inside of you that steps up and says, "NO! No more. I will not live this way." And that's exactly the force you will need to propel you right through the bars of the nice person cage.

In just a moment, we are going to turn our attention to exactly how to do this. How to break free finally to become the most powerful, free, confident and authentic version of yourself. This version of yourself also happens to be the most charismatic, charming, attractive, loving, and successful one as well.

However, before we do, we must take one moment to see if you're ready. Because here's the truth. Breaking out of years of nice person conditioning isn't a one-step instantaneous process. It isn't an easy quick fix that involves no discomfort or effort. It isn't a machine that shocks your stomach muscles while you sit on the couch watching TV until you have rock hard six-pack abs.

Instead, it's a process. It's a process that can transform your self-esteem, relationships, and life, but it requires commitment. Let's take a moment to determine your level of commitment before we move to the next chapter.

FIVE LEVELS OF COMMITMENT

The five levels of commitment are a way to assess how committed you are to any process. They are described quite well by Dr. Robert Wubbolding, who is a pioneer of Reality Therapy, along with William Glasser.

Level 1: Lack of Commitment

Strong resistance characterizes this level and statements like: I don't really want to do anything different. I like ____ (smoking, drinking, pleasing others, etc.).

Level 2: Outcome without Effort

This level is full of wish, hope, and fantasy. I want to lose weight and get in great shape. I want to be able to walk up to any attractive stranger and just casually start talking to them. I want to start my own business, get a promotion, or make X amount of money (insert large number here).

We do want all these things, but we don't want to make the effort. We don't want to take action consistently over time. We don't want to do any work at all for the outcome. We just want it now, quickly and easily. This level is characterized by a lack of any significant action. Instead, we have numerous reasons as to why we can't get what we want, because either the outside world is preventing us (excuses), or we are not capable to make it happen (stories).

Level 3: Trying

This level of commitment indicates we're actually willing to do something. We're willing to try things, take action, and begin to take steps in the world to create the outcomes we want. However, as I say in *The Art of Extraordinary Confidence*, trying is weak. It means we will take action until we hit something difficult or challenging, and then we'll quit.

This level is characterized by phrases like, "I'll try," "Maybe," and "Probably." We might say, "Ok, this week I'll try to start conversations with some people at that networking event," or "I'll probably approach some women at the party. Maybe, if I feel like it."

Underneath this language is this mentality: *I'll do just enough to get by.* I see this level of commitment all the time in clients. If they're uncomfortable speaking up in meetings, they'll think: *Ok, I'll work on this confident speaking up thing just enough to get a little better at it, to not be completely silent. That's good enough.* Or, if someone wants to work out, they think: *what's the minimum I have to work out per week to get into ok shape?*

The bare-minimum-to-get-by standard is the calling card of the dabbler and never leads to mastery. It also rarely leads to great outcomes, consistent results, wealth, love, or happiness. By rarely, I mean never.

Level 4: Do My Best

This level is where things really start to heat up. This is when we start to take consistent action, face our challenges head on, and step up in life. This is where we start to notice progress and results, which feels good. This might even seem like the top level of commitment; however, it still leaves the door open for giving up.

We may put our all into something for weeks or even months. We put in effort, energy, time, money, and our motivation and intention. We do our best. However, we still aren't getting the results we want. When this happens, many people will say, "Well, I did my best. I guess I'm just not meant to get X or achieve Y."

This of course is false, but it does make a plausible story. We now can quit, stop putting in the effort, and go back towards the safety of our comfort zone. We may even feel good about how hard we tried, and how we "gave it our all." However, little do we know that we are actually worse off than before. Now, back in the safety of the center of our comfort zone, we also have this poisonous belief: *I did my best and I couldn't get the result. That means I never will.*

That's why you need to step up to level five.

Level 5: Whatever It Takes

This level of commitment leads to results. Period. This was my level of commitment many years ago when I decided I was going to turn off my video game and start looking for solutions on how to become more confident approaching women and dating. It's the level of commitment you've made on any major endeavor that you've stuck with and succeeded. Anything that required effort over time, required this level from you.

The reason this level is so powerful is that it cuts off all exit routes. There is no escape. If I don't know something, I'll need to learn it. If I'm scared to do something, I'll need to face it and overcome it. If I believe I can't, then I must.

This level is so powerful because it shows us repeatedly that our mind's predictions about what is possible for us are completely arbitrary and usually wrong. We stop believing in the predictions of our Safety Police and start getting into more and more action, faster and faster. Moreover, that's when we achieve incredible breakthroughs in short periods.

So, when it comes to shedding the unhelpful elements of your nice person patterns, how committed are you? What is your level of commitment to take consistent action to break free and live as your most powerful, expressive, authentic self?

Really, take a moment to slow down, breath, and check in with yourself. Don't just instantly say "Five!" and keep reading. See where you actually are. Are you going to "try this out a little and see if it works right away"? (Level 3) Are you secretly hoping that you'll find the magic bullet in a chapter later in this book and it will instantly remove all discomfort and fear forever? (Level 2) Or are you willing to step up, face fear and discomfort, do new things, and experiment with being in the world in different ways until you truly discover who you really are? Are you willing to do whatever it takes?

In any area of life, dabbling will get you very little. In case you aren't familiar with the term, dabbling is when you try a little, then quit when it gets difficult or uncomfortable.

We all dabble in something. I've dabbled at learning Spanish. I get a book, get excited, and dive in... until chapter three. I buy a course like The Rosetta Stone, and practice it passionately... for four days.

And guess what? I don't speak Spanish. I never will. Not unless I decide, deep down, that I am going to speak Spanish. That I must do it. Then, I'd be on the path of mastery and it would only be a matter of time until I became fluent.

The same goes for shedding nice conditioning and stepping into your authentic, powerful, loving, and successful self. Reading a few chapters will get you virtually nothing. Maybe some excitement, hope, or insight. But nothing will truly change, or profoundly transform, unless you decide you are going to do this. To commit to this. To master it.

Take a moment right now and ask yourself, "Am I going to dabble or decide?"

Am I going to read a few chapters, feeling the excitement of promise and the sparkle of possibility that a new book brings?

Or am I going to dive in fully, go deep, and *use this book to transform* how I show up in the world? Am I going to read it, study it, underline it, do the activities and exercises inside it, and keep returning to it until the job is done?

Take a moment now to ask yourself these questions. The answers you come up with determine the course of the rest of your life.

In fact, take a few minutes to write out a list of all the ways that being too nice is holding you back in your life. What is it costing you? What has it caused you to miss? What pain does it force you to live in on a daily basis?

Then consider the flip side. Write out what it would be like to be free of all this. What would your life be like if you weren't afraid of other's opinions? What if you could freely be yourself without worry about what they would think? What if you could say no when you needed to without guilt or fear? What if you could ask for what you wanted, and receive it much of the time? What if you could handle confrontations with calm and bold assertion? How would all this feel? What would this powerful version of you be able to create in your life? What kind of relationships, business, or personal success could it bring?

Take some time to consider the cost of nice and the benefits of being more powerfully yourself. Write them down and focus on them. This will allow you to get leverage on yourself, so you're fully committed to do whatever it takes to break free.

If you're in, continue on to the next chapter, and dive into Part II of this book. You will find a wealth of insights, activities, and strategies that will guide you to achieving your freedom.

If not, I'd suggest re-reading the first part of this book, especially this chapter about the costs of nice. Honestly take in just how limited your life is, how anxious or depressed you really feel on a daily basis, and how powerless and hopeless you feel about your love life, friendships, or career. Let yourself feel the pain and discomfort of it all until it reaches a breaking point. Until you get so fed up that you decide with force and conviction, "That's it. Forget this. I'm done living this way. I'm ready. I'm ready to do whatever it takes."

Then your life will never be the same again...

Once you're clear in yourself, take it one step further. Find a friend, your spouse, or someone in your family who is supportive of you growing and becoming the best version of yourself. Don't go to

Uncle Frank, who spends all day watching TV and thinks personal growth "is for wimps who need to man up and see that life is tough and then you die." Find someone who is on the same page, and share your commitment with them.

Share what you are learning in this book, and how niceness is causing pain and holding you back. Share your vision for how you want to be in the world, and who you want to be. This act of sharing with someone close to you is significant. Once it is spoken and known, it becomes real. It sets things in motion inside of you that are not even visible until months or years later. It's powerful, and it's worth it. After all, you're willing to do whatever it takes, remember?

Thank you. Thank you for your courage, your honesty with yourself, and your desire for freedom. I honor and respect you for it, and I see you as a brother or sister on the same path. I love you, and I am so excited to share the way out with you now.

ding niceness is the answer. If you read each chapter that follows, and apply what you learn, there is no end to the quality of life you can create for yourself.

And, to remind you, this section is not about making you a "self-centered asshole who just takes whatever you can get from others." This is the common misconception about breaking out of nice: That you will automatically just flip to being some sort of terrible sociopath who hurts others.

The reality is that making these changes will make you a *better* person. You will become more powerful, more direct, and more assertive. Others will notice your strength and authenticity and be drawn to you, which will open doors in your business and personal life. Because you know yourself, can ask for what you want, and can say "no" when you need to, you are not overtaxed, overwhelmed, and resentful. You can actually give more joyously, connect more easily, and love much more fully.

Not only that, but shedding your excessive niceness and being more authentic actually brings out the best in others as well. It frees them up to be more genuine, encourages them to advocate for their needs, and treats them like the powerful creators they are in their lives. It creates clearer communications, more productive meetings, and better resolutions for conflicts and disagreements. You being less nice truly does make the world a better place.

I'm like you. I want to be successful, but I also want to be happy. I want to be loving and patient with my kids instead of cold, angry, or irritable. I want to have harmony, intimacy, deep sharing, and passionate sex with my wife. I don't want to be distant, live like roommates, bicker, criticize, or have hurtful fights that involve attacking each other's vulnerabilities. I want to be an inspiring leader in my business. I want my team to speak freely, challenge me, support me, and have fun working with me. I don't want them to fear me, secretly dislike me, degrade me behind my back, and wish they had a better job. I want my clients and customers to feel cared about, inspired, challenged, and respected. I want them to feel like they got so much value out of their investment that they can't put a dollar amount on how much better their lives are now. I don't want them to feel let down, uncared for, like a bother, and that their growth and success is irrelevant to me. In short, I want to be a "good person" too. However you define that in your world, I'd imagine it's pretty similar.

And here's the big secret: The path to doing all the stuff I just mentioned is different than what you've been taught. Going down nice-guy or nice-girl lane will not get you there. It's counterintuitive, but being less nice will actually create a more positive impact in your life and in the lives of everyone you touch.

For example, I have more boundaries, more directness, and speak up for myself in my relationship with my wife more than I ever have in any other relationship. I speak my mind, share my perspective, bring up things that are bothering me, and ask for what I want. I'm more aware of my own needs and I find ways to prioritize taking care of myself, even though we have two small children. And in spite all of this assertiveness, which in the past I would have thought of as "mean," "pushy," or even "selfish,"[3] we have a truly extraordinary relationship filled with love, sweetness, passion, growth, and mutual support.

And that's not just me saying this, Candace would agree. Watch:

ME: Honey, do we have an amazing relationship?
CANDACE. Yes. Yes we do, Aziz.

There you have it. Indisputable evidence. If you would like to find out what she says in more detail, go to NotNiceBook.com. There you will find an interview with Candace about niceness, authenticity, and extraordinary romantic relationships.

Trust me, this path truly will completely change your life for the better, and I am so glad you are joining me on it. Let's begin by describing the 30,000 foot view of how this whole process works.

---

3. Ahh! The dreaded "S" word. More on this in chapter 10. Look out.

BOLDNESS TRAINING BOOT CAMP (BTB)

As I was writing this book, I had many conversations with Candace about nice versus not nice. She, like me, grew up with a large amount of nice programming and had done quite a bit of personal growth to become more free and powerful. Whenever something would come up that involved being assertive or confronting someone—friends, family, construction contractors, etc.—I would encourage her to speak up for herself.

One night, during a discussion about being more assertive and direct with others about her views on parenting, Candace exclaimed, "Whew! This not nice stuff isn't easy. It's like a boldness training boot camp!" That name was too good to pass up, so behold! Welcome to your Boldness Training Boot Camp.

To liberate yourself from niceness and unleash your boldness and power, you do need to recondition and train yourself. You have countless unconscious, habitual responses to situations that might cause you to respond with niceness, submissiveness, guilt, approval-seeking, and conflict-avoidance before you are even aware you're doing it. That's why we highlighted all the core features of niceness in the first part of this book, so you can become better at catching when you flip back into nice mode. Then you choose differently, again and again.

Here is a high-level map of how this process will work in your life:

HOW IT WORKS

Here is the three-step process for eliminating excessive niceness and becoming a much more authentic, confident version of you:

1. Decide to be not nice.
2. Do the not nice stuff that makes you scared and uncomfortable.

3. Work through the internal backlash (guilt, anxiety, doubt, fear) afterwards.

Then do it all again. If you continue in this process, and do not stop, over time you gain more power and stop being so anxious about other people's opinions of you.

Most people never make it that far because they get stuck in Step 1. They never decide to "not be nice" because they equate that with being a bad human. You, on the other hand, may have already decided to be less nice and more bold after reading Part I of this book. Or, you may not quite be there yet, and you may decide to be more authentic and direct after reading Part II and gaining more clarity.

Even if someone decides they don't want to be nice, Step 2 often trips people up. How many times have you decided you are going to be more assertive and direct, or speak your honest opinion in a situation, or confidently approach people at a party, only to get there and stay small, quiet, and on the sidelines? Right in the moment of action our boldness and resolve leaves us, and we quickly revert to our nice and safe behaviors. Then, afterwards, we might beat ourselves up about it, which in no way moves us forward. It's just an unhelpful pattern that operates outside of our conscious control.

But let's say you're on a mission. You are not going to be stopped. You decide you're not going to be nice. You face your fear and speak up, or say no, or put yourself first for once. Success! Right? Sure, but it doesn't feel that way.

What I saw in myself, and in clients who are breaking free from niceness, is an intense discomfort after being less nice in a situation. This can arise as guilt for what we said or did: *Oh my God! They must be crushed after I said I didn't like their favorite movie!*

It can show up as fear, anxiety, or worry: *What did they think of me for speaking up like that? Hector did not look happy. He thinks* anyone thinks of you. You are completely relaxed, comfortable, and confident in yourself no matter what… What would you do? Take two minutes now to really think about that.

Now, let's turn some of those images and ideas into a quick list. Just write out a list of things you might do if you had no fear, no guilt, and no doubt in yourself.

For example, maybe you were seeing images of yourself smiling at others as you met them, being charming and smooth. Maybe you saw yourself interrupting and shutting down Andy, that jerk who always interrupts you at work, or telling off Janet for all those times she lied to you. Maybe you imagined yourself being a head honcho or powerful leader in your work or career.

If this were the case, then your list would look like this:

I'd smile and be charming with people I just met.
I'd interrupt Andy and give Janet a piece of my mind.
I'd be a powerful leader in my company.

Make sense? Don't overthink it, just keep it quick and simple. And don't censor it or make it look pretty. This is not for anyone else, and this isn't a polished mission statement or ten-year plan. This is just for you. As always, I'll play along too. Because if I'm not getting a little uncomfortable, and getting my hands dirty, then how am I growing right alongside you as we do this? So here we go. Let's both go make our lists. Start with this phrase at the top of the page:

"If I had no fear, guilt, or doubt, I would…"

Ready? Let's do it now.

Good. How did it go? Was it easy to come up with things? Hard to imagine? Did it make you uncomfortable in some way even to create the list? Sometimes just imaging being more fearless, badass, and guilt-free induces fear and guilt.

Don't worry about that. As long as you were able to create something, you're in good shape. If not, then I'm afraid you will die a terrible, terrible death. No, I'm kidding. But you won't get nearly as much out of this section, or this book if you're just a passive viewer along for the ride. If you step up, play full out, and are willing to do whatever it takes, then you will break through to a new level of power and confidence that will make all the work worth it.

I noticed that my list was just a few things at first. I sat back and smugly congratulated myself. It must be because I've done so much boldness training and confronted so many of my fears that I indeed do most of the things I'm scared of. I clearly am awesome. And then I thought of something else to add. And then something else. And I started to reflect on my recent interactions—with colleagues, clients, and people I just met. I started to see the subtle ways I still hold myself back out of fear, or niceness. And my list grew. Here's what I came up with:

I'd email my list about group openings.

I'd email my list about things more often in general.

I would personally invite 10 people to my Mastermind program.

I would more passionately tell people about what I did for work, what my mission is.

I would talk more about my accomplishments.

I would be even less nice.

I would change the subject more often.

I would end conversations more quickly with some people.

I'd say what I was perceiving more during conversations, even with people I just met.

I would be even more irreverent, and make more jokes, even with people I just met.

I'd amuse myself more in conversations.

CHAPTER 7:

HAVE BOUNDARIES

As you will see in the chapters to come, boldness training is all about speaking up for yourself, saying "no" when you want to or need to, and prioritizing yourself instead of always putting others first. These, and many other behaviors, will transform your sense of power and freedom. However, if you don't understand boundaries or, worse, don't have any, then all of these liberating behaviors are just a fantasy. They're science fiction. Things you wish you could do, but seem far off, impossible, and maybe even "not allowed."

Now I know the topic of boundaries might sound a little boring. *Why are we starting here? Shouldn't we dive into the "say what I want and tell others to shut it" part of the book?*

Here's the thing: If you don't have boundaries, you won't know when to tell others to shut it. You won't know what you actually want, because all you're aware of is other people and what they want. Without boundaries, there is no you to speak up for!

BOUNDARY-LESS

"Imagine there's no countries, it isn't hard to do."
- John Lennon, *Imagine.*

I spent a long time with very few boundaries. Although I didn't consciously know this at the time. In fact, if you would've asked me what my boundaries were, I would've given you a blank stare. In fact, I prided myself on how flexible I was. I thought of myself as someone who was easy going, who could "go with the flow." And then, after reading books like *The Power of Now,* by Eckhart Tolle, and other eastern philosophies, that idea of myself was reinforced. *I'm not identified with my mind and my beliefs, man. I don't need to hold any strong opinions, or debate anyone. That's all just ego stuff anyway, and I'm above that now.*

Sounds good, right? Except it wasn't true. I wasn't easygoing and at peace most of the time. I was tense inside. I had chronic stomach problems and pain in my neck, wrists, and shoulders. I disliked certain coworkers and colleagues, even though I was jovial and easygoing on the outside. And I couldn't sustain a romantic relationship longer than several months. All of this was related to a lack of boundaries.

The truth is I didn't know where I ended and other people began. I didn't have a clear sense of who I was in any given moment. That might sound abstract or philosophical, so let me give a few examples to make it clear. If I was in a conversation with someone, I would be very aware of what *they* were feeling, and what *they* were wanting. I'm very perceptive and sensitive, so I was quite good at this. In fact, most nice people are. You probably are. It's like having some kind of x-ray vision where you can see through people's outer layers, their outer personas, and see how they're feeling underneath.

If I noticed sadness, frustration, anger, tension, disappointment, or any other painful feeling in them, I would instantly feel obligated desire and ask for it. In some instances, you may decide to override your want and let it go. But that comes from a place of self-love and choice, not fear and shame.

It's time to stop smashing down this piece of who you are. It's time to turn inwards and re-discover what it is you *really* want, across all situations in your life. Below are some empowering beliefs you can choose to adopt right now that will help you get more in touch with what you want.

It's good to discover what I want
It's good to ask for what I want.
It's good to say what I want.
It's good to say what I don't want.
It's good to be able to put myself first.

(That last one might be a doozy for you. We'll talk more about that in Chapter 10, which is all about the dreaded S-word: Selfish.)

These statements are all true. These are a part of your upgraded, more accurate map of human relationships. In any relationship, whether it's with a colleague, boss, friend, or your life partner, identifying what you want and being able to express it will enhance your relationship. A chronic pattern of being unsure, never knowing what you want, looking to others, letting them make the decisions, and always putting them first will create resentment in you, frustration and resentment in them, and eventually create distance that erodes the relationship.

In addition, if you perpetually look to meet the needs of others, and disregard what you truly want, you diminish over time. You have less energy, vitality, and passion. You feel less happy and fulfilled. Over time you whittle away and have little to offer others because your cup is so empty.

Hence, if you want great relationships, and you want to feel better in those relationships, it's good to discover what you want, ask for what you want, say what you don't want, and be able to put yourself first sometimes. You may be nodding your head as you read this, intellectually realizing that this is all true. Let's take a moment, though, to bring these ideas out of your head and into your body and emotions, because that's what makes the difference between information and transformation.

In fact, give yourself some time to focus on these new empowering beliefs. Write them out ten times in a journal, or fifty times. Repeat them often to yourself. Put them on a note card and carry it in your back pocket. Then throughout the day, when you have a few moments to kill time, instead of flicking on your phone and compulsively checking news, sports stats, social media, or something equally unproductive, take a few breaths, slow down, and read through your little note card. You'll be amazed how much this will open up the floodgates. Because, being aware of your desire and expressing it freely isn't some unnatural new ability you have to train yourself to do, like juggling. This is one of your most basic, innate, hardwired abilities that is right there underneath the surface as soon as you stop pushing it down.

WHAT IF I DON'T KNOW WHAT I WANT?

This is a common question that arises as you begin to look inward and pay attention to what you actually want. At first it can be quite confusing because so much of your life may have been based on what other people want, and what you "should" want in order to be a good son, daughter, employee, friend, spouse, and so on.

At first you may be confused and uncertain. Your mind might say: *I have no idea. I don't even know what I want!* If so, that's perfectly normal. It's a natural part of the process. You'll get better at identifying your desires over time. Until then, don't be fooled by your mind's hasty conclusions that you don't know and will never know what you want.

Sometimes, when we say, "I don't know," we don't really mean, "I don't know." What we really mean is "Ack! This is uncomfortable. I feel uncomfortable and don't like what's happening right now. I want it to stop and I want to just go back to how I felt before, even if it was kind of miserable!"

I see this all the time in sessions with clients in my coaching and group Mastermind programs. When someone says, "I don't know" in response to a question, there often is a tone of frustration or irritation. They are conveying either, "I don't know, and I'm frustrated that I don't," or "I don't know, now back off. I don't want to know."

We push against discovering what we want because it can be uncomfortable to do so. First, we bump up against our negative beliefs about desire, so we can feel a subtle sense of shame just for paying attention to what we want. *That's so selfish and bad!* Then there's fear about what we might discover. What if I don't want to spend time with that friend anymore? What if I'm secretly feeling disengaged and bored during sex with my partner and I want something to be different? *Bad! Selfish! Wrong!* And then we're scared about what we've discovered because that might lead us to speak up and actually say no to somebody, or bring up an uncomfortable conversation with our partner or anyone else. *Eek! That's freaky. You know what? I just don't know what I want. I don't know. I said, I don't know. Now back off!*

Yes, it's scary. And it's worth it.

To help in this process, we want to adopt an attitude of lightness and curiosity. Instead of *I don't know!* try out Hmmm, I don't know… Invite in curiosity and wonder. You're about to learn something, to discover something, to uncover something fascinating and valuable in your life. *I wonder what it could be. I wonder what I'll find out.*

And it's OK if you experience confusion. We are complex creatures and made up of many different parts. Part of you wants to spend time with that friend, and part of you would prefer to be alone. It seems like no matter which one you choose, there will be some sadness or missing out by not having the other option. That's OK, too. Let yourself miss the other option, even as you pick the first one.

The sense of freedom, ease, power, and confidence we want doesn't come from picking the "right choice" in all situations. It comes from looking inward, asking ourselves what we want, and honoring what we discover. Even if we don't choose it, or we don't get what we want, the simple act of valuing your own desires creates positive feelings of power and freedom.

WHAT DO I PERCEIVE?

Right up there with knowing what you want is knowing what you think, believe, and perceive. When our boundaries are weak, we tend to have a very shaky hold on these sorts of things. We automatically look to others to determine what our thoughts and opinions might be. We look to others to determine our reality for us.

You may experience this as a lack of certainty in your perceptions and convictions. You may not have a strong opinion on much of anything. You also might feel quite a bit of self-doubt about what you say, whether it's right, or if others agree with you. In fact, you might even pride yourself on this. I know I did for years.

I would tell myself: *I'm just a more flexible and open-minded person. People's opinions and beliefs are all based on their ego's need to be right anyway. I just don't buy into that as much.* Never underestimate our ability to make ourselves feel better than others when we unconsciously feel inferior and insignificant.

While some of this is true—I am a very curious and open-minded person and don't tend to lock into debate battles with people about their opinions—I also didn't have a strong sense of myself. I didn't value what I thought or perceived in that moment. I assumed others' opinions were more intelligent, better researched, and more valid than my own.

Part of having solid boundaries, and being less of a nice person involves owning your perspective. Valuing it, acknowledging it, and being willing and able to share it. It doesn't matter if someone in the company has been there longer than you, or that person has read more articles on the subject than you. That doesn't mean you don't have insight, ideas, or a unique and valuable perspective.

The first step to boldly and confidently share your perspectives in any setting begins internally. If you have a negative habit of valuing other opinions too highly, and as more valid than your own, then you'll never really be sure of what you think in a given situation. It leaves you feeling confused and unable to express yourself, limiting your happiness and impact in the world. Imagine if Martin Luther King didn't stand up as a leader of the civil rights movement because he didn't trust his own perception that oppression was unacceptable. What if Tony Robbins stayed working as a janitor because he didn't think his ideas mattered?

It's time to interrupt any nice-person habits that keep you from owning your perspective. Stop hypnotizing yourself with the story that you don't know enough about the subject, or that other people are smarter and you should just agree with them and keep silent. Uncovering what you think about a situation is the first step in being able to assert yourself.

Start looking inward in all settings–at work, in meetings, while speaking with your boss, with your spouse, your friends, and your parents. Ask yourself, "What do I think about this? What's my opinion? What's my perspective? How do I see the situation?"

You don't have to even voice this at first. You just have to assess where you stand internally. Notice if you agree with what someone is saying, or disagree. If you disagree internally, don't immediately push that away with rationalizing and telling yourself to be more flexible and open-minded. Instead, honor that difference. Let yourself think: *Hmm, I don't know about that.* Again, for now, you don't need to worry about speaking up, what to say, and how to disagree in conversations. We'll cover all of that in Chapter 9.

SMARTER, BETTER, MORE CERTAIN

Sometimes it is hard to honor your perspective because you're not so sure inside yourself. Maybe you don't know what you think about something, or where you stand on a topic. This might be from a lack of practice of discovering and honoring your perspective. In fact, you may have years of habitually assuming your thoughts, opinions, and feelings about a subject don't matter much. But as you examine what your perspective is more and more, your sense of certainty will grow stronger.

You also might be automatically assuming that other perspectives are more valid because you deem them as smarter and better. Part of this might be due to their age, experience, or status. It might also be a response to the level of certainty they have when they communicate. If they sound confident, it can automatically create a sense of uncertainty or doubt inside of you.

But remember this: Certainty does not correlate with accuracy. Just because someone *sounds* certain, it does not mean that what they're saying is accurate. It also doesn't mean that it's more thought out, researched, or backed by anything at all.

People Just Say Stuff

I remember one moment in graduate school when this became glaringly obvious to me. I was in my third year of doctoral training to become a clinical psychologist and had a good deal of uncertainty about my skills, knowledge, and ability to help people. Other people were more confident in their approaches, their theories, and what they would do in any situation. They had strong opinions about different methodologies, medications, and treatments. Everyone seemed to have it all together.

One morning I was sitting in group supervision with a seasoned psychologist and several other practicum students and interns. We were in a community clinic where we provided counseling to a wide variety of clients of all ages and backgrounds. One of my colleagues was confidently asserting a theory about how to intervene in a specific situation involving children. She was saying something to the effect of, "The research shows that you must do A, and not B." Her tone was decisive. She implied that if you do B, then you're an idiot.

Something sounded a little fishy, though. I didn't think that B was quite so bad, and I was curious to learn more. So, I said, "Interesting, I haven't heard that before. What research did you read that said that?"

"Well…" she replied, sheepishly, "I saw it on *Supernanny*."

I kid you not: *Supernanny*! The British TV show starring Jo Frost who does dramatic turn-arounds of naughty children. Nothing against Jo Frost, and I don't doubt that she's helpful, but that is hardly "the clinical research" that my colleague was throwing around moments earlier.

In that moment the curtain was pulled back and I saw Oz was just a little gray-haired man, frantic and uncertain, hastily manipulating controls in order to look all-knowing and all-powerful. I realized this is happening behind everyone's facade, from doctors, to TV experts, to your seemingly confident boss or CEO. Those people might have a lot of experience, insight, and factual knowledge on various topics. And, they are prone to bias like the rest of us, are uncertain about all kinds of things, even in their field of expertise, and often just fill in the gaps with as much certainty as they can muster.

I remember another conversation I had with the head psychiatrist in another clinic one morning before a meeting. He was the clinic co-director and the head honcho. He sat drinking his coffee and eating a scone and he said, "This whole anti-gluten craze just boggles my mind. There's no scientific evidence that gluten impacts people in all the ways they say it does." He continued to strongly and assertively share his opinions about the foolish people who avoided gluten.

I found the topic fascinating and had been personally exploring the effects of gluten on my body. I had not come to any strong conclusions yet, but I was curious about what his sources were, because he was indicating that it was a well-researched medical opinion.

That weekend I was spending time with a good friend of mine who had just completed his medical school training. I asked him how much research and training students had around the topic of diet and nutrition and its impact on health.

"We had one seminar on that." He said.

"Like one ongoing class? For how long, like a quarter or a semester?" I asked.

"No. One, three-hour seminar on diet, nutrition, and how food impacts disease."

Now, I have no idea if the psychiatrist at my clinic studied dozens of hours of nutritional information on his own time, although I highly doubt it, given his seemingly poor diet and general appearance of sub-optimal health.

The truth is people just say stuff. They package it in certainty and lean on their education, experience, or status to make it sound like it's highly researched and valid. Start to pay attention to this phenomenon around you. Question the sources of people's knowledge, and start to see through the illusion that others' opinions are more intelligent or important than your own. Start to look inward and find your own thoughts and feelings about the subjects you encounter in your daily life.

MINE AND YOURS

One of the most empowering and liberating benefits of having boundaries is to know where you end and someone else begins. More specifically, you know what is your responsibility and what is someone else's.

Without boundaries, this distinction is completely unclear and leads to the over-responsibility challenges we discussed in the Guilt-Bubble chapter. The sum of this problem can be described in this simple, highly inaccurate belief that we carry into all our relationships: *If something is happening in you, it must be due to me.*

If you're upset or angry, it's because I've done something wrong.

If you're disappointed or sad, I must have fallen short or done something to let you down.

If you're hurt, I must have said it wrong or done something wrong.

It's all my fault. Your feelings are my fault, I did this to you. And now it's my responsibility to fix them, and fast.

This is a reality that many people buy into. You can have entire relationships where both people are completely hypnotized by this illusion. They have lots of fights that consist of volleying accusations back and forth at each other: "You did this to me, and then you did that to me, and you made me do this, and made me feel this way!"

If one person is honest and shares a challenge they're having in the relationship, the other person exclaims in pain and horror, "How could you say something like that to me?!" This is a defensive maneuver that is designed to shut down any sort of scary or uncomfortable conversations. Nine times out of ten it will work in the short term, especially if the person bringing up the complaint is nice. They will feel bad for bringing up their challenge and stuff it back down, going into apology and damage control mode. Now the conversation is about how mean or bad it was to share that hurtful thing, instead of addressing the underlying issue. Problem solved!

In all seriousness, this pattern doesn't really work in the long term because the problem is never addressed or resolved and doesn't just go away by itself. The one who uses guilt to shut the other person down is doing so because they're scared of painful feelings, criticism, or being left. Of course, by blocking communication they are inadvertently bringing about the very thing they are trying to avoid. Over time they are much more likely to experience more painful feelings, and the other person most likely will leave them.

In order to have thriving, healthy romantic relationships, solid friendships, and effective and enjoyable work relationships, you must find a way out of the trap of over-responsibility. You must be able to distinguish between what is yours and what is somebody else's.

"One often meets his destiny on the road he takes to avoid it."
- Master Oogway

YOU ARE NOT RESPONSIBLE

I am going to make a bold, simple claim here that might seem extreme or absolute. In fact, it might go against every nice-person bone in your body. You might challenge it, or have lots of questions about it. And that's all OK. Ready?

You are not responsible for other people's feelings.

Take a moment to sit with that one. Breathe in and out. Re-read it several times. Try the personal version out: *I am not responsible for other people's feelings.* I am not responsible for my coworkers' feelings, my boss's feelings, my client's feelings, my friend's feelings, my wife or husband's feelings, my kid's feelings, my mom or dad's feelings—anyone's feelings.

How does that feel to say that to yourself? Liberating? Relieving? Perhaps a little uncomfortable or wrong, as if you're saying something bad or cruel? Whatever is happening inside you, simply slow down, breathe, and notice.

We want to slow way down here because our minds, and nice-person programming, can fire up quickly and try to shut down this line of inquiry. Nice Police sirens start wailing and this dissenting, Not-Nice idea must be captured and removed immediately! *Bad! Wrong!*

In fact, your mind might start sputtering: *Wait, wait, what if I just told my kids to shut up, and told Barry at work that I hated his fishing stories and didn't want to hear them anymore, and told my husband to step up and stop whining so much? I mean, doesn't what I say and do matter? What if I say critical or hurtful things? I can hurt people. I am responsible!*

Or, you may not be having such a strong reaction. You might be calmly thinking that you agree with the statement above. It intellectually makes sense to you. But if you imagine actually being more direct, saying what you really think in specific situations in your life, you feel anxiety or guilt. This might indicate that you intellectually agree that you're not responsible, but emotionally you feel responsible for the feelings and actions of others.

You may think this is part of being a good, kind, thoughtful person. And there is some truth to that. To have the awareness that your friend is self-conscious about the fifteen pounds he's gained and not say, "Geez, Larry, you've really let yourself go. You look like a tired, bloated old man!" is probably a good thing. Some containment of our immediate thoughts and reactions is valuable in relationships. Sometimes, if we're seething with rage or resentment, it's best to just be quiet for a few minutes in order to calm down. To not send that text, or email, or storm into the kitchen and start ranting at our partners.

But we can take this too far. Way too far. We can start to assume that *anything* that might lead to a negative reaction or uncomfortable emotion in someone else is inherently wrong and a bad thing to do. So instead of having only more extreme things on our "bad list," like yelling or harshly criticizing others, we start to add things like: asking for what we want, disagreeing with someone, telling someone we don't like something or are upset, changing the subject during a conversation, or speaking up for ourselves and challenging someone in a meeting.

Thus, more and more behaviors become taboo. We start to view others as fragile creatures who couldn't possibly handle any discomfort or upset. We start to view ourselves as extremely powerful demigods who can crush the hearts of others with a few simple words. We think to ourselves: *I couldn't possibly do that to her; that would break his heart; he'd be crushed; she couldn't handle that.*

The reality is *you* couldn't handle that. Or, to use more accurate language, you don't want to experience your own discomfort about another person having strong feelings. It stirs up too much. It pushes your buttons and you don't like it.

There are two main problem with this approach. First, it will never create lasting and satisfying relationships. This is because close relationships inevitably include discomfort. It's impossible to not have moments of disappointment, hurt, conflict, sadness, and anger. When we believe a relationship should only involve happy, loving feelings, and never include discomfort, we avoid all topics and conversations that are uncomfortable. This keeps relationships superficial, distant, and lacking passion. We keep everyone at a safe distance. While this might avoid a certain kind of immediate discomfort of going into messy feelings and conversations, we also miss out on the deep joy, happiness, and fulfillment that can come from fully connecting with other humans. We end up feeling deeply alone inside, in spite of having loving people all around us.

The second problem with the avoid discomfort approach is that it keeps you and others stuck as victims of circumstance in life. I discuss the difference between being a Creator in your life and being a Victim in more detail in my book *The Art of Extraordinary Confidence.* The short version is Victims see life happening to them. Forces outside of their selves determine how they feel, what they do, and whether or not they have the life they want. *I'm mad because my boyfriend's a jerk. I'm stuck in my job and my boss sucks but I can't do anything about it.* That sort of thing.

A Creator, on the other hand, realizes this: If my life is not the way I want it to be, then it's my responsibility to change my attitude and approach to my circumstances. Over time, and through consistent action, I can create the life I want. I won't get there by blaming others, telling myself that I suck, or any other avoidance maneuver. I must step up, face my fear, and take bold action again and again.

When you treat others as fragile, as if they can't handle the truth about what you want, how you feel, or how you think, you are perceiving them as Victims. When you take responsibility for them, you are keeping them in this Victim stance. *How will they feel if I say this?*

Here's another question for you. Are there people who don't want to be connected and similar to others? People who want to be different? Want to be more significant? Or people who create their identity by challenging others, debating, disagreeing, and proving others wrong? People who want to be certain, want to be right, more than they want to get along? Absolutely. And I'm sure you've met a few of them.

How on earth could we possibly meet these people's needs? What if their rules for how their needs can be met are completely unrealistic? What if they are prioritizing significance and certainty and it never feels like enough to them? In all of these cases, it's going to be very difficult for them to feel at peace. They themselves will have a very hard time making this happen. How are you supposed to do this for them? Impossible. Insanity.

It's time to let it go. You will never be able to make anyone and everyone feel happy. At best you can temporarily meet some of their needs, sometimes. Which is fantastic news. Because you are not responsible to meet all their needs—they are! What a relief.

Now that you have even more clarity around what you are not responsible for, and what you can just let go of, let's turn to some practical tools that will help you do just that.

Peace Process

This is an extremely helpful tool that I learned from one of my mentors, Christian Mickelsen. It's a specific type of meditation that can be done sitting with your eyes closed, lying in bed, or as you drive, walk, and carry out other activities.

You can use this every time you feel guilt, anxiety, or any other upset about someone else's feelings. Actually, you can use this anytime you feel any unpleasant feeling at all, but for now let's focus on using it to release over-responsibility.

Take a moment now to think of a person or situation that tends to provoke a sense of guilt or anxiety. Perhaps you are afraid of hurting their feelings, over think what you will say, and feel afraid of upsetting them. Maybe whenever you meet someone new, you tend to take responsibility for their feelings and you get very tense. You worry how you're coming across and if you're making them uncomfortable. Once you start to feel that uncomfortable, guilty, anxious, unsettled feeling, congratulations, you're right on track.

Now, simply bring your attention out of your thoughts and into your body–right to where you feel that uncomfortable feeling most. It might be a tightening in your stomach, a squeezing in your solar plexus (the area in the center of your body right below your sternum), or a burning feeling in your chest or throat. Take a few breaths and scan your body with your awareness until you find the feelings and then bring your attention right to the center of them.

Breathe. Soften and relax your belly, soften and relax your jaw. Often times we unconsciously tense up our bodies in response to an uncomfortable feeling, trying to brace ourselves or get away from it. The Peace Process is the exact opposite of that habit. Instead, we move towards the uncomfortable sensations in our body. Right into the center of it. Like slowly easing yourself into a cold swimming pool or a hot bathtub. Our impulse may be to pull back, but if we just relax our bodies, we can ease in a little further.

As you breathe and move towards the sensations in your body, notice your attitude towards these feelings. Most commonly, we don't like these feelings because they're uncomfortable, and we want to be rid of them as soon as possible. Our stance towards them is one of frustration, impatience, and irritability. *You again? Uggh. I don't have time for this.* This frustration, resistance, and avoidance is the very thing that keeps us stuck in the feeling for hours or days. The key is to surrender.

Surrender to the feeling. Just let it be there, without trying to fix it, figure it out, or solve it with your mind. Each time you notice yourself thinking about the feeling, or anything else, gently bring your attention right back to the sensations in your body. Just breathing and feeling, nothing else to do right now.

You can experiment with the statements above or come up with one that works best for you. The key is to remind yourself of what is actually true. Much like when we first catch on fire, our default pattern when someone is upset is to frantically scream in our minds, "They hate me! We're all gonna die!"

Remember, what really makes someone upset is the perception that they're not meeting their needs. If you've let go, and don't feel responsible for "fixing" their feelings and making everything instantly better and smooth, then you can consider if there's something you can do to help them meet their needs. This is coming from a very different place than the approval-seeking pleaser who is scared of the emotions of others. This isn't coming from fear, it's coming from a desire to connect, love, and contribute.

From this place, we can ask ourselves, *What might this person need?* Do they need a sense of certainty or security? If you notice they seem anxious or unsettled, this might be what they need. Are they feeling unappreciated, not good enough, unsure of themselves and their abilities? Perhaps they need some significance. Or maybe they just need some love and connection. Just take your best guess and then experiment with ways that you might help.

For example, in the case of someone needing certainty, you might provide reassurance: "I can see you're worried about not getting the project in on time. I know it's a high-pressure situation. And I also know that you've done so much amazing work for this company, and that they need you. Even if you miss this deadline, they're going to want to keep working with you for a long time."

If someone is needing significance, you can acknowledge or appreciate them for something specific. Give them a compliment for something they did well. Highlight a quality or characteristic in them that is positive, that you admire. Give them praise.

If it's love and connection, you might lend a listening ear. Hear them out. Empathize with them, and share your own experience so they realize they're not alone.

If you're not sure what they need, guess what? You can ask them! This sounds so simple, yet I didn't realize it was a valid option for years. It's not only valid, it can be the most supportive and effective way to help someone when they are struggling. In a curious and patient tone, ask them, "Do you know what you need right now?" or "What do you think would support you best right now?"

These are just a few examples of the dozens of ways you can support, help, and contribute to others. **Once we've let go of taking responsibility for others' feelings, it frees us up to focus on them and really give them what we can in the moment.** We're no longer focused on ourselves, tense and worried about whether they'll like us or not. We can show up more powerfully, and serve more deeply.

This is yet another example of the Not Nice paradox. When we're trying to be nice, please others, and be a "good person" who everyone likes, we end up becoming way more self-absorbed. We don't approach the person who's struggling in an effective or helpful way. We either avoid them because we're scared, or we come out guns ablazin', trying to hastily fix their feelings because we can't tolerate their upset. But when we let all this go, we end up being way more attentive, focused on others, loving, and helpful. We end up being better people by letting go of trying to be "better" people.

SURRENDER
THE APPROVAL QUEST

*"You can be the ripest, juiciest peach in the world,
and there's still going to be someone who hates peaches."*
- Dita Von Teese

By now you are probably aware that an endless quest to get people to like you is somewhat misguided. You might be seeing how strong your desire for approval has been, and how this desire has reduced

What is your purpose?

I am here to eradicate social anxiety and instill confidence. To smash through fear, doubt, hatred, and criticism. To bring power, boldness, authenticity, humor and love for myself, and for as many people as I can on the planet. I am here to take care of my family, to create an extraordinary love with Candace, and to give my children all I can to support them in becoming powerful leaders in their own lives. I am here to be a Warrior of the Light. To positively impact as many people as I can during my life, and afterwards through what I can create. I am a force for good, a force for God.

If you have not done this exercise, I highly encourage you to stop now and do it. Strengthening your reality and sense of self has a powerful effect on your inner confidence and self-esteem. It also directly impacts those around you, as they see you as more self-assured, powerful, and as a leader.

<u>YOU WILL BE DISLIKED</u>

"This book is trash. I wish I'd purchased the paper copy so I could wipe my ass with it."
- Audible Review for *The Solution to Social Anxiety*

At the time I'm writing this, there are 7.4 billion humans on this planet. And that number just keeps going up. Barring massive calamity or world order collapse, estimates for the year 2100 range from 11 to 14 billion people. That's a whole heck of a lot.

We hear numbers in the billions, and even trillions, quite a bit these days, as it relates to national spending and budgets. But few people actually grasp how large these numbers really are. If you were to take a single US dollar bill and lay it on the ground, it will measure just under 6 inches. If you laid out 100 bills just like that, end to end, it would be 614 inches or about 51 feet (or 15.5 meters for my international friends). So far so good. Do you know how long 1,000,000,000 (one billion) dollar bills would be? Take a guess now.

96,900 miles (about 156,000 kilometers). This would be enough to wrap around the entire earth almost four times. A billion is a huge amount.

There are 7 billion of us humans running around. The vast, vast majority of these people will never even know of you and your existence. If 500 people know you, which is a lot of people if you think about it, that means you're interacting directly with .00005% of the humans on the planet. If you do something that brings more attention to yourself, such as writing a successful book or being in the media, that number may be slightly higher. In any case, the majority of humanity doesn't know about you, and doesn't really care.

And when it comes to the people you do know and interact with, how much control do you really have over what makes them like you? It's way less than we'd like to admit.

THE MAGIC NUMBER 62

Once I was working with a client named Mira who really didn't like the idea that some people could dislike her. She intellectually understood that this was inevitable, but she hated it emotionally. She also kept asking, "Yes, but doesn't how I show up determine whether people like me? If I am charming, or funny, or warm? This will make people like me more, won't it?"

That's when I came up with the Magic Number 62.

"Imagine you walk into a room that has 100 people in it that you don't know," I said during one of our private sessions, "total strangers. Let's say you had the confidence to approach each person in that room over the course of the day and talk with them. With each person you were able to be relaxed, open, curious, and comfortable. You shared who you were, what you liked, and found out more

CHAPTER 8:

OWN YOUR SHADOW

For the last few months, my wife and I have noticed an interesting pattern with our first son, Zaim. He's just about to turn three years old and is, as most three-year-olds, a little wild man. Each Monday and Friday we have a nanny, Alexa, who comes for five hours to help watch the boys while my wife takes care of essential tasks and her own needs. We noticed that after the nanny left, Zaim would go on a mini-rampage. He'd scream, knock things over, try to throw items off the counter and be much more likely to hit his younger brother. Full-on destructo-mode.

At first my guess was that he was upset that Alexa left because he enjoys playing with her. I would ask him about it and empathize that it was hard to have her go. This seemed to help a little, but it certainly didn't make a big difference. Neither my wife nor I had a better idea, so we stuck with the "contain and empathize" approach for a little while, until one day when my wife was home while the nanny was over. She overheard a fascinating conversation that changed everything.

While my wife was taking care of tasks in the kitchen, she overheard Zaim and Alexa playing a game with stuffed animals in the living room.

ZAIM: Arggh! T-Rex is going to fight you. Fight!

ALEXA: Let's have T-Rex hug instead.

ZAIM: T-Rex is going to fight you. He's going to kill you.

ALEXA: Oh no! I don't like killing games. Let's have them be friends.

This is by no means a rare occurrence. I'd known for a while that Alexa was a very nice person, in all the ways described in Part I of this book. Of course, she would want to guide Zaim to be nice too.

As soon as I heard this, I had an idea. The next time Alexa left, I ran over to Zaim and said, "Let's play a chasing game!" He was intrigued and his eyes brightened as a big smile expanded across his face. As we raced around the house, I came across the T-Rex stuffed animal. I picked him up and abruptly stopped to turn towards Zaim. "T-Rex is going to fight you!" I announced dramatically.

"No, I'm the T-Rex!" Zaim declared, grabbing the stuffed animal out of my hand.

"Ok, I'm the Triceratops!" I replied as I grabbed another stuffed dinosaur.

We fought it out so hard with those dinos. They flew in the air at each other, smashed each other, cast magic spells at each other, and killed each other. It was glorious. And it was extremely calming for Zaim.

How come? Because he'd just spent five hours with someone who represses her own shadow and unconsciously guides him to repress his. This creates a pressure that he then needs to release in the form of agitated, destructive, and aggressive energy.

The one major difference between a three-year-old and an adult, is that the adult can be much better at stuffing their shadow and keeping it out of sight for much longer periods of time. This makes it subtler, often out of our conscious awareness, and takes a much greater toll on our lives.

WHAT IS THE SHADOW?

Nineteenth century Swiss psychiatrist Carl Jung was the first person to coin the term "shadow," although many before him described the "darker impulses" of humans. **Your shadow is made up of all the qualities that you learned are unacceptable in society.** This includes thoughts, feelings, impulses, and actions that you learned are bad, unacceptable, and bring on disapproval and a loss of love.

Each person's shadow is slightly different due to the unique messages they received from their family, school, religious community, and peers. These specific messages shape what you see as acceptable attire, how to speak with others, what's OK to say and not say, and so forth.

There are also certain qualities that are generally held in the shadow for most people in most societies. These include things like anger, aggression, physical violence, sex, masturbation, selfishness, and greed. Basically, think The Seven Deadly Sins from Catholicism (pride, greed, lust, envy, gluttony, wrath, and sloth).

From a very young age we begin to pick up on what is good and what is bad. Sometimes this is directly taught to us through reprimands or punishment ("Don't hit your brother! Hitting is bad!"), and other times it is learned through observation of adults and listening in on their conversations. Regardless of how we learn it, we quickly realize there are ways we should be and ways we must never be. Sounds a bit like the Nice Person training we talked about earlier in this book, right?

Well, there's one interesting twist here. All of those things that you learn not to do don't just disappear. The desire to hit your brother, take his cookie, and eat it right now is still inside of you, you just learn how to suppress the impulse.

In this chapter, you are going to discover much more about your shadow and how it holds the key to liberate you from the cage of excessive niceness. First, we have to expand who you think you are...

<u>YOU ARE NOT JUST</u> <u>A "NICE PERSON"</u>

I'm sorry to break it to you. You're not just a nice person. You're not *only* kind, loving, generous, good-hearted, patient, wise, smart, pro-active, and responsible. I'm not saying you aren't these things. In fact, you may have many or even all of those qualities. But guess what? You're also selfish, self-centered, judgmental, impatient, impulsive, greedy, and careless.

Ouch.

Now before you throw this book across the room in defensive disgust, hang on for one moment so I can explain. I am all these things, too. We all are. Because we humans are animals, even though we often forget this fact, and we are extremely complex. In fact, we share a large amount of our core brain structures with reptiles. This part of our brain is primarily concerned with keeping ourselves alive, securing a mate and having sex, and maintaining power and domination over others so that we can secure said mate and sex.

We also have a highly advanced emotional brain that we share with all mammal species. This makes us focused on deeply connecting with others, helping them out as they help us out, and devoting ourselves to taking care of our young children. And then we have some super advanced stuff going on in our neo-cortex that no one fully understands yet. This sucker evaluates scenarios and acts with higher order reasoning, ethics, and other abstract concepts. It allows us to time travel to the future and envision things that do not yet exist so that we can create them. And it taps us into something so miraculous that we experience self-aware-ness and consciousness.

This combination is incredible and makes us a most miraculous species. And at the same time, it can be quite confusing, especially if you think you are just supposed to think or feel only one particular way, that your mind is just one singular entity rather than a collection of parts that can vary greatly in their desires and intent. Once you realize this, and start to accept and own your shadow, you become more clear, and more relaxed with all parts of yourself. This reduces guilt, fear and anxiety, and greatly increases your power in all areas of life.

YOUR INNER DREAM TEAM: ID, EGO, SUPEREGO

Alright. It's time to get Freudian on yo ass. Back in the day, Sigmund Freud spent large amounts of time speaking with patients who would candidly reveal their deepest secrets, desires, and impulses. It was during the Victorian era, when there were especially strong societal pressures to repress sexuality, vulgarity, aggression, and anything else that was deemed lewd, crude, or otherwise uncivilized.

Freud discovered that while people followed the rules of the society and outwardly seemed docile, pleasant, chivalrous and civilized, inside they were full of all kinds of desires and impulses. It appeared that each person had what Freud referred to as the "Id." This was a part of people's psyche that was made up of unrefined and unfiltered instinctual impulses. This includes sexual impulses and desires, and all forms of anger and aggression, including rage, violence, the desire to dominate, and the urge for revenge.

The Id is driven by what Freud called the "pleasure principle." It wants instant gratification and pleasure, and it wants it now. The Id is not concerned with societal rules, what others will think, and what the impacts of our actions might be. It is raw feeling, desire, and impulse. And it's inside all of us. Yes, even you.

This is apparent if you've ever spent any amount of time with a three-year-old child. He wants the cookie and he wants it now. If he doesn't get what he wants, he can feel strong emotions of sadness, frustration, and anger. He gets enraged. He has an urge to break or hit things. Look out little siblings, a storm is coming. No patience, all pleasure.

Of course, the vast majority of humans are not running around immediately gratifying their impulses, raping and pillaging, and generally running amok in society. This is where the Superego comes in. Your Superego is your internal moral police force. It carries all the rules you've learned about what it takes to be a good, moral, and respectable person. It knows how you should be. Thou shalt not hit, steal, hurt, take for yourself, disregard others, be offensive, rude, etc.

When you feel guilty, that's Superego at work. *How could you do that? That poor person. You just walked over them and took advantage of them by being so direct and forceful with your tone. Bad, bad, bad!* When you have a million things you "should" do, that's your Superego doing its thing.

Then, to mediate and manage the whole situation, enter your Ego. This is the part of you that takes into account the impulses of the Id and the commandments of the Superego and tries to figure out how to operate in the world. This part of you knows the reality of the world around you, that you can get in trouble if you act out of line, and so he restrains many of the Id's impulses. He also knows that if you only did what the Superego wanted and completely cut off the Id that you would go insane or be utterly depressed and miserable. So he brokers deals.

Id sees someone you're attracted to and says, "Sex. Now!" Superego sees the same situation and says, "Sex out of wedlock is bad," or "Wanting sex right away makes you promiscuous and bad," or "Sex without getting to know someone first is hurtful and wrong" (depending on whatever your unique conditioning has taught you). Ego says, "How about we walk over, introduce ourselves, get to know them and see what happens?"

As you walk towards them, you see an attractive, charming person swoop in and start talking with them first. Id says, "Kill them! Throw your drink on the floor and scream!" Superego says, "Violence is bad and wrong, be nice." Ego says, "OK, showing any sign of anger or jealousy will reduce your appeal in their eyes. Stay cool. Wait a few minutes until they're done talking and then move in."

And on and on it goes. All day, every day. Your Ego is hard at work, managing the wide disparity between your Id and Superego.

So, what does this trip down Freudian lane have to do with being less nice and more boldly yourself? It turns out quite a bit. Because guess which of these three parts is the biggest proponent of "nice"? That's right, your Superego. And most nice people are completely identified with their Superego. They think they are that completely nice, loving, generous, gentle, patient, serene, "good" person. Any evidence that creeps into their awareness that shows they might not be is threatening and met with strong internal pressure to shape up, and get back to being good. As a result, the Superego runs the show, attempting to completely deny and eliminate the Id. After all, that's what a good person does, right? Overcomes her animal impulses and acts like a good and moral person should?

In theory. That's what we're taught by well-meaning parents, school, and religious communities. But it doesn't work in practice. It breaks down, and leads us to be outwardly good and nice, and inwardly a mess. Inside we are tense, anxious, upset, sad, depressed, irritable, uncertain, full of doubt, and full of guilt.

Let's be honest, it's not really working. We need a new, practical approach that works much better, leads to greater ease, fulfillment, authenticity, and happiness. And don't worry, this new way actually makes you more free, expressive, loving, generous, and all the other ways you'd want to be as a "good" person in this world. It's just a very different path to get there.

WELCOMING THE SHADOW

One of the biggest challenges most nice people face is the intense internal pressure to be a nice person. Our Superegos have completely taken over and our sense of self, our identity, is that we are a nice guy or a nice girl. To even consider that we might not really be as nice as we think, or to have a desire to be less nice is morally unacceptable and it's offensive to even consider it. This is why many people become defensive and upset when you question the idea of being nice. It threatens the very core of their personality and how they've organized their entire lives.

Yet regardless of how much we deny it, or how upset we get at someone for suggesting it, the reality remains that we have an Id inside of us that is not so nice. True freedom begins when we acknowledge this fact and stop making it wrong, stop fighting it, and stop fighting with ourselves.

During my doctoral training at Stanford, I had an amazing opportunity to work closely with Dr. David Burns, author of *Feeling Good* and one of the world's leading cognitive-behavioral experts. I was involved in a small training group that would meet weekly with him to learn, practice, and master the skills of helping people change their beliefs and experience greater freedom and joy. One of the best parts about this training was that David insisted that the most effective way to learn was on real challenges that we were having, not abstract or made up role plays. I am deeply grateful for the insights and growth I experienced in those meetings.

On one evening a colleague of mine, Jeff, was discussing a challenge he was having in his workplace. He was in the advanced stages of his training as a psychiatrist and was completing his residency. There was a fellowship position opening up in the very same department he was working, and he was excited about getting the highly

TOP 10 THINGS OFTEN LURKING IN OUR SHADOWS

1. Frustration, anger, or resentment with people closest to you (partner, kids, parents, etc.)
2. Anger and judgmental thoughts about friends, colleagues, boss, customers, and clients.
3. Sexual desire of strangers, friends' partners, and other people you "shouldn't desire."
4. Sexual feelings and desires you or others might deem strange, bad, or inappropriate (use of pornography, fetishes, bondage, etc.).
5. Dissatisfaction with big life situations (your job, being a parent, your spouse, your city, etc.).
6. Grief, sadness, and pain of loss (both recent losses and all the way back to your childhood).
7. Deep uncertainty or doubt, including self-doubt, doubt of God, doubt of purpose, doubt of any meaning in life.
8. Strong sensitivity to people's comments, feeling deeply hurt and sometimes secretly enraged by them.
9. Desire for and fantasies about vengeance, retaliation, getting back at someone, or hurting someone.
10. Desires and impulses for physical violence (hitting, attacking, killing).

Rage Ball

Most people repress feelings of anger. Whether it's the irritation we feel with our boss, or our child as he pours milk all over the counter, daily life is full of small irritations that we need to suppress our reactions to. In addition, there's all the demands and pressures of our lives: showing up to work each day, handling projects, dealing with coworkers and customers, being a parent, paying your bills, making healthy food choices, fixing things and solving problems, and on and on. Being a responsible adult in this world involves many demands on your time and energy. This too produces anger. Remember, that Id in there wants fun and pleasure now. She doesn't want to sit in that two-hour meeting where you have to force yourself to stay awake and look alert as your boss tells another extended story about his past glorious escapades as a salesman for some company that no longer exists.

And these are just the *external* pressures. We also have all the *internal* pressures to contend with as well. The pressures from our Superego to be good, to be nice, to be giving, to be loving, to be generous, to forgive, to put others first, to do a perfect job, to not slack off, to give it our all and do our best all the time on everything, to do better at work, earn more money, spend less and save more, eat better, cook more at home, work out more, get in better shape and look better naked, be funnier, more outgoing, have more friends, not drink so much, not eat sugar, and for heaven's sake, just be better than you are right now!

What do you think all that pressure does to your little Id? Makes him as big as the Hulk. Each of those demands enrages your Id, it's the complete opposite of everything he wants. And the more pressure we pile on, the more he tantrums inside of us, the more enraged he becomes.

Even if we aren't aware of it, this buildup is happening inside. Consciously we put on our best smile and try to push through the day, being a good person. Sure, we may be aware of some annoyance or irritation at a coworker, or someone in traffic, but we handle things well. This is the image of the Superego, the image we want to portray to the world, and to convince ourselves of. But it's just not true.

If you are in physical pain, you're not "handling everything fine." If your low back hurts on and off for years, if you have plantar fasciitis and foot and ankle problems, if your neck and shoulders always hurt, if your jaw is tense and you grind your teeth at night, if your old knee acts up, or your stomach is acting funny again... you're not handling it well. If you feel anxious in the morning, stressed and irritated during the day, and depressed and negative about your life and don't know why because you have so much and you "should be happy," then you're not handling everything fine. If you compulsively check your email, your phone, stats online, social media feeds, the news, anything to absorb your focus, then you're not handling it fine.

You're agitated, uncomfortable, and hurting inside, and you need to face it. But don't worry, it's not all those dramatic thoughts that you might scare yourself with sometimes. Thoughts like: *I must be depressed and have something wrong with my brain; life is just hard and everyone is miserable; I'll never really be happy again.* These are all just another form of avoidance, albeit a scarier and absorbing one.

What you need to do is acknowledge your shadow and start paying attention to these feelings. You need to carve out time each day to go for a walk, or to write in a journal. You need to pay attention to your shadow and your Id, and to listen instead of pushing it further down. You need to finally own this part of you, so you can truly feel more alive, happy, and free.

CRAWLING SKIN

Just the other day I was writing in my shadow journal, which is something you'll learn about soon. I keep mine in a locked file on my computer so no one will ever read it. Heck, I don't even go back and read it. It's just a place for me to express everything inside of me that needs to get out. It's not meant to be pretty, read well, or make a point. It's full of typos and fragments.

It had been several weeks since I'd last written in the journal, and I was noticing pain in my shoulder and foot over the last few days. My mind, of course, dove at the chance to say I'd been running too much and working out in the gym. That's why I'd "injured" myself. Spontaneously, for no reason. But I know better by now, so I went digging around in my shadow to see what I was upset, hurting, sad, or angry about.

Sure enough, just below the surface was all kinds of messy stuff. Part of me was angry with my kids, my wife, my work, and my life. So, I let it speak and share whatever it wanted. This part of me was enraged when my one-year-old son, Arman, screams and screeches. He is in a phase where he expresses himself through screeches. Wanting more food, attention, or a nearby ball. It all requires an ear-piercing screech. While I generally handle it with patience outwardly, inwardly my Id was not happy about it. He wanted me to yell at Arman, and scream back in his face to make him stop. That was sure uncomfortable to imagine.

He went on to tell me how he didn't like how demanding the breakfast routine was, how much he hated taking care of the kids and being a parent in general. He hated all the responsibility, all the work, and the lack of time to do pleasurable activities.

This, of course, is the toned down version for you. When it came out in the journal it was full of misspelled run-on rants and expletives. It was not something I would want to show my wife or kids, or anyone really. But that's not the point. The point is to show myself. To acknowledge that part and meet him with patience, acceptance, curiosity, and love. To hear him out.

And, it sometimes makes my skin crawl. That's why we avoid it and hide in our distractions, anxiety, and physical pain. Because this stuff can be confusing and unsettling. It's uncomfortable to see how much anger is in there, and how enraged that part can

That's why you must own your shadow. You can think of those raw energies of desire, anger, aggression, and sexual impulse as the raw materials you might use to run a power plant. Your shadow is like the coal, the raging river, the natural gas, the nuclear reaction, or the bright heat of the sun. All of those forces are immense and can instantly destroy you if you let them take over. But when you harness them, you can use them to generate targeted, effective forms of power.

This is essential to understand as we move towards one of the core pillars of Anti-Niceness and topics of this book: how to speak up for yourself. Doing so requires energy; it requires power. And that power is going to come directly from your shadow.

For example, if you don't speak up in meetings, are ignored by senior management, and colleagues talk over you when you try to share your ideas, then you need to speak up for yourself. You need power to do so. And that power is going to start deep in your core as anger and aggression. It's going to be your Id saying: *What the f**k? How dare you talk to me that way? How dare you talk over me? Shut the f**k up, Gary! I'll kill you!* Of course, you don't actually kill Gary. Instead, this energy passes through a network of tubes and hoses inside of your body and mind and comes out as assertiveness: "Hold on a second, Gary, I'm not done. Let me finish my point."

Your tone as you say this is calm, yet firm and commanding. There is a power behind it that gives you an authority makes people pause and listen to you, and much more likely to heed your request. If speaking up is something you struggle to do–if you often desire or intend to but fear prevents you from doing so– you may be disconnected from your full power from years. If on occasion you do speak up for yourself, and you are overlooked, ignored, or bowled over after doing so, it may be time to harness the power of your shadow.

HOW TO HARNESS THE POWER

"You don't know the power of the dark side."
- Darth Vader

Don't worry, we're not going to turn you into Darth Vader, or the twisted evil Emperor Palpatine from the original *Star Wars* movies. There's a common misconception that acknowledging our shadow, or giving attention to it, will make it grow stronger. This is a fundamental premise in several dominant religious schools of thought. If you listen to the devil, it will seduce you into making bad or evil choices. Or, in the modern day positive thought or law of attraction movements, people say, "Don't focus on the negative stuff. That will just bring more negativity into your life, man."

While there is truth in these philosophies, and we can use them to better ourselves and our life circumstances, they are also missing a fundamental quality of human nature. **That which we repress doesn't grow weaker, it grows stronger.** If you had a dog that barked loudly or sometimes growled at people and you decided to solve the problem by putting the dog down into the basement and locking him in there for days or weeks, would that make him calmer and tamer? Probably not.

Once something is pushed out of awareness it "goes rogue" and just starts operating beneath our conscious attention. The further down it gets pushed and the longer it's repressed, the more intense, and sometimes twisted it becomes. This is where you get the unfortunately well-known example of the pious priest who only represents goodness and purity, but turns out to be molesting children. He has so disconnected from his sexuality, has pushed it so far down into the shadow, that it starts to become twisted and grows in power until it can take over.

A less intense example that we can all relate to is that of how we eat. Let's say you have a certain food that you don't want to eat because you

It also helps to breathe deeply as you feel the anger and other emotions. Deep, full breaths in and out. Fill your belly and chest with air. I also like to take the fingers of my dominant hand and gently tap on my chest. This, combined with the breathing, helps to move large amounts of anger and other emotions quickly.

Much like the journaling, after doing one of these walks I feel clearer, lighter, and refreshed. I am more resourceful in addressing my challenges and problems, and in dealing with people that may be frustrating or taxing.

THE BENEFITS

As you become aware of your shadow, stop rejecting it, and welcome it in without judgment, some amazing things will happen. You will start to feel lighter, more energized, and freer. That oppressive sense of badness, shame, and guilt will begin to lift, and you just might start liking and loving yourself.

This shift occurs because you've started to really pay attention, in a curious and non-judgmental way, to a part of yourself that desperately needs your attention. Instead of being at odds with yourself, running from and suppressing parts of you, you're becoming self-aware.

In addition, you start to become OK with who you are, and less concerned with what others will think. The things we're most afraid others will judge us for—pettiness, anger, jealousy, insensitivity, greed, sexual desires, and all the rest—we accept. We won't have to vehemently deny or defend the reality that part of us is sometimes selfish, or angry, or greedy. It stops being such a big deal. We become more at peace with all aspects of ourselves. And you will begin to see just how powerful you really are.

As this raw power grows, you will become ready to use it to boldly and unapologetically speak up for yourself. Socially, in your relationship, and at work, you will start to say what you think, ask for what you want, and speak your truth. You will say what needs to be said, even if it's uncomfortable. And as you do this, your entire world will transform.

CHAPTER 9:

SPEAK UP

"I don't want to be one of those spineless people."
- B.B.

Finally! The chapter about how to speak up for myself. Took long enough to get here, geez.

I know, this may have been the very reason you picked up this book. Perhaps you want to speak more freely around others, share your ideas more clearly at work and in meetings, challenge people who try to shut you down, assert yourself with your in-laws, tell your accountant when you have a problem with their work, or respond to your partner when he says something critical. There may be dozens of places in your life in which you are tired of holding back, being silent, playing nice, getting looked over, ignored, disrespected, pushed around, and otherwise "doormatted."

Trust me, you're in the right place. In this chapter, I'll deliver. You're going to learn how to unlock the cage that stops you from speaking up, and how to access your power and voice so you can freely share what you want in any situation. You'll also learn specific strategies on exactly how to speak up in different situations, including examples of what to say, and how to say it. We'll go into detail on how to speak up in the four key areas of life: sharing freely socially, speaking up at work, how to handle disagreements and other difficult conversations, and asking for what you want. In addition, you'll discover practical exercises to strengthen your assertive tone, speak with more certainty so you can influence others, and come across as a powerful authority, no matter what topic you are speaking about.

There's a reason why this chapter is this far into the book. It's because speaking up for yourself is only 10% strategy. Like almost everything in life, your success in this area is based on your inner game, which accounts for 90%. In fact, you can know exactly what to say, have it all planned out intellectually, but then in the moment, hesitate, hold back, and stay silent. Or say it in such a soft, tentative, and hesitant manner that no one takes you seriously.

Can you relate? Has this happened to you? This was a regular occurrence for me. I'd know what I wanted to say, and even how I should say it. Whether it was speaking up in a group or asking a woman out, I'd have it all mapped out in my head. But then, in the moment of action, the moment of truth, I'd hesitate, pull back, and say nothing. It was so frustrating and I often felt confused and stuck. I thought it was all about the "what." *What do I say?* I need to know what to say. I need to know the phrase for being assertive, how to interrupt people, and the "pickup line."

But the truth is, the "what" to say is very easy and can actually be quite varied. There are a million ways to do it. The inner strength, courage, boldness, and willingness to take a risk–that is what determines our ability to speak up more than anything else.

If we're living in a world where we think we *should* be pleasing and nice, we *should* take on responsibility for the feelings of others, we *should* only feel loving and never angry, then we're lost before we begin. We'll never be able to speak up. Because doing so will break our internal rules and leave us feeling anxious, guilty, and ashamed. We'll feel like a bad person who is unworthy of love and belonging, which is a pretty intense form of pain. And so, despite our desires to be bold, get results, be authentic, have great relationships, and create the life we want, we won't speak up and go after what we want.

However, now that you're shedding all those layers of nice-person programming, and liberating yourself so you can show up as your authentic self, you're ready to start speaking up.

To do this, we're going to uncover the reasons you're holding back, and help you upgrade your model of relationships so you have more permission to freely be you. Then we'll dive into how to be assertive in general, and in specific situations such as meetings, in romantic relationships with your partner, and when interrupting others. We'll also cover an extremely important topic, which is how to ask for what you want, and how to do so without feeling bad or guilty.

Are you ready? I'm excited. As you study this chapter, and apply what you learn, your life will never be the same again.

THE PEACEMAKER

If you've noticed that you have a pattern of hesitating, holding back, and not speaking up for yourself as much as you'd like, there's probably a reason for it. No, it's not what your inner critic says. You're not "weak, spineless, messed up, broken" or whatever other garbage stories you've told yourself. The real reason is that it probably made sense for you to act that way at some point in your life.

Most people who are nice were the peacemakers of their family. They weren't the loud, defiant, confrontational ones. On the contrary, they were the ones who hated that discord and found ways to minimize it as much as possible. When very young, this may have just involved holding back and not sharing needs, or not asking for as much to avoid being too demanding or putting too much pressure on others. As we got older and more sophisticated, it may have included talking with family members, trying to get others to understand each other, and doing whatever was in our power to keep peace and harmony in our families.

As an interesting side note, I've found with many nice people I've worked with, that they often have a sibling who is much more outspoken, direct, and naturally assertive. Their sibling didn't have to study how to be that way, learn assertiveness techniques, or how to speak up for themselves. It just came out of them. If anything, their sibling could benefit from holding back sometimes!

Clients will often ask why this is the case. *Why did I end up this way, and my sibling was so different? Why did I have to be the peacemaker?* That's a big question, and I'm sure a million different experts have a million different opinions. I'm not so sure having a story about the why would enable you now to be more bold and free. But, to satisfy your intellect (somewhat), I can share two very simple explanations. These are very practical and not based on deep academic theory, but simple observation.

WE ALL COME OUT DIFFERENT

First, we all come out different. As in, out of the womb. Having two children myself, I am amazed at how different they can be, starting at such a young age. This last Christmas we spent time with my wife's family in her hometown out in the desert in Eastern Washington. At one point, we drove to her grandfather's house for a short visit. We pulled up to the house, unloaded the crew out of their car seats, and crunched across a thin layer of snow on their lawn to the front door.

As we approached, some relative-in-law who I didn't know opened the door with an excited look on her face.

"Candace!" she said energetically.

As they hugged, we all bustled into the door. The house had a great layout with a large living room joined to the kitchen, creating a spacious, open feeling. This was a good thing because there were about thirty people in the house. Kids of all ages, uncles, aunts, grandparents. There was a big TV in the living room blaring a Seattle Seahawks game that was in the fourth quarter. There was a lot going on in there.

Within ten minutes, my three-year son Zaim was in a bedroom of the house, as far away from the noise and chaos as possible. He wanted me to go in there and play with him, away from all the commotion. If someone wanted to talk with him, he'd be hesitant and wary. "I don't know you," he'd say to them, before turning away.

After playing with him for a bit in the room, I convinced him to come out with me to get a snack. As we walked into the bustle of the living room, I saw my younger son, Arman (or "Mani" as we call him) surrounded by a circle of adults, kids, and onlookers. He was standing up, waving his arms in the air, then falling back down. He had a huge smile on this face. He was the center of attention and the life of the party, and he loved it.

We all just come out differently.

Another key factor I've noticed is tolerance. To illustrate this point, I'll use a fun example we can all relate to. Have you ever lived with a roommate or family member who had a different cleanliness standard than you? Perhaps they had no problem leaving a dish in the sink for a day or two. Or maybe you were the messier one. Either way, let me ask you this. Who did more of the cleaning? That's right, the one who could tolerate the mess less. Regardless of conversations about the topic, requests, plans, chore grids, or anything else, at the end of the day, the one who hated seeing that nasty dish in the sink would eventually break down and just clean it up. Because they hated seeing it in there. (Guess which one I'd be…)

The same is true for conflict. Across the board, when I speak about this topic with clients, they will all tell me how much they hate that feeling of conflict. When someone is upset with them, the sensations it generates in their nervous systems are strong and unpleasant. It's very hard to just ignore them and go about their day as if nothing were the matter. They have an overwhelming urge to make the feelings go away by "fixing it" and making things right (aka removing the other person's upset).

While feeling tense and uncomfortable when there is discord between you and others, especially someone close to you, is natural, we all feel it differently. Nice people tend to be more sensitive. We tend to feel things more strongly. We might even hear sounds more loudly, be more sensitive to smells, and our other senses. And we feel our emotions, and the emotions of others more intensely. There is nothing wrong with this, it's just how we came into this world. Just like there's nothing wrong with Zaim for wanting to get away from the noise and big energy and go somewhere quiet.

I happen to be very sensitive, which is something I would not admit for a long time. Because, as a man, is being "sensitive" a desirable trait? Absolutely not. At least not in my upbringing. When I was growing up, being sensitive was weak and shameful, and made you worthy of ridicule. So, I learned to hide and deny it. My wife has been extremely helpful in letting me see this in myself, and the beauty and strength in this quality. It helps me be more present and loving with her, my children, and do the work that I do in the world.

As you're reading this, and reflecting on your own experience, what are you seeing about yourself? Did you hate conflict, tension, or discord in your family? Did you try to stop it and make things better? And, most importantly, are you able to have a bit more understanding and empathy for yourself? Both then, and now?

Because we both know that you're not stuck in any way. Just because you've hated the feeling of tension and avoided conflict in the past, doesn't mean you'll never be able to tolerate those feelings and break through. In fact, with all you've learned so far in this book, and the tools you'll discover in this chapter, your capacity to speak up for yourself is going to transform. If, you go easy on yourself. If you're able to hold yourself with empathy, respect, and compassion. Because if you're beating yourself up, calling yourself a spineless, overly-sensitive wimp who should "just get over it," then you won't make it far. That won't give you the energy and power you need to expand, take risks, and grow. So, in the spirit of love, self-compassion, and infinite patience for yourself, let's look at why you don't speak up now.

TOP 10 REASONS WE DON'T SPEAK UP

1.	I don't want to offend people or hurt their feelings.
2.	I don't want to feel guilty afterwards.
3.	I don't want people to think I'm rude, mean, arrogant, pushy, or "an asshole."
4.	I don't want people to say yes because I made them.
5.	I don't want people to get angry and retaliate (directly or later on).
6.	I don't want to make things worse.
7.	I don't want to get flustered, show strong emotion, start crying, or show they "got to me."
8.	I don't want people to see me as needy, demanding, or "high maintenance."
9.	I don't want people to judge me (for how I'm feeling, what I think, or what I want).
10.	I don't want to do it wrong, lose my train of thought, look stupid, or lose others' respect.

THE THREE MODES OF COMMUNICATION

Which of these reasons resonate with you? Which two or three are the ones that hold you back most? Can you think of any others that are not on this list that keep you from speaking up?

Regardless of which particular ones influence you most, they all lead to the same result: staying silent. This puts you into the first major category of communication: passive.

Passive Pants

Being passive is really your only option if you don't want any of the feared outcomes listed in the chart above. If you've been taught, or convinced yourself, that speaking up is high risk with many possible negative outcomes, you will avoid doing so.

This forces you into the passive stance. In this mode of communication, you don't speak up for yourself, say what you like or dislike, or ask for what you want. But this poses a dilemma, because you are a human animal with natural desires and needs. So how do you attempt to meet these? Why, passively of course.

This means we silently hope people will know what we want and give it to us. We have internal hopes and silent agreements such as: *If I'm nice enough to you, then you'll give me what I want, without me having to ask for it. If I give you attention when you want it, then you'll give me the same when I want it. I won't say I want attention, I'll just imply it or suggest it and you'll pick up on the hint and give it to me.* So, goes the plan at least…

If we don't get what we want, or if someone does something we don't like, we get angry. This anger remains internal, however. Because to share it or show it leads to painful or threatening outcomes, so we dare not do that. So where does it go? Down into our bodies, messing with our energy levels and overall mood. But it also comes out. It has to. As humans, we must find a way to get what we want and express ourselves, no matter how much we fear the consequences.

The only way to express anger while in the passive mode is indirectly. This way we can always deny that we were angry. For example, we might let out a heavy sigh when asked to do something. If the person asks us if something is wrong we say, "no, I'm fine." We might be more distant, share less, be harder to get a hold of, or otherwise withdraw from the relationship. Or we might make slightly cutting comments or jokes that have an edge or sting to them. Or we may say things that induce guilt in others, subtly implying they're taking too much, not appreciative, or otherwise hurting us.

When asked or confronted about any of this, we simply deny it. And for many people who are rooted in the passive mode, they might not even be aware they are doing it.

This kind of behavior has been labeled "passive-aggressive" and has a negative connotation in our culture. No one wants to be accused of behaving that way. But that way of being is inevitable if we don't have permission to speak up. Someone who's communicating anger passively is not a bad person. They're just scared. Actually, they're terrified. Terrified that if they were to freely share what they think, directly ask for what they want, and reveal themselves, that they will be harshly rejected, ridiculed, abandoned, or some similar terrible consequence. This creates an invisible prison that limits all interactions and is a great source of suffering. I would know, since this was my mode of choice for more than ten years.

The core mindset of the passive mode is this: *Other people's wants and needs matter more than my own. Speaking up is dangerous and generally leads to bad outcomes. It's best to be nice—extra nice—and then others will give you what you want and life will flow your way. Besides, I don't want to be one of those aggressive assholes anyway.*

Aggressive Asshole

The other side of the spectrum is to be aggressive. This is a take-no-prisoners, no-holds-barred approach to communication. The core mindset of the aggressive mode is: *In life, you figure out what you want and you just take it. Don't let anyone stand in your way or treat you without the respect you deserve. My needs matter, yours are inconsequential.*

Of course, most of us don't think of it this way when we're in the aggressive mode. Very few people consciously identify as an "asshole." Instead, we have a good rationale for how we're behaving.

This person didn't get that report back to me in time. My kids were screaming too much. He showed up an hour later than he said he would. I deserve this position more than she does, I've worked harder to get here. Regardless of our reasoning, we are in it to win it. We're there to control the situation and the outcome as much as possible. We say and do what we need to, long term consequences be damned.

We berate our assistant for giving us the report late, yell at our kids to make them shut up, tell our friend he's always late and an inconsiderate jerk, and launch a calculated campaign to smear the image of our colleague. *It's only fair. I deserve it. They didn't do it right. They should have done this or that instead. My treatment of them is the result of their poor actions.* Or so our story goes.

It's rare for someone to spend their entire lives in just one mode. Hence, many people who are predominantly passive will hold all their anger and frustration inside, only to go crazy-balls Hulk at a random time in their life. Often times the aggression comes out most with family, children, spouses, and other people who are unlikely to leave us (at least right away). Passive with our boss, aggressive with our kids, for example.

Some people do spend the majority of their time in the aggressive mode of communication. It's unlikely they would pick up this book, however. Most likely you are more passive than you'd like to be in many situations and sometimes blow up and act aggressively. And that's OK. It doesn't mean you're a bad person. It means you're human, and similar to the vast majority of people. As your self-awareness grows, your courage increases, and your map of relationships upgrades, you'll find your way more and more to the third mode of communication: assertiveness.

The Middle Way: Assertiveness

If passive is on the far left of the pendulum swing and aggressive is on the far right, then assertiveness would be in the middle. It combines the beneficial elements of both the passive and aggressive modes of communication. The core mindset of assertiveness is: *My needs matter and so do yours. Let's have a clear discussion about what we both want to see, what might work best for us both. Sometimes I will choose what serves me, even if it upsets you. And sometimes you will do something for yourself, even if I don't like it. That's just how relationships work.*

This realistic approach to communication requires that we know what we want. Hence the focus earlier in this book on helping you cultivate a habit of identifying what you want in a given situation. Once we are aware of this, we speak up to actively pursue our wants and needs. This is similar in some ways to the aggressive mode of communication. We know what we want and we go for it. The major difference is we are more aware of others as we do so. We want to know what they want, and we want to see if we can create a win-win agreement. If that's not possible, and a decision we want to make generates negative feelings in another, we want to hear the other person and acknowledge their feelings.

This capacity to hear another's perspective and be influenced by it is similar to the passive mode. The difference is when we're assertive, we don't instantly change what we're doing to please them. In fact, you might decide to proceed, even though they're upset. This is a key area where assertiveness differs greatly from passivity. When we're passive, we don't go after what we want in the first place, let alone continue forward when someone wants us to stop.

There is great power in the assertive mode of communication. We can be more direct, more up front, and clear. We reduce patterns of beating around the bush and implying things, and instead simply say more of what we really mean. This makes us much more effective communicators. It also helps you get more of what you want. And, surprisingly, it actually makes others like you more.

This last insight is your key to liberating your voice so you can speak up freely and powerfully in any situation that matters. Most of us who lived in the passive mode learned that this is the "best" way to be. This makes you a nice person who is good and will be liked and loved by others for that goodness. You have the distorted idea that to veer off that path means you're instantly an aggressive asshole who is despicable and hurtful. The truth is there is a third way that is respectful, increases your self-esteem, and creates healthy, mutually rewarding relationships in your personal and professional life.

In order to give yourself permission to step off the passive path and fully dive into assertiveness, however, you're going to have to upgrade your map of relationships.

UPGRADE YOUR MAP

It's time to upgrade your map my friend. Like those old globes that have the Soviet Union on them, yours might portray things that no longer exist. The map I'm referring to in this case is your internal map of relationships. Just like a map of a city on your computer screen represents some real place in the outer world, you have an internal map that represents the terrain of relationships. It's our understanding of relationships: how they work, what things mean, and what we predict will happen based on how we behave.

For example, let's say you're driving somewhere new and following the GPS directions on your phone. It is using a map to guide you to your destination. When it says, "turn left and your destination will be on the right," most likely you will turn left and your destination will be there on the right, just like the robot hive-brain predicted (which will most likely someday be our tyrannical overlord in a twist of irony, but that's a different story). This map accurately predicted what will happen when you turn left, and so you got to where you wanted to be.

When it comes to our internal map of relationships, however, I'm afraid it's often not so accurate. In fact, we have dozens of errors in our map that guide us all over the place, far from our destination. Our map might say: *If I express anger, others will find a way to hurt me*, so we avoid all actions that might lead to conflict or difficult conversations. Or our map tells us: *If I disappoint someone, they'll fire me, dump me, or leave me in some way.* This guides us towards people-pleasing, leaves us permanently on edge, and makes us a nervous wreck anytime we think someone might be let down.

These kinds of directions steer you farther and farther away from healthy, empowered relationships with others. The more you follow this kind of map, the worse you feel–trapped, powerless, anxious, resentful, in pain. These feelings are usually not the destination we set out for in our love lives, friendships, or business relationships.

Let's discuss the mindset, beliefs, and map that actually works for relationships. The map that empowers you and others and creates a sense of freedom, autonomy, cooperation, fun, and joy.

5 RELATIONSHIP TRUTHS

1. People Aren't Fragile

Your old map might tell you that if you speak up, say what you want, or share directly, you'll hurt others, perhaps deeply. But when you slow down and examine your fear of how you'll hurt others, you'll discover how it holds you as all-powerful and the other person as extremely fragile. They just can't handle it.

Do you see certain people in your life that way? Do you imagine your honesty would crush them?

The truth is people are not fragile. They are strong, powerful, and resilient. Most of us can endure so much more than we realize, so much more than we've ever had to. Humans survive extremely intense experiences and brutal conditions, like slavery and prison camps. Humans are fierce in their determination and will to survive, thrive, and liberate themselves.

So, can Terry handle you telling her that she needs to get that email to you once per day or you're going to have to let her go? Yes. Can your husband handle it if you start a discussion with him about who does what chores in the evening after the kids go to bed? Yes. Can your girlfriend handle it if you tell her that you want to end your relationship? Yes.

Others may not like these things. Heck, *you* might not like these things. You don't want to have the conversation either. But you know the cost of not speaking up, so you're willing to do it anyway. And you know that **people are not porcelain dolls that will shatter if you speak the truth.** People are strong and can handle life. And when you treat them that way, you're treating them with the respect and dignity they deserve.

2. Upset Is Temporary

One major roadblock that prevents people from being more assertive or direct is the fear of upsetting others. This is reasonable enough, because directly addressing a conflict is more likely to result in upset than avoiding it and stuffing it inside (at least in the short term). But it's important to remember that upset is temporary.

When you bring up a challenging topic, ask a difficult question, or share something directly, the other person is going to have feelings. That's OK. That's normal. That's good! We want to stop seeing feelings as bad, scary things that shouldn't occur. A healthy range of emotional responses includes anger, upset, sadness, and many other feelings.

Keep in mind, however, that the person you're speaking with is only upset now, in this moment. Time passes and feelings shift. Nothing is permanent, especially in the ethereal realm of human emotion. You can also remind yourself that the upset is in service of creating a richer relationship, deeper connection, a better professional environment, etc.

Sometimes when my wife is upset about something and we have a discussion about it, I'll imagine she's still upset hours later. I'm studying her as she moves about the house, reading deep into her nonverbal signs, interpreting body language and voice tone, and continuing to conclude that she's angry. When I get out of my head and simply ask her, I am surprised to hear her response, "Upset about that? That was hours ago. I've let go already."

The upset was temporary, but I was perceiving it as permanent. I was keeping it alive and making it real in my own mind, which impacted my feelings and nervous system. How often are you imagining others are upset with you? Is it once in a while, or do you do it all the time? Is it one of your favorite pastimes?

It can be helpful to take a moment to slow down and really see the truth about people and relationships. Upset really is temporary.

This can create relief and spaciousness to be yourself and share more freely. Even if someone is temporarily upset by what you say or do, it's not permanent.

If someone does get upset and then withdraws and turns it into a permanent grudge or hatred of you... look out. That is not someone you want in your life. They have a strong need to feel certain and significant by making others bad and wrong, and are unlikely to meet their needs in more healthy, positive, growth-oriented ways. They're probably not the optimal person to be in any sort of relationship with.

3. Truth Is Not Bad

If, in the past, you've lived a life of over-responsibility for the feelings of others, then you've done everything you could to avoid hurting them. This most likely included withholding the truth. In fact, you may have concluded that being honest is bad, it hurts others, and it's better to keep that inside and be nice. I mean, "if you don't have anything nice to say, don't say anything at all," right?

This is another aspect of our relationship map that we need to update. Truth is not bad. It's good. Honesty is what connects us with others and creates deep, healthy, lasting relationships in our personal and professional lives. If there is a consistent pattern of withholding what's actually true, people begin to drift apart. They may stay in the situation because they feel obligated to, or because leaving the relationship seems too scary and difficult, or they've worked that job for twenty years and don't know what else they'd do. But they won't feel connected, engaged, and fully alive. They won't thrive.

The truth brings energy and vitality back into our relationships. It breaks us out of certainty and predictability and brings us into the realm of uncertainty, where all energy and passion comes from. When we're being fully honest, we no longer know exactly what's going to happen next. We can feel nervous, excited, or terrified. Yes, some of these feelings can be uncomfortable, but they also tell us we're alive!

We're no longer trying to control the other person by withholding information so they'll stay near us. We're no longer playing life like a game of chess where you must calculate seven moves out to avoid all pain. Instead, we're jumping in, being real, and fully living. It's edgy and it's invigorating. *I'm not sure what I'm going to say next, and I have no idea how they will respond because I haven't shared this before...*

If you make a habit of doing this, all of your relationships will improve. People crave real connection and authentic communication. Most of them are just too scared to initiate it themselves. And yes, there is a way to be skillfully honest and tactfully express ourselves when it comes to difficult subjects. We'll cover more about how to do that later in this chapter. But the how comes second. First, we must fully realize that the truth is not something to be avoided. That is simply old, fearful, inaccurate thinking based on painful moments we've had in the past, or messages we learned growing up. It's time to start sharing the truth—with yourself and with others. Because the truth will set you...

4. Others Aren't Victims

When you *really* get this one, and it just becomes part of how you see others, your communication power and social freedom skyrocket. It's similar to the truth that people aren't fragile, but it goes further. This mindset says, not only are people strong, they are the owner and creator of their lives. They are the captain of their ship and the master of their destiny. So am I, and so are you. Everyone is, whether they recognize this or not. And many people, unfortunately, do not recognize this and actually fight to maintain the viewpoint that they are not the owner in their life. They are, in fact, a victim of circumstance. Their feelings, actions, and results, are all determined by forces outside of themselves and outside of their control. Their challenges, pain, and struggles are everyone else's fault.

We discussed this earlier in the book: the importance of not seeing others as victims of circumstance, even if they see themselves that way. The key now is to upgrade your map so you stop subconsciously assuming everyone's a victim who can't handle things, blames others for everything, and doesn't take responsibility for their life.

You can *decide right now* that you are going to give everyone the gift of seeing them as a powerful creator in their lives. They have an infinite, untapped power and potential to grow, break through challenges, and create the life they want. They may or may not choose to do that, and it's not your job to make that happen for them.

As you see others in this light, the background fear, over-responsibility, and excessive care-taking urges dissolve. This allows you to create healthy, lasting relationships that bring great value to your life and the lives of others.

5. Speaking Up in Itself Is Good

Just like the truth is good and serves relationships, so does speaking up, in and of itself. Regardless of whether the other person receives you well, agrees with you, or gives you what you were hoping for, speaking up is good.

When you speak up about something, you can get a sense of closure. If you don't, your mind has an unresolved, unexpressed energy that drives you nuts. It can create pent up feelings, resentment, and endless rumination about the situation. But speaking up in the moment, or soon afterwards, can dissipate all of that, even if you don't reach a perfect resolution and solve everything immediately.

Speaking up is about self-expression, and the more you express yourself, the less bothered you'll be afterwards. I didn't understand this truth for years. My old relationship map guided me to keep quiet, hold back, and not say anything that could be seen as angry or defensive. So, I was pleasing in the moment, but I'd leave a hot mess of pent up anger, resentment, frustration, hurt, and confusion. I'd ruminate about conversations for days, feeling more and more wound up.

Then I realized that if I'm really bothered after an interaction, and it lasts for more than a few minutes, that's a sign of suppression. It means I held myself back, played nice, and didn't speak my mind. It's a signal to speak up more and, most likely, be *less* nice.

Once you internalize this belief, you will find way more freedom to speak up. Instead of mentally grinding away for hours on how to say something, or the "best way" to say it so you do it right and get the result you want, you simply share more in the moment. You are able to put your perspective out there, disagree with others, and offer your opinions. Because you know that if they get upset, it's temporary. They're not fragile, and they're not a victim. Speaking the truth as you see it is healthy for the relationship and brings energy and vitality, and speaking up in itself is good, regardless of the outcome.

When you can do this, you are free. Free to speak up for yourself, free to share who you are, and free to just be you. And that freedom feels amazing. Let's turn our attention now to specifically how to do this in the most skillful, effective way.

HOW TO SPEAK UP FOR YOURSELF

Until now we've been discussing speaking up in general terms. Now, let's get into the details, specifics, and how-tos of actually doing it in the situations that matter most to you in your life. Overall, there are four kinds of speaking up for ourselves.

1. **Sharing Freely Socially:** This includes speaking your mind, sharing about yourself and your life, asking what you are really curious about, speaking up in groups, and generally feeling empowered to throw in your two cents in any social situation.

2. **Speaking Up at Work:** This includes speaking up in settings like meetings, among colleagues and peers, with potential clients and customers, or with supervisors, bosses, executive members, and other

"higher ups." To be able to clearly and directly ask key questions and share your ideas so you can add value and make an impact.

3. **Objections, Disagreement, & Other "Difficult Conversations":** This can be in any relationship–business or personal. It involves noticing when you don't like something, or are upset, and being able to clearly and directly communicate this with the right person or people.

4. **Asking for What You Want:** This involves approaching others and asking for what you want, without shame or guilt. This can be in a work or business setting, with family and friends, or with your spouse or romantic partner.

As you read this list, which ones stand out to you? Is there one area where you already feel free to speak up? Perhaps you crush it at work and boldly share your ideas there, but are extremely uncomfortable and restricted sharing yourself when meeting new people, or out on a date. Or maybe it's the other way around. You're great at asking for what you want in your relationship, but you're terrified to speak up in a room of "senior management" and other people who have more experience than you.

And, if you are thinking, *man, I need to speak up in all of these areas!* Well then, you're in the right place. Let's dive into each one with specific strategies and examples, to give you a clear sense of how you can begin speaking up for yourself in any situation, starting right now.

But before we do, I have to mention one *extremely important* thing. If you don't get this one distinction, your progress towards speaking up for yourself will be slow or nonexistent. How important is it? Super, duper important. Are you ready to know what it is, so you can finally break free and become the bold, expressive, unapologetic, fulfilled person you're meant to be?

You learn this by doing. **You learn the skill of speaking up for yourself, by practicing speaking up for yourself.** There is no other way.

Below you will find guidance, strategies, and examples. Things you can do and put into practice today. But only if you're willing to step outside the familiar comfort zone and actually do them. Reading about them, accumulating more knowledge on the exact right way to do it, and all the rest, will not set you free. Only action will.

Like all skills, if we're new at it, we might not be awesome at first. It might be a little clunky, or messy, or awkward a few times. Or a lot of times. And that's OK. That's the only way to really get good at this. Could you learn the guitar without ever missing a note, without ever messing up a chord? Absolutely not. That would be an insane expectation and would severely limit your progress. Yet that's how many people approach learning to speak up and be assertive.

Let that go now. Let yourself be a beginner. Let yourself learn, and be messy, and make mistakes, and keep going and growing. That is the path to mastery, and that is the path you are on.

Now that I've banged the Action-Drum yet again, let's turn our attention to the ins and outs of speaking up.

SHARING FREELY SOCIALLY

This topic in itself could be an entire book. In fact, my book *The Solution To Social Anxiety,* my in-depth confidence training course, *The Confidence Code,* and my live event, *Supremely Confident Conversation Master* are all focused on breaking through social fear, maximizing self-esteem, and mastering all the ins and outs of being able to comfortably and confidently talk with anyone.

If you suffer from social anxiety, or if this area is a major challenge for speaking up, and you really want to master it, I encourage you to explore these other resources. You can find information about all of them on my website: www.SocialConfidenceCenter.com.

Since this book is all about shedding excessive niceness and people pleasing, that's what we'll focus on here. We'll explore the key shifts you need to make now to start boldly saying more, sharing more, and simply being yourself around others. The earlier chapters in this book have set you up to implement these strategies quickly and easily. By asking yourself what you want, and owning your perspective more, speaking up will now come much more naturally.

YOU GET WHAT YOU THINK YOU DESERVE

When it comes to social interaction, what do you deserve? This might be an unusual question that you've never really asked yourself. But unconsciously you have a set of beliefs that tell you exactly what you deserve. And socially, as with all areas of life, you get what you think you deserve.

Most nice people don't think they deserve much attention or focus when interacting with others. They tend to keep the conversation focused on the other person, asking them questions, and sharing less about themselves. They don't want to be an egomaniac or attention hog who just talks about themselves. In fact, being the center of attention is often uncomfortable, even when they're just talking with one person, let alone a group. It can lead to a squirmy, I'm-on-the-hot-seat-and-want-get-off feeling that causes them to wrap up and stop sharing themselves with others. Enough about *me*, let's get back to *you*.

What would serve you more is to have a healthy expectation of attention in a conversation. This means you think you deserve attention, for others to be present with you, and listen to what you are saying. What you say is significant and it matters, because it's about you. Even if it's you simply sharing something you read, or an experience you recently enjoyed in your life. That matters, because you matter.

One of my Mastermind clients recently shared about a first date she went on. She had been working on her dating confidence for the last several months and was starting to go on more dates, which the group celebrated with her. On this particular date, she said that she was very attracted to him physically, however whenever she shared about herself, he would listen briefly and then bring the conversation back to talking about himself.

"Did that feel good to you?" I asked.

"No, I didn't like it," she replied instantly.

I knew this would be the answer, because it doesn't feel good to anyone. We all want to receive attention when we're sharing, we all want to feel like we matter. Yet here's the fascinating part. She didn't enjoy the conversation that much, but she wanted to go out with him again, and she was anxious about whether he would follow up or not. Have you ever been in that situation? I know I have. And it baffles our conscious minds. *Why do I care so much about whether this person calls me back? I'm not even that into them!*

Yet we get what we think we deserve. On some level, my client still believes she doesn't deserve full attention, focus, and interest from a man she is attracted to. On some level she still believes she's not worthy of it.

This is something I really get. For years, whenever I was speaking with someone and they didn't seem interested, I would instantly conclude it was because whatever I was talking about wasn't interesting. The topic was stupid, or I was a boring and unengaging person. I wasn't good enough to keep their attention and I didn't deserve it.

Regardless of how long you've felt this way, now is the time to let it go. Raise your standard. You do deserve it. What you want to say and share matters. It is interesting. Own it. Expect more. Not in some crazy entitled prima donna way. In a healthy way that allows you to create the relationships that you really want, the ones that really nourish you.

So, the next time you're speaking with someone and they don't seem that interested in you and what you're sharing, pound the table with your first and loudly shout, "Do you know who I am?!"

No, I'm kidding. Actually, just notice it. Acknowledge that it's happening and notice that it doesn't feel good to you. Remind yourself you deserve better than this and act accordingly. Maybe you end the conversation and go talk with someone else. Maybe you decide not to pursue a second date even though he or she was really hot. There are tons of amazing, attractive, compelling people out there. Find one that excites you and gives you the attention that you deserve.

Side note: There is one caveat here. If virtually everyone you talk with seems disinterested, most likely you are doing something that is creating that response in others. It doesn't mean you're a boring person, it means there is some snag in your communication style that is blocking your connection with others. If that's the case, I strongly urge you to explore the resources I mentioned at the beginning of this section so you can rapidly identify and change that pattern.

SELF-INSERTION

"Here I am, Rock you like a hurricane."
- Scorpions, *Love at First Sting*

Please join me in a moment of reverent silence to appreciate the awesomeness of that song, and the era of hair-metal. Thank you.

So, if you deserve attention, connection, love, and all the rest, what are you waiting for?

That's not a rhetorical question, I'm actually wondering what you are waiting for. Usually, we're waiting for someone to invite us in, give us permission, or tell us it's OK. We're waiting for someone to ask us a bunch of questions and draw us out. And we wait, and wait, and wait...

Unfortunately, this passive approach doesn't work and never will. We have to insert ourselves–into conversations, into groups,

SHARE WHAT INTERESTS YOU...

...Not what others ask you. We have all been trained to respond to the questions people ask us. If someone asks us a question, we'll usually instantly answer it without thinking twice. Or, if for some reason we don't want to, we still feel a strong pressure to do so. And the nicer we were taught to be, the stronger that pressure is.

But speaking up is not about doing what everyone else might want or expect. It's about doing more of what you want. One key way to do this is through what you share in conversations with others.

Most people don't realize the wide-open frontier that conversations are. Instead, they're usually just a predetermined series of standard questions that you have predetermined answers for.

What do you do? Where do you live? Where's your name from? (well, maybe only some of us get that one). And to each of those standard questions we have a default response. Think about that for a moment. Do you have standard phrases in response to common questions? Do you say virtually the same thing every time? And, if so, how engaging is that? How fun is that for you? Of course, your mind says: *Well, I have to answer their questions...*

Do you? I'll never forget the breakthrough insight I had while working at the Homeless Veterans Rehabilitation Program in California during my clinical psychology training. There was one crusty old psychologist who'd been at that treatment center for four decades and was gruff, direct, and had a huge heart. His name was Don, and I really admired him.

I remember after one group therapy session with some of the veterans he pulled me aside. I was new at the center, relatively new in my training, way too nice, and generally a softie. These guys in the treatment center had been in the army, addicted to drugs, and lived on the streets. Many had spent time in and out of prison. I was no match for them. During this group, one of the guys started asking me questions—where I grew up, what my training was like, my experience with substances. As the questions continued, I started to get more uncomfortable, yet continued to answer them, because what else could I do? Not answer them? Gasp!

After the meeting, Don pulled me aside and said to me, "Aziz, when someone asks you a question, you don't have to answer it." In that moment, a lightning bolt hit a light bulb in my head.

"Really?" I asked. "How do you do that? What do you say?"

"Well, it depends on the situation, but anything I want really," he replied.

"Like what?" I needed specifics. I needed the exact words. I needed the "pick-up line," the script that'd keep me safe.

"I don't want to answer that question," he offered.

Whoa. That blew my mind. So simple. So obvious. Yet so outside of my world at the time. And the way he said it mattered. It had no edge to it. No defensiveness, no push-back, no guilt. It was very matter of fact, relaxed, and friendly. As if someone said, "Do you want fries with that?" and you said, "no."

Flash forward a decade and I now teach people many different ways to do the exact same thing Don taught me that day. Here are some specific examples so you can see how to use this in your life now.

One time I was in line at a restaurant where you order at the counter. I struck up a conversation with the woman in front of me by asking her what she was going to order. We ended up talking together while we waited for our burritos to be prepared. Soon into the conversation she asked me, "So what do you do?" Standard question, standard answer, right? No, let's try something different.

So instead I replied, "Ahh, the old 'what do you do question...'" I said this in a playful tone, like a kung fu master might respond to a student who asks him how to do the Flying Dragon Kick of Death. (As you can see my entire knowledge of kung fu is based on the *Kung Fu Panda* movies.)

I paused for just a second, and she had a slightly unsure, slightly confused look on her face. "I can answer that one, but let's mix it up first. Something different. Something fun. How about I ask you two random questions, and then you ask me two random questions?" I gave her another playful look, like a street vendor who is holding out a plush handbag, saying "Who are you to resist it, ehh?"

"Sure," she said as she cracked a smile.

That's just one way you can ask or share what interests you more in conversations. Once you've given yourself full permission to do this, there are an unlimited number of ways to steer a conversation towards something that engages you more. Yes, engages *you*. The purpose of a conversation is to connect, have fun, build trust, and possibly form some kind of relationship. And if you're not having fun, and only pretending to be engaged, then no real relationship will form. And if you can't steer it, or the person gets freaked out and wants to follow the standard conversation protocol, then how fun is your connection going to be in the long run? How much are you really going to enjoy talking with them as the months and years go by?

Another way to share what interests you is to simply do so spontaneously, without even being asked a question about it. If you just saw an amazing movie, or had an intense thing happen, and you were meeting up with a friend, what would you do? Would you immediately jump in and say, "Dude! You are not going to believe what just happened!" Most likely. Although you might not start all your conversations with the word "dude" like I do.

Dude, the key point to remember here is you can do this with people other than your best friend. You can share freely and spontaneously with someone you just met, a work colleague, or when you meet your friend's girlfriend.

If a colleague at work asks you, "Hey, how's it going?"

Instead of, "Good. And you?" You can say something like, "I'm doing good. I just got back from the mountain yesterday. There is so much snow up there. It's crazy!" Or, if you didn't have any big adventures the day before, you can simply share something from your life.

"I'm doing fine. I talked with my brother last night. He met a guy at a party who was really into the topic of cattle mutilation. Have you ever heard of that? It's crazy."

Yes, that's a real thing. You can look it up on *Wikipedia.* It's a strange mystery and no one knows exactly what's happening, but some people think it's aliens. I'm using that as an example because I did just speak with my brother yesterday and that is what he told me about.

And if that's too wack-a-balls crazy sounding for you, you can share about a book you're reading, or a show you saw, or a hobby you're into. Something. Anything. The key here is to spontaneously put more of yourself out there so others know you better, and you feel freer to express yourself.

Even if someone asks you a question, you can minimally answer it and then share about what you find more interesting.

"So, what do you do?"

"I'm a coach and an author. And one thing I'm super into these days is something called heart intelligence, have you heard of it?"

Now, instead of answering standard questions about who I coach and what I write about, I can share about something that I'm actively interested in right now. To see free video demonstrations of these ninja moves, and others, go to NotNiceBook.com.

How can you start doing this in your life more? Are you aware of what you're most interested in? Just as a little drill, I mean game, let's try this. On the count of three, come up with the first five things that pop into your head that you're interested in, or did recently, or learned, or watched, or heard. It could be anything. Don't filter any of them out as boring, or too strange, or insignificant. This is just a game to practice building your spontaneous sharing muscle. Ready, 1...2...3. Go!

What came to your mind? Your dog, a movie you watched yesterday, working out? Don't dismiss anything like this as irrelevant or uninteresting. **Anything about your life that is interesting to you,**

is interesting. It matters. If we see it this way, and share it this way, it tends to have a different impact on others as well. If you let your natural enthusiasm, passion, or interest for something show, other people tend to be way more engaged and responsive.

For example, if someone asks you what you did yesterday after work, and you say in a flat, dismissive tone, "nothing much, just went to the gym then home," then not much will come of that. They'll get the message that you don't want to talk about it and the conversation will stall out, or you'll have to scramble to find something else to talk about. Or you can just direct all the attention to them (which is usually the nice-person's comfort zone anyway).

Instead, what if you knew that your life was fascinating and interesting? What if you stopped dismissing and criticizing yourself and your life as boring and lame? Are you engaged in it? Are you excited about the things you're doing? If the answer to that is no, then it might be a sign to start doing some things you're interested in. If your life is dull, repetitive, and you feel bored, it means you have too much certainty and you spend too much time in your comfort zone. You need to step up, try new things, explore, grow, challenge yourself and get scared. That will bring back energy, passion, and vitality fast.

What I often find is that people are actually interested in their lives. They do like the things they do. But they're telling themselves others won't find them interesting. For this, I suggest you take a page out of the book of Zaim, my three-year-old son. Or your inner three-year-old. When I get home from work, he'll scream, "Daddy!" and run over to give me a hug (which is the best feeling in the world). Then he'll launch into a completely random story from his day, usually right in the middle of it so the context is not entirely clear. "We went to Mountain Land! Teddy and T-Rex came across, but Triceratops didn't. I found my little guys!"

"Your little guys?" I ask with a big smile on my face.

"Yeah! My little earplug guys. They were swimming and swimming, and over here, and over there, and one said, 'aggghh!'" He pauses for a moment, looking a little sad, then continues. "Those guys didn't go to Mountain Land…"

"Aww, they didn't?" I ask.

"No, 'cause they were with me in the bath!" he says, enthusiasm fully returned.

This can go on for a good long while… in three year-old-time, which is two minutes. Then it's time to sit down and play doctor, stat!

What I love about these exchanges is his complete lack of hesitancy about my interest in the topic. He just assumes that of course I'd be interested in this because it happened to him. He doesn't even have the evaluation of whether something is interesting or not. It's something that occurred and he loves me and wants to share it with me. He wants to be seen, to be known. To connect these interests with others. We all do, no matter what our age.

So, when you share about what you did the night before, what if you brought back some of your three-year-old self? What might you say?

"After work, I went straight to the gym. I have all my gym clothes ready to go in my trunk so I don't have any excuses. I had a great workout! I've been going consistently for about four months. And my goal is to go four times per week this entire year. So far it feels awesome."

How does that feel? Completely different than the first response, right? And it's so much truer. It's your actual experience instead of some downplayed, muted, stuffed down, I'm-not-interesting-so-let's-not-talk-about-me act. And guess what kind of response that's going to get from someone? Do you think they'll be less engaged than with the first response, or more engaged? That's right, much more. Usually.

If for some reason, you share this and it gets no traction and the other person gives a minimal response and changes the subject, what does that mean? That you're boring and what you shared is stupid? No! Watch out for those old stories. It means that person is not in-

I don't know enough yet.
I'm not as smart as others.
Everyone is more skilled and better than I am.
I am a fraud.
I am an impostor.
I should know more than I do.
If I say I can do something, I'll fail.
It's best to avoid more responsibility and play small.

These stories are toxic sludge. They aren't true and they don't serve you or anyone in your company or life.

They come from this strange phenomenon: you comparing the inside of you to the outside of someone else. Let me explain. You're aware of your inside–how you feel and what you think. If you're nervous or insecure, you feel it in your chest, your throat, or your stomach. Your breathing is tight and your mind is full of worried thoughts. Outwardly, you probably don't say all of those crazy thoughts and you try to keep it cool. That's your outside, your persona, your mask. We all have it and we all do it.

The problem is we don't see the inside of other people. At best, we get their report of what's happening inside. If someone is open and vulnerable with us, they may tell us what's going on inside, but in most work settings, people are not that vulnerable. They put on their suit, get their game-face on, and show up looking put together, no matter what they think or feel.

Hence, the strange comparison. Outwardly, Jimbo looks strong, bold, confident. He speaks with authority and certainty. He seems to know what he's talking about. Internally I feel unsure, doubtful, and have conflicting thoughts. I must not be as smart as Jimbo, or know as much. I must be a fraud, an impostor!

But guess what's happening inside Jimbo? The same kind of stuff! Uncertainty, doubt, confusion, fear. He feels them all. He just has a very practiced and polished exterior. Now, we don't know to what degree he's feeling all those things in any given moment, but I guarantee you that as a human, he feels all those things and more.

Once we understand this, and see the truth of it, we can begin to relax. We see ourselves as human, just like everyone else. We are no longer less-than, weak, flawed, or broken. Our thoughts and feelings are OK. We're OK. And from that place of relaxed, deep self-acceptance, tremendous power emerges. The power to speak up, to share, to express yourself and your ideas freely.

You, as you are right now, have something to contribute. It's time to start owning that and stop dismissing it. It's time to stop disrespecting and diminishing yourself based on some weird, erroneous comparison to another's persona and image. What would happen if starting today, right now, you decided that your perspective mattered? It didn't require years of experience or some higher level of intelligence. It didn't even require you to be the smoothest or best communicator. What if your perspective mattered right now, just as you are?

My guess is you'd start to share it more, wouldn't you? What do you notice as you imagine that? For many people who've held back for too long, fear is waiting for them at the doorway to freedom. "Don't step through," it whispers. "You will surely die out there." It paints a vivid picture of embarrassment, failure, public humiliation, and shame. It does everything it can to keep you from taking those risks, to keep you small, and safe.

But you can just walk right through that door, you know. That voice is just like a recording on the loudspeaker at an airport. "If you notice any unattended baggage, please report to a TSA security agent immediately." You can pay attention to that voice, or not. It's just there, part of your experience, as you get your snacks, walk towards your gate, and prepare to board the plane.

Now is the time to start sharing. It can be scary at first, but guess what? It won't be less scary six months from now... Or six

Qualifiers

Qualifiers are phrases we use before or after we speak up that are designed to soften what we say. When we're insecure we can begin or end our statement with qualifiers that are apologetic and submissive. They are designed to diminish what we say, so as to not produce conflict, disagreement, or anything else we perceive as threatening.

Some examples are:

I'm sorry to put this out there, but… (statement)

You'll probably think this is wrong… (statement)

I have an idea. It might not work, but… (statement)

I'm sorry, but can I add something?… (statement)

(statement)… I don't know.

(statement)… but that's just my opinion.

(statement)… but I don't know as much about this as you do.

Have you used any of these? Do you have other ones that are your go-tos? Pay attention the next time you're in a social group or business setting. Notice what qualifiers others use, and which ones you tend to use.

Then, eliminate them.

Certainty Rant

If you want to be a person who is taken seriously and seen as a leader both in business and socially, you must learn how to communicate with a tone of certainty. The good news is it's not that hard. You don't have to become smarter, gain twenty years of experience, or achieve anything else first. You can just start doing it now.

Speaking with certainty is just a pattern of voice tone and body language. First, start paying attention to when you are certain about something. I had a client who was hesitant when speaking socially, especially with people he didn't know very well. He was a successful business owner, who knew quite a bit about business building, but even talking about this was difficult. He was concerned about saying something with certainty because he feared someone could find a counterargument and disagree with him. Or he could see that there's always another perspective and he wanted to acknowledge and honor that every time he spoke. The result was a halting, hesitant sounding manner of speech that was filled with the qualifier, "I don't know."

To begin, I asked him some questions about a topic he was completely certain about: football. I asked him a series of basic questions about which teams were favorites this season and why. I asked him what their weaknesses were and who the best quarterback in the league was. No matter what my question, he answered immediately, with a tone of absolute certainty.

Next, we had him study other people in his life who spoke with certainty. He noticed their body language and voice patterns. He began paying a little less attention to *what* they were saying, and started paying more attention to *how* they were speaking.

I encourage you to do the same thing. Discover in your own life what you are certain about and notice how you communicate when speaking about it. Where are you naturally most certain? Is it in your knowledge about sports, movies, or video games? Perhaps it's your opinions in politics, finances, or another field.

Once you've identified it, do the following exercise. The next time you're alone, perhaps driving somewhere in your car, go on a "certainty rant." This is where you speak out loud, with complete and total conviction about anything you want. Start out with the topic you know well. It doesn't matter what the content, or how eloquent or thought out it is. That's not the point. The point is to begin practicing speaking with authority. Think of it as vocal training for an actor.

Once you're going, start talking about anything and everything in your life. What you did yesterday, what you're going to do that day, a particular situation at work, your opinion on an issue in your team, what you think of someone's performance, what you liked about the dinner party last night (or didn't like). Don't censor yourself. This is not a time to be nice or polite. No one's going to hear this, it's just an exercise to flex your certainty muscle.

Notice what happens as you do this. Where do you sound most certain? Where do you falter or become hesitant? As you practice these once per day in your car, do you slowly become more and more certain sounding in the areas where you once sounded unsure of yourself?

What are the qualities of a certain voice tone? What is your volume like? How quickly do you speak? What is your tone like? It's slightly different for everyone, so you want to discover this for yourself. And the only way to do this is to get into action and start practicing. Once you do, you just might find that the certainty rant is actually fun and generates a confidence in yourself that lasts for hours afterward as you go about your day.

To see a demo of how to do a certainty rant and a breakdown of some of the components of a certain voice tone, go to NotNiceBook.com.

MEETINGS: COMMAND THE ROOM

Once you give yourself permission to ask questions and really start to acknowledge the value of your perspective, you'll naturally start speaking up more in meetings. The next level is to command the room.

This doesn't require being the highest level of authority in the room or being the boss. It also doesn't have to come across as condescending or like you think you're better than others. Rather, it's a natural way to communicate when you believe in yourself and aren't focused on harvesting approval and pleasing everybody. Instead, you say what you think and you stand behind what you say.

The more you practice this, the more natural it will become. It will simply be what you do and how you communicate. It will become who you are and how you show up.

In order to command the room, you need to really internalize the mindsets presented in this book: letting go of the need for approval, taking care of others, and feeling overly responsible for their feelings and reactions. That might mean going back and reading those chapters again, and practicing all the suggestions and exercises. If you read through those sections passively without doing the exercises, you may have an intellectual understanding, but that's very different from generating massive power to step up and be who you are. That only comes from action.

Let's cover two key abilities you must have in order to be able to command the room. You must be able to hold the center of attention without freaking out or collapsing in upon yourself, and you must be able to handle interrupting others and being interrupted.

If you want to accelerate in your career and go beyond a basic technical position, you will most likely need to manage others, lead, and run meetings. If you run your own business and you want to expand beyond a solo-shop where you do everything yourself, you will need to lead and manage others. To reach any level of significant influence, impact, and income, you must be able to be the center of attention and handle interruptions.

While it's most essential in your career, developing these two skills will serve you greatly in your personal life as well. Being the center of attention allows you to share a story at a dinner party, give a toast at a wedding, or approach a group of strangers to initiate a conversation. Being able to interrupt radically improves your social experience, prevents you from getting stuck in one-sided conversations that drain you of energy, and helps you guide conversations to be more fun, engaging, or productive.

In short, you want these skills. You *need* these skills. And it's worth facing the discomfort of learning how to build them, as they will serve you for a lifetime.

Holding Court

Back in the day, as in ye olden times, royalty would gather their loyal dukes and whatnot and hold court. This term later evolved to mean being surrounded by and commanding the attention of admirers, subordinates, or hangers-on.

That's what you want to do. As you become less nice, and less concerned with how every single person will respond to every single thing you say, you can command the center of attention more easily.

The reason this is difficult for most people is because they have low self-esteem and have many things about themselves they dislike or think are inadequate. When others pay attention to them, they imagine they're being criticized and judged for their shameful inadequacy. Combine this with a hefty dose of approval seeking and fear of upsetting others and you find yourself nowhere near the center of attention, ever.

But this negatively impacts your life in multiple ways. Without being the center of attention, you can never command a meeting, give a powerful presentation, or do anything in the business world that could produce significant results. Even when it comes to socializing and dating, if you can't be the center of attention, then you can't tell stories, speak up in a group, or walk over to people you don't know and jump into the conversation.

It's time to start thinking of speaking up in work settings as if you are holding court. Start by paying attention to people who already do it and study them. How do they hold the center of attention, how do they speak, how do they look at others? Instead of instantly putting up some false barrier between you and them, thinking *I could never do that*, pay attention to what you can emulate.

Then, combine your newfound certainty tone with stepping up and taking some risks in a few meetings. Own it. What if you were The King? The Queen? How would you speak to your subjects?

Would you have any qualms about taking time or space? Of course not, you're the ruler and you are surrounded by your loyal subjects.

This isn't some narcissistic stance where we think we're better than everyone else. It's just a playful way to bring our self-esteem back up to where it should be—where it originally started when we were young: knowing you are awesome.

It's you giving yourself permission to hold the floor and own the room. *Yes, I want your attention. It's important for you to give it to me right now. Of course, my idea is worth sharing; it's my idea. Of course, it's worth contributing this, I created it. Of course, they need to hear this, it's important!* This healthy perception of your value allows you to speak up and command the attention of the room.

During one of my live events, after a segment where participants went out in the world to practice what they were learning, one client shared this: "As I walked down the street, I felt like I was the king out on a stroll and I was lovingly looking at all my loyal subjects." The room laughed in surprise and delight at this fun image. It was especially significant for him, because he had spent decades uncomfortable meeting new people and avoiding eye contact with all but a few that he knew well.

Make a mini-project out of studying how people hold court. Notice it at work, and any time you see it on TV, at a party, or anywhere else in the world. Watch the person's face, their body language, and listen to their tone. Then mimic that in your own life until it becomes familiar and a part of who you are.

HOW TO HANDLE BEING INTERRUPTED

Jump to your feet, pound the table, and yell, "Sit down and shut up!"
   Next section.

No, no, that may cause some problems down the line. Instead, let's discuss how to handle this situation in meetings at work. Once you learn how to do this, however, it extends way beyond just this setting. You can use it with friends, when communicating with your lawyer or accountant, or even with long-winded Uncle Thorpy at Thanksgiving dinner.

When you are speaking and someone tries to cut you off or speak over you, it's important to respond right away. If we consistently stop speaking, quiet down, and let the other person take over, we create a negative pattern that communicates the message: *It's OK to speak over me. I don't value what I have to say that much anyway. Your viewpoint is probably more important than mine. Besides I don't really deserve to hold the floor anyway.*

This is not the message we want to send, and it's not true. The truth is your opinion matters and what you have to say needs to be heard. As soon as someone jumps in to speak over you, raise your volume just slightly and keep going. If needed, gently raise your hand slightly, palm out, and say, "Hold on a second, Jim, let me finish my point." Then keep going without hesitation and finish your point. No apology, no hesitation, no niceness. Just you owning the floor while respecting both yourself and others.

If the same person continues to interrupt you it can be helpful to call out the pattern. Some people would approach the person one-on-one, but I would call it out right when it's happening. "I notice you have been speaking up as I'm speaking, Jim. It seems like you're eager to share your perspective, yet I haven't finished mine. My preference would be to give each person space to finish their point, then to have a discussion about it. How do you imagine we could solve this problem?"

If you're feeling empowered reading this, good! You can absolutely speak to your colleagues and coworkers this way. The sooner you speak up, the better because you will have less of an emotional charge and sound more neutral as you do this. If you've been stuffing it down for months, building resentment, your tone will most likely sound harsh or angry. However, if you speak up right away, it will be an assertive statement about what you want in the moment.

It's worth mentioning the flip side of stopping someone from interrupting you, and that is interrupting others. I know, it seems ironic to teach you how to stop others from interrupting you and then encourage you to interrupt others. But there is a time in a meeting when you need to tactfully interrupt to share your viewpoint or keep things on track.

In order to do this skillfully, you must give yourself full permission. Then, carry it out with a solid volume that is slightly louder than the volume at which others are speaking. This will command attention and give you an in. It helps to acknowledge what is being said, or that you are interrupting. "Hey guys, you both are making important points here, and I need to interrupt you to keep us on track in the meeting. We need to determine exact next steps for this week before we complete today."

When you can tactfully insert yourself and gracefully block others from interrupting you, you gain an ability to command any meeting. This makes you feel better, reduces resentment, and improves your happiness and performance at work. It also establishes you as a leader, which is important for career advancement and living life on your terms.

DEALING WITH "SUPERIORS"

Superior is defined by Google Dictionary as "being higher in rank, status, or quality." While this definition includes three very different things, our subconscious minds can blur them together. Hence, we consciously know that our superiors in business just have a higher rank or status than us, but we *subconsciously* think they have a higher *quality* than us. Higher quality equals "better than me." Just like when people hear the term "net worth," it's hard not to subconsciously equate that with your worth as a human.

As a result, we often approach people who are of a superior standing in the company as if we are inferior human beings. This can amplify any pre-existing habits of approval seeking, people pleasing, or hesitation to anxiety-producing levels. This generates fear, worry about meetings and presentations, and more hesitation and avoidance, none of which is you owning your power and freely being who you want to be in the world.

It's important to realize that company status or position does not equal smarter, more talented, or better. There are many reasons someone achieves a high rank in a company. They could have been there earlier, or in the right place at the right time. They could be good at talking, connecting, and schmoozing. They could be good at sounding certain even when they're unsure of what they're talking about. They don't necessarily know more or have some secret quality that makes them better.

The key to being less nice around your boss, senior management, and anyone else is to see through the company strata and look right at the person in front of you. The human being. The soft, fleshy pile of bones, organs, and skin. The one who has hopes, dreams, and fears, just like you.

To help you do just this, let me share a little story about the "Executive Committee."

The "Executive Committee"

The key to boldly speaking up around anyone at work is to remember this key insight: Everyone you work with, no matter how high up in the company, how successful, how experienced, or how rich, is still just some person. Some dude. Some gal.

They sleep in a bed, poop in the morning, and sometimes get terrible gas that they try to hide from others. They sometimes feel happy, excited, confident, and totally on fire. And sometimes they feel confused, uncertain, insecure, or inferior (even if you've never seen them act that way). They have challenges in their relationships and sometimes struggle with their spouse or kids. They will get old, they will get sick, they will feel afraid at times, and eventually they will die. They are just a human animal moving through this mysterious life, trying to figure it all out and have some purpose and happiness before it's all over.

The more you see through the suits, the jargon, and the "I got it all together" facade, the more relaxed and confident you will become.

For example, one client I was speaking with was anxious about an upcoming meeting she had with the executive committee in her company. She was preparing for the meeting and feeling tense, worried, and unsure of herself, despite decades of experience at the company.

I noticed every time she referred to the meeting and the people there, she called them "the executive committee."

"How many people are on this executive committee?" I asked.

"Two," she replied.

"Two!" I exclaimed, "I was imagining a boardroom full of nine stone-faced, old guys in suits."

"No," she laughed. "It's just two. And I actually know them both well."

"What are their names?" I asked.

"Tim and Glenn," she said.

"Tim and Glenn," I repeated. "That's a lot less intimidating sounding. What's Tim like?"

I asked her more questions about the people she was meeting with until they once again became people in her mind. She has a long history with them both and could see that they cared about her and they had great working relationships.

So, the next time you're going to meet with your "supervisor" or "the CEO," what if you started thinking about your meeting with Sunil or Linda? Because that's all that it is.

Serving Versus Pleasing

Have you ever been on the opposite side of the pleasing dynamic? Perhaps you meet someone socially or at work, and you can instantly tell they like you and are impressed by you. They want you to like them. They are engaged, energetic, and… a little too much. They laugh too hard at what you say, they agree too quickly, and they smile too much even when the topic is serious. How does this feel when it's happening?

In my experience, it's unpleasant. While there is an appreciation or admiration present, there is also a lack of authenticity. It's hard to really trust that person because they're not showing who they really are. And there is the palpable sense that they want something from me. They need something from me (specifically my approval).

This is not the kind of impression you want to make on senior management, or your boss, or anyone else for that matter. Your boss doesn't want you to please her. She wants you to add something of value that benefits her, the customers, and the company. The executive team doesn't want you to agree with everything and smile. They want you to boldly share your expertise to help them make the best decisions possible.

The difference between serving and pleasing comes down to what we are focusing on. When we are pleasing, we are focused on ourselves. Sure, we're paying attention to the other person and the situation, but all so we can get a gauge on our performance and how others are liking it. *Do they like me? Is this going well?* We then say and do whatever we need to so that they are pleased with us. This leads to over-agreement, not pointing out challenges, and often taking on too much so that we end up over-promising and under-delivering.

Instead, we want to serve. Serve your boss, serve the company, serve your customers and clients. Service is one of my core values and the more I live it, the better I feel, and the more abundant my life and business becomes. When we serve someone we ask questions, share our input, and try to do whatever's best to help the situation. We're focused on the other person and their needs, and the larger situation as a whole. We can disagree if we think that serves the person. We say what needs to be said, even if it's uncomfortable.

And when you do this, guess what happens? People respect you. Your boss admires you and trusts you. The executive team appreciates your honesty and imagines you will be a powerful member of their team one day. And your clients and customers benefit greatly and want more.

As you are reading about speaking up at work and in your social life, you may be feeling more and more liberated and excited. It might seem possible for you to bring more of yourself to the table so that you can be more expressive and free. You can be out on the field and a major player, stepping into the life you actually want for yourself.

And you may have a part of you that is cranking up a little nervous energy and worry: *Yes, but what if I say that and someone doesn't like it? What if they challenge me publicly? What if someone shuts me down or mocks me? What if they get angry and criticize me? What if all my goals and dreams go terribly wrong??*

These kinds of fears are a sign that you need to have a road map to handle objections, disagreements, and other difficult conversations.

OBJECTIONS, DISAGREEMENT, & OTHER "DIFFICULT CONVERSATIONS"

Imagine these scenarios...

You are working on a big project with a coworker, and all of a sudden you realize that he lied to you and to the customer. This is going to cause a big problem for the company, but you've been working on this project together for months and you don't want to make him look bad...

One of your employees frequently has a disgruntled attitude that she communicates with voice tone and body language. Sometimes she's warm in her responses, but often it seems like she's pissed at everybody, including you. She also is resistant to change and doesn't consistently implement new strategies to grow the business...

You had an agreement with a subcontractor and they failed to deliver on an aspect of the project. You had a conversation with them about this and they promised they would send you weekly updates of their progress every Friday. It's 9p.m. on Friday evening and you haven't heard anything from them...

These are just a few of hundreds of specific examples clients and myself have faced that require objecting, disagreeing, or initiating an uncomfortable conversation. And these examples are just from a work setting–we haven't even gotten started on dating and relationships yet!

The reality is we come across situations on a weekly basis that would be better to address than avoid. But so often, avoiding is our primary response to any potentially uncomfortable conversation. All our fears from the chart earlier about what will happen if we speak up, come back with a vengeance. And sometimes we don't even let ourselves imagine speaking directly and assertively. Instead, we fill our minds with excuses and rationalizations. We explain why the other person did what they did, and tell ourselves we need to be more flexible, patient, and relaxed. *I should just let it go...*

Of course, sometimes it is good to let things go. But most of the time this is a fear of a direct conversation. In fact, that direct conversation where you address the challenges head on is the fastest and best way to actually let it go and move on. And since the need for these conversations arise at work, in your friendships, with family, and in your romantic relationship, learning how to handle them is essential. In fact, **the quality of your life depends on how many of these uncomfortable conversations you are willing to have.**

If you can skillfully talk about sex, money, how to raise your kids, and all the other hot-button topics in a relationship, then you will have an extraordinary relationship. If you cannot, then you will avoid these topics, reduce intimacy, grow distant, and live together-but-separate lives of loneliness and quiet desperation.

If you can say what needs to be said, call out problems, and directly ask people what's going on at work, you will quickly rise to the rank of leader. If you run your own business, or manage others, you will create effective teams that get the job done quickly with minimal drama. If you avoid the uncomfortable conversations, you will never be recognized as a leader who can handle challenges and solve problems. You will also likely feel angry and resentful inside, blaming others for your frustration, and seeing it as unfair when others get promoted.

So, let's just say this skill is important. Here's how to do it right.

ADVANCED CONVERSATION STRATEGY: 7 STEPS TO HANDLE ANY SITUATION

Sometimes we don't speak up because we're too scared to in the moment. We know exactly what we want to address, but our body hits the override switch and we stay silent. But sometimes we don't speak up as often as we'd like simply because we don't have a clear strategy. If it's something you haven't done many times before, you just might be unclear about how to do it effectively.

Below you'll discover a clear 7-step approach you can take to handle any difficult conversation. These seven steps have come from years of practical research in the field that has been tested with hundreds of clients and thousands of conversations. I've seen it help people resolve disputes with their neighbors, manage their employees better, deal with an upset boss, greatly enhance their romantic relationships, and bring them closer to their families and parents. In other words, This Stuff Works (TSW).

The key with these steps, as with any skill, is practice. Start by reading them over and getting a basic understanding of them. Then begin applying them in all the situations in your life that could benefit from more assertiveness.

Step 1: I Don't Like It.

This actually occurs inside of you before you open your mouth to say anything. It involves paying more attention to your own internal response to situations, and then acknowledging and honoring that response instead of dismissing it. If someone you work with always tells you really long stories about his home remodel project, and you feel bored and restless, notice that. If you feel irritated each time your partner behaves a certain way, pay attention to that.

Notice that moment of internal resistance. It could come as irritation, impatience, or some other internal feeling of: *Hey, I don't like that.*

This is the exact opposite of the nice person's habit of over accommodating and assuming any dislike or upset is your problem. You might tell yourself to be more patient, more flexible, less judgmental, and more relaxed. *I should just let it go and not be so bothered by it.* This might sound like you aspiring to be a more enlightened person, but it's actually a sneaky way to avoid conflict.

Instead, notice that internal resistance. It's trying to tell you something. It may be indicating that there is a need for you to speak up.

Step 2: What Do I Want?

The next step is to tune into that internal resistance and get curious. Ask yourself: *What's happening here? Why am I upset?* And, most importantly: *What do I want to be different?*

In the examples I shared above in Step 1, ask yourself what you want in that conversation where your colleague shares in depth play-by-plays of his remodel decisions. Perhaps you want them to talk about something else, or pause for several moments to just be silent. Maybe you want to be sharing more and you want them to listen.

In the example with your partner, pay attention to the behavior that bothers you. Perhaps they put too many paper bags in a drawer so it makes it hard to open, and you want there to be fewer paper bags. Or, once you slow down and really feel what's happening inside of you, you realize that it has nothing to do with the paper bags. What you actually want is more of his attention, or you want her to touch you more and hold your hand when you sit on the couch.

Because you read about the power of asking yourself, "What do I want?" earlier in this book, and have been practicing it, your ability to do this step and uncover what you really want will come more and more easily to you.

Step 3: I Noticed...

The first two steps are internal preparation for speaking up. This is the first step when you actually open your mouth to say something. And that's when we come out of the gate swinging, right? Actually, it works much better if you approach the other person from a curious, neutral stance. It's OK to feel upset inside, but if you charge at them with accusations and hostility, the most natural reaction in the world is going to be defensiveness and fighting back.

Instead, you can simply point out what you noticed to enter the conversation:

"I noticed that you share a lot of the details of your remodel with me..."

"I noticed that you like to put paper bags in that drawer..."

"I noticed you scheduled eight appointments for Barry this week and only 3 appointments for me."

"I noticed I sent an email on Monday and you responded to me on Friday."

These are just a few examples among the millions of things you could notice in your interaction. **The purpose is to bring up the challenging topic directly in a curious and neutral way.** Using the phrase "I notice" removes an accusatory tone and allows the other person to be more receptive. Notice how all the examples above are very specific, and devoid of interpretation or judgment. This is a key point that is sometimes difficult to remember when we're upset about something. Instead, it might come out like this:

"I noticed that you just go on and on about your remodel project..."

"I noticed that you always stuff that drawer so full of paper bags that we don't need and never use anyway."

"I noticed that you favor Barry and give him way more appointments than me."

"I noticed it takes you way too long to get back to me on emails."

Can you see how these are different? They're loaded with more frustration, judgment, and blame. You can almost hear the unspoken part of the sentence that says, "What the hell is wrong with you?" This tone and language more often than not creates a defensive reaction in the other person, or at the very least makes them less open and receptive to resolving the issue.

Once you've broached the subject, then you can get more information. Why do they do that thing? What happened that it took so long to respond? What's their idea of what to do with the paper bags? Ask questions and try to understand their model of the world, and why they are doing what they are doing.

Again, tone is important here. You're not a prosecutor cross-examining a witness: "Why did you give more appointments to Barry? I see. I see. And did you think that was OK to do such a thing? Has anyone ever accused you of being a *racist*?"

Objection your honor!

Our job here is to actually inquire and find out what's happening. To see if we can get into their world and gain a better understanding, and to be open to the possibility that our knee-jerk interpretation might be slightly inaccurate. But only slightly, of course. We could never be completely wrong, could we?

Step 4: Reflect

As you are exploring the situation with the other person, slow down and pay attention. As you listen, reflect on what you are hearing to make sure you understand it clearly:

"So, you like to have a lot of paper bags around because you can use them for garbage or recycling?"

"This remodel is a huge deal for you and your family and it helps to talk it through with someone, is that right?"

In certain situations, the other person may challenge what you noticed, stating that didn't happen. In response, our urge might be to immediately fire back and provide our evidence, but this will only entrench the other person further. Because difficult conversations are not about who has the accurate facts. They're really about connecting and being heard, which is how people positively influence each other.

Let's take the example of someone in your office scheduling more appointments for Barry than for you. When you say you noticed they scheduled eight for Barry and three for you, imagine they deny this or have some explanation. In that case, you'd simply restate their explanation:

"So, you were just scheduling people as they came in, with whatever times worked best for them. And you weren't paying much attention about if it was with me or with Barry. Is that right?"

Notice the "is that right?" at the end of several of these examples. That is a simple, yet very powerful question to ask. First, it helps you know that you're accurately reflecting what they're saying. If you're missing key details or misconstruing what they said, they will say "no." If you are accurate, then they will say "yes." This has them verbally affirm that you are understanding them, and that you are getting what they are saying, which causes people to be more open and receptive in any discussion. Remember, we all just want to be seen, heard, and understood.

Step 5: Impact

Now, *this* is the time you can come in swinging. Finally! I'm still kidding in the sense that accusations and criticisms will never influence someone in the long term, or ultimately feel good to you. But it's essential to share the impact of their behavior on you, and your reactions. It's even more important to share what you want and work together to create a powerful agreement that works for you both, which we cover in the following steps.

If you skip this step and the next two, then you just have a 4-step process that makes you a way more skillful, nice person. It won't feel satisfying to have these conversations because you won't have fully expressed yourself and the situation won't feel resolved.

In order to really speak up for ourselves, we must share the impact someone's behavior is having on us. Are you annoyed? Hurt? Angry? Sad? Disappointed? Feeling insignificant or unwanted? Then say so. Tell the other person what happens inside of you when they do X, Y, or Z.

This step trips many people up. When I work with clients, they're often with me for the first four steps. It doesn't involve revealing much and while it's a little uncomfortable to broach a touchy subject, it still feels relatively safe. Still under control. But this step is where you lose control. You reveal what is actually happening inside of you. You show that you are not some perfect, impenetrable being that no one can get to. Instead, you reveal the truth, and use this as a powerful force for connection and influence.

Just like with the previous steps, be aware of using blaming language that makes the other person bad or wrong. They're not responsible for your feelings and they didn't "make you angry." In fact, it's worth getting curious about yourself, what buttons they pushed inside of you, and what you may need to address and heal. Instead of blaming, we want to take responsibility for our feelings and simply share what is happening. Here are a few examples to help you get the difference.

"When you put the bags there, I feel agitated. Whenever I try to open the drawer, bags pop out and fall on the ground. I get annoyed and don't like cleaning it up each time."

"When you go deep into the specific details about your house model, I have a hard time following what you're saying. It feels like too much to me and I lose interest and feel less connected with you."

"When I send out an email that requires a response and you do not respond for days, I feel uncertain about what's happening. My mind keeps trying to figure out what's going on and why you're not responding. I feel frustrated and angry when days go by and I don't hear back."

How do you feel reading these examples? Excited? Neutral? Scared? Do you feel nervous about saying things like this? These are honest and direct, yet kind ways of expressing our feelings. Notice how I am taking responsibility for my own feelings and reactions and not blaming the other person or calling them names.

It is also important to be congruent in your voice tone, facial expressions, and body language as you share the impact they've had on you. If you're frustrated or hurting, let it show in your voice and body. Sometimes, in an attempt to soften what we are saying, and not rock the boat, we smile or use a soft tone while sharing our upset. This sends a mixed message and confuses everyone. To see video examples of voice tone and congruence, go to NotNiceBook.com.

This way of communicating is more vulnerable, and thus less common. Many people are too scared to speak this way, so instead they skip this step entirely. Or, they don't *really* reveal themselves, instead choosing to keep the blame focused on the other person. For example:

"When you put the bags in there it annoys me so much. You keep way more than we need and it makes no sense to me why you want to do that."

"I can't handle listening to you go on and on about this remodel any more. You talk so much about it. It's all you talk about. You're obsessed. I'm sick of it."

"Your response time is terrible. I'm fed up with you not getting back to me and having such bad communication. Why don't you respond more quickly?"

These are definitely forms of speaking up for yourself. And they might even sound tough and confident. But they usually do not lead to productive discussions that resolve problems. They end up pushing the other person away, creating defensiveness and tension, and failing to effectively change anyone's behavior in the long run.

Step 6: Desire

Once you've stated the impact, you then move on to sharing what you actually want. Since you discovered this in Step 2, it will be a breeze to simply share it out loud. Unless, of course, you have some shame or judgment about what you want. Then you're screwed. No, I'm kidding. Then it's just a bit more difficult and requires some willingness to be uncomfortable.

One desire I had shame and judgment around for years was wanting attention from women. I wanted them to notice me, approve of me, be impressed by me, and want to be with me. However, I imagined if women knew I had this desire, they would see me as needy, insecure, and otherwise repulsive. Hence, I either acted aloof or hoped that if I was charming enough, then women would give me all the attention I wanted.

Flash forward to my relationship with my wife, and there are times I'd want her direct attention. I'd want her to be curious about me, pay attention while I shared something, and give me her input or feedback.

Instead of sharing this desire, however, I would feel ashamed of being so "self-absorbed and needy." I *should* be more attentive to her, and demand less for myself. I *should* be nicer, right?

No. Less nice. More honest.

Say what you want. Say what you don't want. Share what you would like to be different in the situation. Find the courage to be more direct and vulnerable, and express what you really want.

"Baby, I notice I'm missing you right now. I would love to have your attention for just a few minutes. There's something I'd like to share with you."

To relate it to the examples from earlier:

"My preference would be to keep just four or five bags in that drawer. That way, it would open easily and not spill out. If you wanted more bags, I would like it if we could keep them downstairs in the laundry room."

"I would love to talk with you about more things beyond the remodel. I'm curious what else is going on in your life. I would also like to share about what's going on in my life and have you listen and ask me questions."

"I would prefer it if you responded to emails within 24 business hours. I want more communication in our team, as it helps me know what is going on and feel more connected."

How do you react as you read these examples? Does that level of directness or vulnerability feel edgy or uncomfortable to you? Good! That's a sign of increasing your discomfort-tolerance and growth. For many years I had a difficult time expressing anything I wanted directly, for all the nice-person reasons listed earlier in this book.

But if you're willing to take the risk, and begin experimenting with taking this step, you might be amazed at how inaccurate your predictions are. Instead of being turned off, offended, upset, and withdrawing from you, people are surprisingly responsive, adaptive, warm, and loving. I believe this is due to the powerful connecting nature of this seven-step process. When we follow these steps, we're not pushing others away or hiding, we are openly and courageously expressing ourselves to create authentic human connection.

Step 7: Powerful Agreement

Saying what you want doesn't necessarily mean you'll get what you want. You'll often find, however, that simply the act of bringing something up, asking the other person questions, and then sharing what you want makes you feel completely better. In other cases, the behavior is an issue and each time it happens, you feel angry, hurt, or frustrated. In these instances, it's essential to form a powerful agreement.

I am a huge fan of agreements and I create them with everyone on my team and all of my clients. Agreements take things out of the realm of secret expectations in my head, and turn them into mutually decided actions.

Forming an agreement is simple once you've done the step of sharing what you want. You simply ask the other person how that sounds to them. Can they agree to do what you want? Do they have any hesitations or concerns? Do they want to do something different? The key here is to create a conversation that aligns everybody so each person takes ownership moving forward.

If someone agrees to do something, and they chose to do so because they wanted to, they're much more likely to do it. If there is no discussion and they simply agree out of fear, then they're much more likely to drag their feet, resist, "forget," or otherwise exert their true will.

After stating what you want, follow up with questions to see if that works for them:

"How does that sound to you?"
"Would you be willing to do it that way?"
"Is there any reason why you wouldn't want to?"
"Is there anything that might get in the way?"

And then, depending on the situation, I might specifically use the word "agreement" to highlight that we're making an agreement. I personally do this more with team members, colleagues, and clients, rather than in my personal life. It seems to fit better there, and seems a little intense with my wife and friends. Yet I am still creating agreements with them, I just don't use that word. To continue with the three examples we've been using throughout these steps:

This example is involving a spouse or romantic partner:
"My preference would be to keep just four or five bags in that drawer. That way, it would open easily and not spill out. If you wanted more bags, I would like if we could keep them downstairs in the laundry room… How does that sound to you?"

After they respond, you could say, "Would you want to do it another way?"

This fully engages them in deciding a solution so they will take ownership and feel inspired to follow the new plan.

This example involves a colleague at work:

"I would love to talk with you about more things beyond the remodel. I'm curious what else is going on in your life. I would also like to share about what's going on in my life and have you listen and ask me questions."

Then I'd wait for a moment to see how they react or respond.

"How does that sound to you? Would you be open to that?"

The final example is a work example, and I would be more likely to make it clear that we are creating a strong agreement.

"I would prefer it if you responded to emails within 24 business hours. I want more communication in our team, as it helps me know what is going on and feel more connected. Is that something you would be able to do?"

Then, even if they said yes, I would ask more questions.

"Does that feel too fast for you?"

"Is there any reason why you wouldn't be able to do that?"

The purpose here would be to flush out any hidden resistance or challenges that might get in the way of them following through with the agreement. As you become less nice and a more bold, authentic, powerful leader in your life you will start to see just how many other people are overly nice, scared to speak directly, and afraid of your disapproval.

Then, I would conclude with, "Great. So we can make an agreement that you will respond to my emails within 24 hours on business days?"

Approaching any challenging situation or difficult conversation using this seven-step strategy will radically increase your ability to speak up. First, it gives you a clear how-to, which provides a sense of certainty and makes it easier to take action. Second, following these steps will generally produce much better outcomes. Even if you don't pull off all the steps perfectly, you'll feel better having brought up the subject and been able to address a challenge head on. The more you practice this, the greater your confidence will become, and the easier it will be to speak up, thus creating a positive cycle that moves you forward.

Before we move on to asking for what you want without guilt, there is one kind of difficult conversation that can be particularly challenge for recovering nice people. And that is disagreeing with others. Let's explore that now.

HOW TO DISAGREE WITH SOMEONE

The quintessential nice person move is to smile, nod, and say "yes." Not in an empowering, I say "yes" to life, have crazy adventures, and face challenges head-on kind of way. More of the "I'm too uncomfortable to say what I really think so I'll just agree" approach.

I used to avoid disagreeing so much that I never did it. I even had a number of beliefs and philosophies to back me up. I believed it was wrong to disagree. I thought it was just people and their egos battling. I told myself I wanted to be surrounded by "positive people."

But the truth was I was just very uncomfortable with disagreement. I disliked any difference in opinion because this felt like friction and tension, which was the beginning of conflict, anger, and the destruction of all things good.

I have since upgraded my perception of human interaction. Disagreement between people is inevitable if both people are being authentic and honest. It is impossible for two humans to have the exact same thoughts, feelings, perceptions, and desires at the exact same time, always.

In short, it's healthy to disagree with others. Not only do they not crumble or explode, as you might fear, they actually end up respecting you more for being honest, outspoken, and bold.

If, like me, you have spent years not disagreeing, it may take a little practice. But don't worry, it's a relatively easy skill to pick up, and becomes quickly reinforcing because you'll feel so much freer and bolder in all your interactions. Here are some simple ways to effectively disagree with others.

Casual Disagreement

When I first decided I was going to give myself permission to disagree with others and be less nice, I studied how confident people pulled it off. I was surprised to discover how casual it could be. It didn't have to be a dramatic challenge that lead to a showdown. In fact, it appeared other people didn't have my internal rules, and disagreement was no big deal to them. It was just part of the normal discourse, and conversation would continue to flow smoothly afterwards. Here's an example to make it clearer:

Them: The biggest thing we have to worry about is the load that this will put on people's systems. Right now it's at threshold and if we add anything else, it will become totally worthless.

You: You think so? I think the biggest focus is whether it can do the things users want. People want function over speed.

My developer friends will have to excuse my obviously limited terminology. I dropped out of my Computer Science major in my junior year of college. Details aside, do you see how you can simply share an alternative perspective? No need to push back hard, make a big deal of it, or make them admit they're wrong and you're right. You simply state your view in a matter of fact, relaxed way. You can do this with anything, on any topic:

THEM: I like chocolate ice cream. It's the best flavor. We should all get chocolate ice cream.

YOU: Ice cream sounds great. I think we should get strawberry.

Casual disagreement is the most common and most important kind of disagreement to learn because it is you simply expressing yourself. You're sharing what you think, feel, want, and like. It's a way of being yourself around others and letting them get to know who you are. When you hide this in an attempt to be pleasing or non-offensive, people are left with the vaguely uneasy feeling that they don't really know you. Sure, you're nice, but who are you really?

Start practicing casual disagreement whenever you see the opportunity. You might be surprised, just like I was, at how little others react. Instead of getting upset and challenging you, most of the time people don't even notice and the conversation and connection flows on.

Playful Disagreement

This is one of my favorite kinds of disagreement. In this kind, you do point out that you're disagreeing, but it's done in a playful way that maintains rapport between you and the other person. This one is partially about what you say, but mostly about how you say it. You indicate you're not too serious with your voice and body language.

THEM: That movie was stupid.

YOU: Whaaaat? You didn't like that movie? I thought it was great.

THEM: I don't know… People who are into self-help books are all just looking for someone else to tell them what to do. I think it's kinda sad.

YOU: Yes, those poor, poor, lost, idiotic fools. *(Playful smile)* Come on, you really think so? As in any reading about how to handle any problem is a bad idea?

The beauty of the playful disagreement is it allows you to clearly disagree with them in a way that reduces tension and opens up a sincerer discussion. You can use whatever your style of humor is to come up with the playful side. Be aware, however, that it must be obvious you are being playful for this to work effectively. If you are dry and sarcastic in your response, it won't connect you with the other person. Instead, it could come across as derisive or condescending.

To watch a video about how to use the playful style of disagreement, go to the book website, NotNiceBook.com.

Direct Disagreement

Sometimes it is important to directly disagree without being casual or playful about it. We might have to speak up, say what needs to be said, be direct, and get our point across. We may have to stop someone from making a bad decision, stand up for what we believe in, speak out against oppression, or steer the course of a project or relationship. Some matters are serious, important, and require us to disagree, even if it temporarily creates some tension.

When directly disagreeing, there are several important factors. First and foremost, what is your objective? What is the outcome you want? Is it to influence a team's decision? Is it to make sure something happens in your company, or your life? Or is it about speaking up against something you don't like, such as racism or a narrow-minded philosophy? Is your goal to make sure they see that they're wrong and you're right?

When disagreeing, it's very easy to get sucked into this last arena and have it turn into a battle to win the "I am right" medal. This rarely works, as most people will never admit they're wrong or rapidly change their viewpoint. Instead, it can be much more empowering and mutually beneficial to have a "side by side" mindset when it comes to differing views. Instead of "I'm right and my ideas are above yours," or vice versa, our ideas are side by side. My perspective and opinion is over here and look like this. Yours is over there and looks like that. And they are different.

When you eliminate the need to convince the other person they're wrong, you instantly become more influential and persuasive. If you are disagreeing with someone to influence a decision-maker who's listening, your impact will rise exponentially. You can focus on the outcome and the needs of the larger whole, and make a more compelling case.

When disagreeing directly, it is essential to be powerful and congruent in your communication. Now is not the time to smile, use softeners and qualifiers, and pull out other people pleasing maneuvers. Now is the time to sound clear, be an authority, and look people in the eye. It's OK to be nervous or have your heart rate increase. That is normal and expected if it gets tense or the stakes are high. Your goal is to communicate clearly, even if your heart is beating fast. And, as with all things, practice leads to mastery.

You will learn more about how to develop this capacity in yourself in the last part of this book, which is about putting everything you're learning into action.

Information Gathering

There is one more kind of disagreement that is valuable, especially in situations where you're dealing with someone who is in a senior position. They might hold some authority over you due to job title, years of experience, and so on.

Instead of coming in swinging, it can be more effective to begin your disagreement by simply asking questions about the process or decision in under scrutiny. As you do this, the flaws in their thinking or concerns they've overlooked can become obvious.

Here's an example to illustrate. Let's say you're in a meeting with your boss, who was advised by the director of marketing to use a particular strategy. You don't think it's a very good strategy, and you also know it will cause logistical problems. You could say that directly, but if your boss is sold on the idea, he may simply dismiss your perspective and order you to proceed. Here's how you might use information gathering to challenge the plan:

BOSS: So we'll go with Todd's marketing strategy. I need you to tell your team about it and map out the plan to execute it with Amar *(the sales manager)*.

YOU: Got it. Can I ask you a question?

BOSS: Sure.

YOU: What's the length of time we're planning on using this strategy?

BOSS: The initial plan is for 6 months. That's enough time to begin evaluating results, and we can decide to expand it, keep it, or kill it.

YOU: Sounds good. And what is the metric for success? What amount of return would tell us it's going well?

BOSS: Hmm. An increase in sales by 5% would be good.

YOU: OK, shooting for 5% sales increase. What about the added cost of the creation and management of all the promotional materials?

BOSS: What about it?

YOU: Well to do Todd's strategy we would need two people on my team dedicated to creating and managing all the materials. And I'm guessing Amar would need to increase sales calls and hire another rep, right?

BOSS: Hmm.

YOU: I'm curious about what sales amount would not only cover all increased costs, but also make enough to make it worth it.

At this point, you can more directly discuss your concerns, or keep asking questions that highlight the flaws in the plan. This method of disagreeing is useful in larger meetings, when speaking with authority figures, or even when exploring a plan that your friend or spouse proposes.

The purpose here is not just to persuade. It is information gathering. Essentially, at first you have some concerns and disagree with the approach. If you gather information and it clarifies things and gives you a sense of certainty that the plan is good, you may change your mind. If you ask the tough questions and you see that the other person has not thought everything through, you have opened a door to express your opinion.

So far the difficult conversations we've examined assume you are dealing with friends, romantic partners, and colleagues. These are people you are working with, living with, and with whom you are generally on the same team. But what about situations where you are forced to deal with people who are not on your team, people who are actually actively against you? Let's discover how you can handle that now.

BULLIES AND CRITICISM

One major plight of the nice person is to deal with criticism or bullying. For some people this was an unpleasant experience from the past that is relegated to the schoolyard. But for many nice people I've spoken with, it unfortunately continues to this day. They may not be shoved in the locker room or overtly threatened, but they do have at least one person in their life who regularly teases, mocks, or criticizes them.

This kind of treatment is different than the teasing banter you may do with your friends or a romantic partner. That kind of teasing involves being connected, and has a playful give and take quality. You're both in on the game and having fun, even though you're poking each other a bit.

What I'm speaking about here is different. It involves someone overtly criticizing you, using a harsh voice, calling you names, mocking you, or otherwise trying to diminish you and make you feel worthless. Sometimes they even have a gang of several cronies, so they can get the attention and approval of others.

If this is not something you experience, good. But if you are currently experiencing this, then you know exactly what I'm talking about.

The key to ending this toxic behavior is to first realize that bullies have a form of "bully-dar." It's their special unconscious form of radar that allows them to select targets for abuse. They can energetically sense who will take their criticism without fighting back. In other words, they pick nice people.

One client in my Unstoppable Confidence Mastermind was recently struggling with being frequently picked on by one colleague at work. This co-worker would make snide remarks, call my client arrogant, and deride or mock the things he's interested in and shares with others.

In one of our group calls, he shared one instance when this colleague picked on him yet again, making fun of what he said, his voice tone, and how stupid he sounded.

"What did you say to him when he did this?" I asked.

"Well, I had an impulse to tell him off, but I didn't," he replied.

I could have asked him in that moment why he held himself back, but I already knew the answer. And he already knew the answer. So, I tried a different tactic.

I asked the group if anyone there never gets picked on. One group member spoke up right away and said no one ever bullies him.

"Why do you think that is?" I asked.

"Because they know I'll fire back. I'll dish out more than I take," he replied confidently.

"Great," I said, smiling to myself. "Let's have you model how you might respond to the criticism."

The specific scenario involved the bully calling my client arrogant for being a fan of a particular football team, among other things. After he shared the details so we could get a sense of what the bully said, we did a short role play. And sure enough, the client who never got bullied dished it out hard and fast. As soon as the bully finished his statement, he said:

"Whatever, man. You think your team is any better? Give me a break. You have no idea what you're talking about. Get the f**k outta here."

His tone was dismissive and strong. He definitely wasn't taking grief from anybody.

"What did you notice about his response?" I asked my first client.

"It was clear and direct," he replied.

"Was it nice?" I asked.

"Ha, no, definitely not," he said.

"Yeah, it was definitely not nice. It was..." And in that moment, I had an insight. I paused for a moment, mid-sentence, then asked the group, "what's the opposite of nice?"

"Powerful," said the client who doesn't take any guff.

"Being an asshole," said the client who gets bullied.

That was it. That explained why he held back, pulled his punches, and let others bully him. It all became clear in that instant.

"So, in your model of the world, the opposite of nice is to be an asshole. And nobody wants to be identified as an asshole. So, to speak up, to defend yourself, to strongly and appropriately push back against this guy would make you an asshole, or in other words, a bad person."

I paused for just a moment, then continued. "The opposite of nice is not to be an asshole or mean person. The opposite of nice is to be bold, direct, authentic, and powerful. It's showing up with the energy and strength that's needed most in that situation."

We then went on to do more role-plays where my client practiced holding nothing back. He practiced speaking with strength, conviction, and certainty. At first his tone was timid, hesitant, and soft. Then, as he called it, he decided to become more "stern." His tone transformed and his attitude went from apologetic and fearful to powerful and dismissive of this bully's unwarranted criticism.

When dealing with bullies, the most important step to take is to interrupt the pattern. The old pattern is they mock and ridicule you, and you passively take it in. Or try to smile and play along, hoping it will stop tomorrow. Or you push back in a timid and submissive way, which doesn't deter the bully.

Instead, interrupt the pattern. Come back with more energy and intensity than the bully is expecting. Put your hand up just as he begins to speak and say in a loud, clear, commanding tone, "Excuse me, Darren, the adults are talking. I'm not in the mood for your high school jokes." This is so different than anything you've probably ever done, it will scramble the hell out of his circuits. If that seems too hard or scary to pull off, practice it fifty times the day before. Say it out loud while you're making dinner, shout it in your car.

Each time you leave a situation feeling like the bully got the best of you, instead of getting stuck in what you should have done, or how it's not fair, or feeling helpless, stand up. I mean literally. Stand up from your chair and move your body around. Do some jumping jacks or push-ups. Put on some rock music, or metal, or EDM, or anything else that reminds you that you have power and juice left in you. Shake your body out and start saying out loud what you want to say. Practice it again and again until you wire it into your nervous system. Until it comes out so fast the next time you're with him that you didn't even consciously choose to speak up. It just happened.

OK, it's time for another pause. Take a moment to breath and notice what you are feeling in your body. You're learning tons of ideas and strategies about how to be less nice and more powerful, expressive, bold, and free. That can feel exhilarating, and it can also feel scary or overwhelming. That's OK too. You're doing great and you're in the exact right place.

If you're wondering exactly how to apply what you are learning, begin practicing the exercises or techniques that are the most relevant to your life. If you want to have more impact at work and be taken more seriously, practice doing a certainty rant once a day on your way to work, for example. Just pick one activity, one action, one thing you are ready to do, and commit to doing it for the next two weeks. Remember, it is only through action that we reinvent ourselves and set ourselves free.

I also want to remind you that at the end of this book, in Part IV, there is a chapter on taking everything you're learning and putting it into action, now. It will guide you through a step-by-step process of how to build up your assertiveness and power muscles.

Before we conclude this chapter on speaking up for yourself, I would like to share one more key area where speaking up is absolutely essential for fulfilling relationships and a happy life. And that is the art and the skill of asking for what you want. Not only how to do it, but how to release any lingering guilt about asking others for anything.

ASKING FOR WHAT YOU WANT WITHOUT GUILT

Unfortunately, many of us learned that asking for what we want is bad on some level. When I ask clients about their early memories around asking, they often have stories of parents being upset or annoyed with them. I used to judge these parents in my head—how could they be so insensitive and cruel? Didn't they see how they were impacting their children?

And then I had kids myself. At each stage of my kids' development, I experience greater compassion for parents and a deeper humbling of myself. I used to secretly think to myself: *My child will never do this. I'll never be like that. I'd handle it way better.* Then six months later, or two years later, when my child is at that stage, I say to myself: *Ohhhh, that's what was happening for those parents...* and I take yet another superiority medal off my chest.

I have seen why asking often triggered our parents' disapproval. Because kids ask for anything and everything all the time. And depending on their age and development, "ask" is a favorable way to say it. It's more like demand. Or screech. And so, despite being a patient and loving dad, there are times when the rapid-fire demands and unpleasant situations mount to threshold capacity. Then I get annoyed. Instead of responding playfully when my son Zaim demands, "Daddy! Tell me a story!" for the fortieth time, I sigh, look tired and exasperated and say, "No. I don't want to." No redirection, no alternatives such as offering to read him a book, just a straight up, exhausted no.

Perhaps your parents were often exasperated by the demands of parenting and didn't have much patience. Maybe they got even angrier and told you to knock it off, shut up, and get away from them. Whether it was subtle or overt, most people got the message that asking is bad. It's too much, puts people out, and you're bad and unlovable for doing it.

Unfortunately, this is absolutely untrue. **Asking is an essential part of connecting with other humans, and is actually *the most effective way to meet our needs in relationships.*** We misinterpreted our parent's frustration and personalized it, thinking it was our fault. We did not understand how demanding life was for our parents and how Jedi-Zen master they would have to be to not get upset with us sometimes.

It's time to upgrade our map of relationships yet again. Why is asking bad? Why do you feel guilty for simply asking for what you want? Do you fear others will judge your desire as needy or strange? Do you fear they'll feel pressure to say yes and dislike you for it? Or is it just some vague, unexamined feelings of "badness" that bubble up whenever you think about asking for what you really want?

In almost all cases, guilt around asking comes down to poor boundaries. It starts with the idea that we shouldn't want so much and that other people's needs are more important than our own. This is one of the primary nice person strategies to stay small, stay safe, and just give everyone else what they want so they'll love us.

Then, we imagine that our request will put undue strain or burden on someone else. And we imagine they have poor boundaries as well and don't have the right to decide for themselves if they want to say yes or no. We fear they'll feel pressured to say yes and be upset with us, resenting our demanding, selfish nature.

So, we either don't ask and try to do it all ourselves, all the while piling up frustration, and repressed resentment. Or we consider asking, and feel guilty and bad, making the whole process painful and unpleasant. Even if we do muster the will to ask, and the other person says yes, we feel uneasy, wondering if they're upset with us or secretly resent us. We have a hard time letting it in and accepting what they're giving us. This can lead to apologizing or over thanking, neither of which makes anyone feel good.

It's time for a new way. It's time to create a healthy sense of entitlement and to be better able to take care of your own needs and self-interest. We will explore this further in the next chapter, which is all about selfishness. For the moment, can you see the insanity of the current plan? Can you see how it only hurts you and doesn't create healthy, happy, sustainable relationships?

The ideal that you are striving for is noble—to be a giver, not a taker. In general, giving more than we take in life is a pattern that creates wealth, great relationships, and happiness. But giving does not mean *only* giving and *never* receiving. That turns an ideal into an extreme that is unattainable and unsustainable. If we only give and never get our needs met, we will soon feel burned out and resentful. This is true for any human, anywhere, at any time. It's just part of the mechanics of the human animal.

In order to truly be a giving, generous, and attentive person, we must be able to meet our needs and receive from others. **The most effective way to meet our needs is to ask directly for what we want.** Once our needs are met, or we feel the other person is responsive and cares about us, we feel energized and motivated to give them even more.

The key to granting yourself permission to ask for what you want is to realize the following core truths:

1. Your needs matter.
2. You must be the greatest advocate of your own needs (no one else can do that for you).
3. Others actually want to meet your needs.

That last one is usually surprising for many nice people. They've lived for so long with the stories that wanting and asking are selfish and repulsive, that they have become their reality. It can be shocking to realize that it's not necessarily how people around you think and feel. Let me share a little story that demonstrates a new reality in which people want to help you meet your needs.

Project: ULTRA

Last summer I got a surge of motivation and inspiration and decided I was going to initiate what I now call Project: ULTRA. It involved completely planning our meals, diet, shopping list, and store trips. It also involved me waking up at 3:30a.m. to write this book, then go workout with a personal trainer from 5:00-6:00a.m., four days per week.

I cooked up the whole scheme one Wednesday afternoon and approached my wife that evening. She was excited about the meal plan, and ready to rock on eating super healthy, home-cooked, wholefood meals. The plan was for me to get back home before the boys woke up, so there would be little to no impact on her. So far, so good.

Project: ULTRA began the very next week, and we've been doing it ever since. However, an unanticipated factor arose within several weeks of kicking off this health mastery initiative... Reciprocity.

"You're working out four days per week," she said one morning as we ate our breakfast of eggs and a mountain of steamed kale. "I want to go to Barre 3 classes."

Barre 3 is a group workout class that mixes yoga, Pilates, and ballet exercises. I went to several with Candace and was the only man among a sea of beautiful, fit, powerful women. Whilst they wore skin tight spandex pants and hit each move to the rhythm of the beat, I flailed around in my baggy Adidas sweatpants, trying not to fall over. Then I was sore for three days. That class is no joke.

I want my wife to be happy. I want her to be healthy and fit and full of energy, and I obviously understand that having equal workout time is a fair proposition. But, I also struggled with solo mornings with the boys. Cooking the breakfast, cleaning up the kitchen, and managing them both was serious business. Plus, Arman, our one-year-old, was in a phase of screeching at the top of his lungs if he didn't get continuous attention.

"Ugh," I replied. "How many days per week do you want to go?" I asked.

"Well..." she paused, sensing my increasing resistance, "I could start with three."

But I could tell she wanted more, so I asked, "How many would you really want to do?"

"Five days per week," she said. Her energy perked up as she said this. The good husband move was clear. So, I decided to do it. Not out of niceness, people pleasing, fear, or obligation to be fair. But because I love her and I want to help her meet her needs. I know if I do this, and she does the same for me, then we create an extraordinary relationship that only gets better over time.

Of course, for the first several weeks of this new arrangement I made sure to get pouty and irritable when she'd leave for class in the morning. Not that I wanted to, I just couldn't help it. I was so miserable and I irrationally blamed her for my discomfort of having to be with my own two children by myself for 90 minutes each morning. Oh, the injustice!

After two weeks she asked me if we should change the plan, since I obviously wasn't handling it well. I stuck to my (mostly) good husband guns though.

"No," I replied. "This isn't a sign that you need to give something up. This is a sign that I need to keep growing and work through whatever is happening that makes me struggle in the mornings."

And that's just what I did. I learned how to relax and let go, how to get in a rhythm with my boys, and still take care of my own needs like eating and prepping food for work. Soon the mornings became routine and I ended up enjoying them more often than not. I felt grateful I got to spend so much time with my children in the mornings and evenings each day.

What's the moral of the story? Ask for what you want. The people around you care and want to support you, even if they complain and fight you on it sometimes. Stand up for yourself and ask for what you need, even if there's some initial friction.

But what if my spouse isn't so good to me? What if he or she doesn't care about my needs and wouldn't do what you did? Well, that's a big question with many possible answers. The simplest might be that you don't really advocate for yourself because you feel guilty and bad for doing so. As a result, you compromise in your own mind long before you ask for a watered-down version of what you originally wanted. This leads to a bubble of resentment that keeps you two apart and makes both of you less generous, loving, giving, and kind than you used to be with each other. Or, maybe he's just an "immature bastard," or she's a "selfish bitch." Who knows?

It doesn't matter, because this is not about him, or her, or any-one else. This is about you. You need to start advocating for yourself and asking for what you want because no one else will. No one is stopping you because you're not a victim of circumstance. You're the owner of your life, the captain of your ship, and the mastery of your destiny.

You are the one who decides what is right and what is wrong for you. You can decide what it means to identify your own needs and ask for what you want. You can decide to see it as healthy and ma-ture, and to reject the old ideas that it's bad, selfish, mean, or wrong to do so.

The next chapter in this book will give you the insight, encour-agement, and mental rewiring to stop always putting others first and to start taking care of yourself. You're going to learn how to be more selfish in the most healthy, positive, and mutually beneficial ways, and it will transform your relationships and your life.

There is just one last thing we need to cover before we conclude this chapter on speaking up.

THE COURAGE TO BE REAL

You have just learned dozens of mindset shifts, new models of relationships, and specific strategies for speaking up for yourself. Armed with clear tools, you may feel excited to test them out. Or you may feel terrified, like a young bird at the edge of the nest, about to see if she can flap her wings and fly. Regardless, you're doing great. This process of breaking out of old nice-person habits and becoming a bolder, freer, more expressive person is not easy. It's not for the faint of heart. It takes practice, commitment, and courage.

What I've discovered, however, is that our ideas of how it will be when we speak up are often more dramatic than how it plays out in reality. We imagine a disagreement or difficult conversation with someone as this intense, extreme, life-threatening experience. Our nervous systems start to ramp up, as if we were about to rock climb a sheer cliff wall with no ropes. *One false move and I could plummet to my death!*

Then, when we're in the moment and choose to step up and take action, it's a very different experience. Instead of a sheer, vertical cliff, it's more like a steep hill. It's kind of hard to walk up it, our legs burn a little, and we get out of breath. Uncomfortable, but not fatal.

The more you practice speaking up, the more you'll realize it's not as dangerous as you'd thought. You say things, people respond, and the world rotates. Once in a while, someone has a strong negative reaction, but it's rare. Generally, people don't seem too bothered by your increased boldness, and many actually prefer you this way. And the more you take the risk to speak up, and find the courage to be real, the better your life gets.

POST SPEAK-UP FREAK-OUT

There is one phenomenon you must be aware of as you embark on your journey of more boldness and badassery, and that is the Post Speak-Up Freak-out. The PSF often occurs immediately after speaking up for yourself. In the moment itself, you may have been direct, powerful, and assertive. You may have actually enjoyed your newfound powers, and even gotten a positive response. But then, on your drive home… PSF.

You start to review the scenario, playing it from different angles. You watch and re-watch scenes of the event, like a football coach who's watching game footage to spot key errors. Soon, the high of breaking free and the peace of being your authentic self in the world starts to turn into unease, then doubt, then full on freak-out.

That was way too forceful. Did you see Jennifer's face when I said that to Charles? She thought I was being so pushy and whiny. Oh geez, Charles probably thought that too. Why did I go on and on about that car engine analogy?? They got the point already. I was too forceful. I came across as desperate. Pathetic. They think I'm so pathetic. They hate me!

Dates, meetings, conversations with your partner, sharing more of yourself with friends or family–nothing is safe from the PSF. It's all fair game. In fact, it's helpful to anticipate this so you know how to interpret it accurately.

The obvious interpretation might be that the voice in your head is accurate. You *did* step out of line, go too far, or otherwise do something to offend others and embarrass yourself. Or, you could see the truth, that this is total hogwash buffoonery. This is actually nothing more than your Safety Police. The part of you that is terrified of taking risks, being bolder, and revealing who you are in the world. In fact, it's terrified of any change, no matter how positive. Sure, speaking up boldly makes you feel more vital and fully engaged in life, but it also opens you up to rejection and other emotional pain. So, your Safety Police causes the Post Speak-Up Freak-out to try to push you back into line.

In order to develop your assertiveness and strength, it's essential to see the PSF as just a reaction to stepping outside your comfort zone. Give little to no attention to the replays and anxiety that follows. See it just as a part of you that is trying to get you back into your nice person comfort zone. Smile and thank it for trying to do its job, and then move on.

What you said or did wasn't out of line, too far, or offensive. Even if your mind is telling you this is the case. Even if it sounds convincing and certain. Because, at this point your sensors on what is OK to say and do may not be fully and accurately calibrated. If they were stuck on the nice-person approval-seeking setting, then anything bold or authentic is labeled as offensive and bad.

In order to calibrate your sensors and really know if you were too aggressive or out of line, you will need more practice. Now is not the time to stop. In fact, you're just getting started.

So, the next time you speak up for yourself, take bold action, and step outside your comfort zone, give yourself an internal high-five. Then, when your Safety Police begins its PSF, follow this science-based, highly researched medical protocol:

1. Open up YouTube on your phone or computer.
2. Look up: "Le Freak" by *Chic* and press play.
3. Dance in your car and sing along!

Aaahh freak out!
Le freak, see'est Chic
Freak out!

Have you heard about the new dance craze?
Listen to us, I'm sure you'll be amazed...

DON'T HOLD BACK

It's true. Don't do it. Because when you hold back, stuff down what wants to come out, and play nice out of fear, you feel bad. Over time you feel less alive, less engaged, more resistant, and more resentful. Your energy drains and you start to feel more tired when you go to work, or spend time with your partner, or wherever you're not speaking up.

In the past, you've probably been aware of the dangers of speaking up. You've worried about what *might* happen, and how people *might* respond. You've focused on the pain of taking action. But have you ever slowed down to focus on the pain of *not* taking action? How do you feel when you leave a meeting where you were totally silent, and not because you honestly wanted to be that way? Rather, you were held back by fear, intimidated, and assuming others would be upset or judge you for saying what you thought.

What's it like to hide how you really feel around your partner, because you don't want to rock the boat? What does that do inside of you, day after day, to pretend? How about smiling and nodding at a party, agreeing and laughing at all the right times while everyone else does the talking? All the while, feeling secretly apart from the group, like you just don't really fit in. These are just a few of the thousands of moments in your life that you experience when you're held back within the confines of the nice person.

For me, the pain started small, and eventually became gargantuan. It was a cocktail of fear, inferiority, shame, and loneliness. It lead to pent up frustration and anger.

How has it impacted you?

It's time to turn down the Hold Back-o-Meter. To say what needs to be said. Or as my coach so tactfully put it in a recent session with me, "Aziz, what happens when you stop playing the weenie and start playing big?" I laughed when I heard her say that, and now that's on my whiteboard.

I have noticed in my own life, and in the lives of thousands of people I've spoken with over the years, this interesting phenomenon: **when we hold back, we feel less alive and less engaged.** Life loses its color, excitement, and promise. It becomes repetitive, boring, confining, and depressing. Whenever you leave an interaction of any sort, be it in business or your personal life, notice how you feel. If you feel drained, down, fed up, frustrated, or otherwise upset, most likely you held back. You didn't say what you wanted to say, ask what you wanted to ask, and act how you wanted to act.

You can then ask yourself, "How did I hold back?" After you ponder that one for a moment or two, ask yourself, "What would I have done if I was holding nothing back?" And then sit back and watch the theater of your mind play some amazing movies. It might be subtle shifts, such as interrupting to insert your opinion in a conversation, or more dramatic shifts, like jumping into that dance floor and doing some Saturday Night Fever moves. Regardless of what you see, pay keen attention, for these visions are guiding you towards your full, authentic, free self.

CHAPTER 10:

BE MORE SELFISH

If you informally polled 100 people and asked them, "Is selfishness a good trait? Is it good to be selfish?" I imagine almost every single person would say, "No. It is not good." The word has such a negative connotation that it's almost like asking people, "Is it good to be racist?" Everybody knows that being selfish is bad and wrong. It hurts others, and it means you're callous, self-absorbed, just in it for yourself, cold-hearted, and a jerk.

But I have a different perspective. One that may go counter to what you learned growing up. It may seem counter-intuitive at first. But, if you're willing to let go of all-or-nothing thinking about purely "good" and "bad" traits, and ready to examine what *really* creates healthy self-esteem, lasting and deep relationships, and true happiness, then this may be the most liberating chapter you'll ever read.

The truth is there is such a thing as negative or destructive selfishness. This is callously going after what you want and not giving a damn about how others feel, or how it impacts them, all so you can have more pleasure for yourself. Sure, that's not the best strategy for happiness or relationship success. And that's not the kind of selfishness I'm encouraging here.

What I'm going to suggest is that there are many things that you could do that would greatly serve you in your life that might *feel selfish*. These things would not only enhance your own well-being, they would also improve your relationships, career, friendships, and personal fulfillment. In short, they would be good for you and good for others.

The purpose of this chapter is to help you move towards the healthier end of the self-interest spectrum so that you can act on your own behalf. You'll learn how to become your own advocate, skilled at taking care of yourself and meeting your own needs. Rather than making you a self-absorbed (or "bad") person, you'll discover that this allows you to actually be *more* loving, generous, and kind. You'll end up being able to contribute more to your family, business, and greater community.

In fact, you'll discover the surprising secret that being self-sacrificing doesn't make you an altruistic, "good" person. It actually diminishes your energy over time, causes you pain, and thus hurts those close to you. If you are depleted and resentful, those you love receive less of you, even if you try to force yourself to show up and be nice. Ultimately, acting in your own healthy self-interest brings you back into balance, where you are taking care of your own needs, and not passively asking others to do that for you.

If you, like me, grew up with a million and one messages that told you advocating for yourself and not always putting others first is bad, selfish, and wrong, that's OK. Some things in this chapter may stretch you, challenge your old ideas and programming, and push some buttons. I'm going to ask that you trust me even more and read these following pages with an open mind.

On the other side of the fear and the judgment is a freer, expressed, happy, fulfilled, and loving version of you. Let's bring them out to play.

Out beyond ideas of wrongdoing
and rightdoing there is a field.
I'll meet you there.
When the soul lies down in that grass
the world is too full to talk about.
Rumi

THE SELFISH SPECTRUM

First things first, we need to define what selfish means. According to the dictionary, it means you lack consideration for others or are concerned chiefly with your own personal profit or pleasure. So far, that doesn't sound super great. But watch this.

Let's say you want to see movie A and your friend wants to see movie B. If you advocate for movie A, is that selfish? If you refuse to see movie B, is that selfish? You may have an immediate answer to these questions, or it might depend on the context.

Do we almost always go to the movies I want and rarely to the movies you want? Did you do something generous for me earlier that day? Do we go to the movies I want because I go to the opera with you once per month? Is your movie choice something I'd kind of dislike, or is it my least favorite genre in the world?

Now it's getting more complex. And subjective. Because the truth is "selfish" is in the eye of the beholder. It's a calculation based upon how much each person is giving and receiving in the relationship, and what is deemed "fair." Hence, selfish is not really a simple category that you're in or out of. Instead, it's a spectrum.

THE SELFISH SPECTRUM

		SELF SACRIFICE
OVERLY PASSIVE & SELF-DENYING	1	Always You, Never Me
	2	You First, Then Me
	3	Sometimes Me, But Only If It's REALLY Important
HEALTHY SELF-INTEREST	4	Sometimes You, Sometimes Me
	5	Usually Me First, Then You
DESTRUCTIVE SELFISHNESS	6	Always Me, Then You
	7	Me And Mine, Screw You
		SELFISH

On the left side of this spectrum, we have no right to our self-interest. We always put others and their needs and wants first. We feel horrible and guilty if we do otherwise. This can be called self-sacrificing or self-denying.

The complete opposite end of this spectrum is the disconnected, self-absorbed person who mercilessly crushes all who oppose his or her will. They'll get what they want or there will be hell to pay.

The middle of the spectrum is known as healthy self-interest. This is where you can take care of yourself when you need to. You're able to put your needs first at times, and you can enjoy some time off without feeling guilty for not doing enough. You can say no, even if someone's upset about it. You can say what you want and need, and you can finally start enjoying yourself more.

Where do you tend to live? What number on the spectrum, between one and seven? Most nice people hover around two—You First, Then Me. They meet their needs only after they're sure everyone else is covered. They ask for what they want only if they think others will want the same thing.

Under stress they drop down to a 1 (Always You, Never Me) and completely forgo their own needs, wants, and desires. They'll tell themselves something like this: *How on earth could I ask for what I need when it's obvious he's struggling so much. Now is not the time.*

Sometimes, they'll move up to level 3 (Sometimes Me, But Only If It's REALLY Important), but only if it's a big deal. On rare occasion, an event or experience that is important to them, they'll advocate for themselves to go to it. Or, if they're reaching the threshold of how much they can give, they'll ask for more support. More often than not, however, they won't ask directly. Instead, some sort of physical condition, such as migraines, back pain, or neck pain, will become so intense that they force the person to slow down and take care of themselves.

Healthy self-interest exists in the range between level 4 and 5. That may surprise you. Perhaps you see four as a healthy place to be: Sometimes You, Sometimes Me. I mean, it seems fair after all. But level 5, Usually Me First, Then You, that just sounds terrible, doesn't it? Way too selfish, bad, and wrong!

Not necessarily. Because being able to identify what you want and prioritize meeting your needs in a skillful way allows you to be more loving, generous, and giving than ever before. The "Usually Me First" means you are frequently looking inwards to discover what you need and want, first. You are considering that before you factor in others' needs and wants. This prevents the old nice-person habit of always putting others first and allows you to get clear on what will help you thrive.

Remember the Project: ULTRA example from the last chapter where Candace and I were figuring out our workout schedules?

It began with me getting clear: *I want to work out four times per week, no matter what.* It started with a strong, healthy impulse of self-interest. Me first. I need to do this. I want this. I'm going to make this happen. Then, from that place, I began to explore how to make it work for our entire family. And that's **the key difference between healthy self-interest and callous selfishness: I consider how to meet my needs in the most skillful way possible that serves the greater good.**

As I did this, Candace became freer to claim what she wanted and needed. As I put myself first and was able to meet my needs, I became able to freely and happily give generously without resentment. So, when she says she can work out just three days a week, instead of saying, "Great! Less work for me," I say, "Really? How many days would you *really* want to work out?" She gets *more* of what she wants and so do I.

This is the real secret of being more selfish. It's moving up the spectrum to the levels of healthy self-interest so you can most skillfully meet your needs. As you do so, you become a much happier, more loving and giving person.

One important note–if you're a parent, especially of small children, self-sacrifice seems to be the name of the game. In many situations with my boys I'm operating at levels two and three—often putting them first—and that feels good for me to do right now. That means I make them meals and snacks, tell stories in the bathroom during dinner time, and wipe poopy butts whether I want to or not. I do this because I deeply love them and want to create a secure sense of attachment and healthy self-esteem. I know that the more they feel held, respected, and loved at this young age, the more it will serve them for a lifetime.

Parenting is the long-game. I see it as a spiritual practice to continually surrender to what is most needed in the moment and set aside many of my inner child's personal preferences. This is what makes me the adult in that situation.

Yet, the resentment formula still applies (you'll discover what that is in just a moment). So here and there I say no to things I don't want to do and offer alternatives, so I feel like I still have some autonomy.

I also take time for myself to process and release any resentment that forms from giving in this way to prevent it from building up and causing problems. I take time for myself every morning between 3:00 – 6:00 a.m. for my spiritual and physical practices to keep me happy, energized, grateful, and healthy. So, while I give a lot to my boys, I'm sure to give a lot to myself too.

YOUR PRIORITY LIST

In order to move up the spectrum towards more healthy self-interest, you will need to shift your priorities. To illustrate this, let's start with a little story about a client named Ellie. Pay attention to what elements of her story may be similar to your own.

Ellie was a highly motivated, successful sales woman who was well respected in her company. She was married to a loving husband, and they had two young children under the age of five. On paper, Ellie's life was perfect. She had love, career success, respect, and material wealth. Yet she didn't feel relaxed, free, or happy.

She spent much of her time feeling anxious, stressed, and guilty. Even though she worked a full-time job, she expected herself to run the household, including shopping, laundry, cooking and cleaning, as well as taking care of the kids. In her opinion, the house was never as it "should be" and she was falling short. At work, she often felt anxious before meetings with superiors, high profile clients, and other executives, despite having been in the field for twenty years. When she spent time with her parents, whom she described as loving, she felt anxious and couldn't bear the idea of them being disappointed with her.

As we explored her world more closely, an interesting trend began to emerge. Regarding maintaining the household, she didn't ask her husband for more help because she worried about putting more on his plate. She worried about whether she was being a good enough mother to her children, and if they were getting everything they wanted and needed. At work she worried about whether the high profile clients were satisfied, and if her superiors felt comfortable in her presence at meetings and social events.

At first the pattern was subtle to her, almost invisible. But then she began to see just how pervasive the pattern was: **in virtually every situation in her life, she was prioritizing others' needs, wants, and feelings over her own.** Her attention and energy was always focused outwards—*What do they want here? What does he need? How does she feel about that? Will they be OK here?*–and on and on.

This was based on the unquestioned belief that it was always right to prioritize other people's needs. After all, that is what a good, selfless, altruistic human does, right? This is the conditioning that most of us received. It can be compounded in families where ethics and morals are based in a strong religious foundation, depending on how that family interprets their faith. In these instances, the dictate to be selfless is not only good, but to do otherwise is a sin and reviled by family, community, and God alike. As a little kid, that's some serious stuff that you don't want to mess around with.

Jesus, Mother Teresa, Gandhi, Martin Luther King, Saint Francis of Assisi, and countless other spiritual and political figures are heralded as models of goodness, virtue, and what a human should be. Meanwhile, overtly greedy and clearly self-interested politicians, corporate leaders, bankers, and other people who gain infamy from bending or breaking rules to enrich their own bank accounts, are universally seen as bad and how a human should *not* be.

And so, you may strive to be like those from the first list, and avoid all actions that push you towards the second. You let the other person go first, give when it's hard, act patiently with demanding people, support others through their hardships, and turn the other cheek. You act as a good person should. You appear loving, generous, altruistic, kind, and good to others. But what happens inside?

It may start small at first, like a few grains of sand that slip into your shoe as you walk on the beach. Barely perceptible. It's a hint of disappointment when your partner seems to take the meal you prepared for granted. It's the minor irritation you feel with your children as they take forever to get ready in the morning. It's the slight sense of emptiness and dissatisfaction you feel as you fall asleep at the end of a long work day.

Over time, these grains of sand begin to grow into pebbles that stab at your feet with each step. This manifests as anxiety, difficulty sleeping, and feeling depressed. *I don't know why I'm depressed, I should be happy. Maybe it runs in my family. It must be genetic. There's something wrong with my brain chemicals.* Your knee begins acting up again from that old injury from fifteen years ago and you start having more problems with your back. Even though you're loving with your family, friends, and coworkers, when you're driving alone and someone cuts you off, the level of instant rage you feel is surprisingly powerful and a little disturbing. You sometimes feel guilty about how angry you secretly get.

This story can go on and the intensity of symptoms and discomfort can continue to build, all with absolutely no awareness of what is happening and why. Millions of people are struggling just like this, and they seek counsel from their primary care doctor who tells them they have clinical depression and prescribes them an antidepressant medication after a twelve-minute consult. The medication kind of, sort of works, maybe. But maybe they need to change to a different one, because "sometimes it just takes a while to find the right one."

All the while, they're missing the true source of their suffering. It's a problem with their priorities. When our needs and wants are habitually and consistently placed as low or last priority, we're going to suffer. It's a recipe for resentment. In fact, it's so predictable it's virtually a mathematical formula.

THE RESENTMENT FORMULA

After working with thousands of people, it's become clear to me that there is a natural formula for resentment in humans, and it goes something like this.

Giving + No Choice About the Matter = Resentment

If we give too much, *and feel like we do not have a choice about the giving*, we will feel resentment (which is just another word for anger). The not having a choice part seems to be the key factor in the resentment formula.

We can give generously and freely, and do so way more than we receive in relationships. In fact, that can be an extremely healthy thing to do and is a key component of creating extraordinary romantic relationships and deeply bonded relationships with our children: to give more than we receive. But, if that giving is done under pressure or demand, we will start to feel angry.

Often times the pressure is not obvious or overt. It's not always the boss yelling at you to "get that report done by Sunday night dammit!" **The pressures are often internal and based on your own need to please others and be nice.** More specifically, the pressure comes from that convincing voice in your held that commands you to carry out your nice-person conditioning. *She wants that, so I'll do it. I know he likes that and I don't want to disappoint him. They'll be hurt if I say no, so I'd better say yes and go.* All of these pressures to be nice and "do the right thing" eliminate a sense of autonomy, freedom, and choice. You've given up your sovereignty. You *have to* do these things. And this is what creates the resentment.

If your nice-person programming is particularly strong, then you may not even realize you're angry. That is not nice, after all, and therefore remains blocked from your conscious awareness. But regardless of your awareness of it, it's there. Because it's part of human nature. We resist pressure, demand, and bondage. Even if we're out-wardly compliant, our shadow does not go silently into that good night. It gets fired up, pissed off, and ready to fight.

If you own your shadow and speak up for yourself, then you can speak about this challenge directly and work through it quickly in your relationships. If you do not, then it will manifest as passive aggressive behaviors, distancing or withdrawing from the other person, secretly judging them, being internally irritable or blaming them, or annoyed by minor things such as how they breathe through their nose or certain faces they make.

If anger is completely taboo for you, then even these signs of irritation will be blocked out of your awareness by more powerful defenses, such as feeling anxious or depressed, having panic attacks, developing chronic pain conditions such as back or neck pain, repetitive stress injuries, or a "frozen shoulder" (from sitting at a computer too much no doubt. *This has nothing to do with my feelings. Nothing I say! It's all structural, my doctor told me so*).

Whether you're aware of the source of your resentment or not, you will suffer the consequences. It sucks away your happiness, peace, and joy in life and leaves you feeling angry and burnt-out, or sad, anxious, depleted, and depressed. When you're struggling in this way, you might turn to others for help: friends, family, parents, or those in our community. This may alleviate feelings of loneliness and isolation and give you some sense of connection. However, most people in your world may have no idea about the resentment formula. They may perceive putting others first as one of your best virtues and encourage you to "stick with it" and "have faith." In other words: keep on going as you always have, try harder, be nicer, and it will all work itself out. But what if it doesn't?

Give and Give

"I know I'm going to break up with her," he said with certainty. "It's not a question of 'if,' it's a question of 'when.'"

I was surprised by his clarity. Many clients I've worked with are often in a more ambivalent, tortured state about whether to end their romantic relationship.

I was walking in my favorite park near my office, having a phone session with a highly motivated, insightful man named Jason. He was in his late thirties and he had been with his partner for six years.

"You sound clear in yourself about what you want to do," I said.

"Yeah," he agreed in a pained voice. "I'm not looking forward to it. It's going to break her heart. When I've hinted about any change in our relationship in the past, it did not go well at all."

I asked him about this and he told me about his partner becoming extremely distraught, crying, and saying, "How could you *do* this to me? How could you value us so little?" and other blaming statements.

And so, he stayed with her. He knew he wanted to move on, to experience life outside of the relationship, to follow his heart. There was no doubt about that. He just didn't want to hurt her. He loved her deeply and he cared about her. He didn't want her to feel so much pain.

He decided to wait for the right time. She was going through some job challenges and was currently unemployed. She also had lost some of her friends recently and he was her main source of social connection. *I'll wait until she's got a job and a few friendships*, he thought to himself, *then she'll be able to handle the end of our relationship.*

As the months passed and she continued to struggle to find work, she eventually cast a wider net for job opportunities. Soon she received an offer from a company in another state. He decided to move with her, since he ran his own business from home and could work from anywhere. *She'll get set up in this job, make some friends, get settled into the new city, and be in a much better place. Then we can break up.*

But then the holidays were coming up, and he didn't want to do that to her right before the holidays. Then she didn't like her new job all that much and was dissatisfied. And now he was having a conversation with me about it.

Jason was an extremely loving and caring person. I could feel how much he wanted what was best for his partner, and how much it pained him when she hurt. I could see how responsible he felt for her feelings and how much guilt he experienced. I could also see how unfulfilled he was in his life, and how much of himself he'd shut down and hidden in order to make his relationship work. And just how much his partner's needs, wants, and feelings mattered more than his own.

This is the plight of the nice-person: to prioritize others, be a good person and do the right thing, only to feel restricted, hollow, angry, and depressed inside, and then to respond to that pain by giving and prioritizing others even more, attempting to dig our way out of a hole by digging further.

You may read Jason's story and see it as extreme. Or you may be shaking your head in amazed recognition at how eerily similar his story sounds to yours. In either case, we're all doing the same thing to some degree. We're all giving too much and perceiving ourselves as not having a choice in the matter, whether it's with our spouse, kids, a boyfriend or girlfriend, with co-workers, employees, clients, or a boss. We all feel like there's certain things we just *have to* do.

That is, until we decide to change our priorities. To change how we approach relationships and other people. To let go of over-responsibility, unhelpful childhood programming, and negative ideas about taking care of ourselves, and step up and take responsibility for ourselves, our lives, and our happiness. To upgrade our understanding of relationships to see what actually leads to lasting love and connection with others, rather than staying stuck in inner commandments about how we "should be." Until we decide to become more selfish.

YOUR REAL RESPONSIBILITIES

You are responsible for meeting your own needs. This means being able to uncover what you want and need in a situation, and then take effective steps to get it. If you want attention, you decide how you can skillfully ask for it and receive it. If you want safety or certainty, you protect yourself or ease your fears. If you want to be touched in a certain way by your partner, you explore what it is you really want and ask them for it.

This may sound obvious and simplistic, but many of us don't operate as if it were. Instead, we ignore our needs, desires, and wants or just keep them to ourselves. We dismiss them as excessive, unnecessary, or burdensome to others. But this doesn't make them go away. We give up our power to meet our own needs, which is one of the hallmarks of being an adult: the capacity to take care of ourselves.

As we deny our own needs and wants, we impair our ability to meet them skillfully and we become more like young children. We're unable to ask for what we want and need. My son, Zaim, who's three years old, is at the age now where he will sometimes groan and yell when he's upset. We have to guide him to slow down, breathe, and tell us what he wants. "Can you say what you want, buddy?" Your parents' might have used the classic phrase: Use your words.

In any case, this is what we revert to when we don't take responsibility for meeting our own needs. Doing this does not make you selfless, altruistic, or a "good person." It hurts you and greatly impairs your relationships, thus hurting others. It makes others have to take care of you more instead of you taking care of yourself, which ultimately frustrates them and pushes them away.

It's time to stop secretly hoping that if we're nice enough and good enough, our needs will magically be met. That others will be perceptive and check in with us: "Hi friend, what do you need today?" While this may happen occasionally, it usually does not. When it doesn't, we become frustrated, hurt, or angry inside. We judge others as selfish, self-absorbed, or totally clueless. And we feel powerless.

It's time to step up and take full responsibility. No one can care as much about your internal, moment-to-moment experience as you can. Because they're not in it. They're not in your body, in your mind, and in your heart, experiencing everything you are. They have their own internal experience to feel and navigate. You are responsible for you.

That means deciding, right here and now as you read this page, that you will shift your priorities and put yourself first. You no longer confuse self-denial with being a good person. You see clearly that always putting others first creates deep resentment, destroys your happiness, and is unsustainable. And you acknowledge that putting yourself first allows you to meet your needs in the most skillful way. This, in turn, increases your happiness, joy, and capacity to love, so you can give freely and create healthy relationships.

Many times per day, ask yourself the questions you've learned so far in this book: *What do I want? What do I need? How can I take care of myself?* Then, instead of dismissing the answers, pay attention to them. Come up with a plan of how to get what you want and meet your needs. With your newfound powers of bold assertion, you have a direct route to do exactly that in a skillful and effective manner.

You just might find that you're better at uncovering your needs and meeting them than you realized. This is often the case with my clients because the main obstacle is simply the belief that putting yourself first is bad. Once they see the insanity of the self-denying patterns, and they give themselves complete permission to take care of themselves, it becomes easy and natural to do so.

As you follow these steps and take more responsibility, you'll let others do the same. As you stop playing the victim of circumstance, you will stop seeing others as victims. You'll think to yourself: *I have power and you have power. Let's both use it.* Thus, by being clear on what you are really responsible for, you will let go of what you're not responsible for.

You're not responsible for other people's feelings, wants, desires, and needs. You do not have to meet everyone's needs. You don't have to do everything that someone wants you to do.

You don't have to do *anything* that someone wants, if it is not right for you. You're not responsible for meeting their needs—they are. You doing something for them is just one possible way for them to meet their needs. If you say no, then it's their responsibility to find a different way.

This last paragraph is worth reading and re-reading many times. Underline and highlight it. Write out the first few sentences on a sticky note and put it somewhere you'll see it often. It's a new way of being in the world, a less nice way, that might take some reinforcement.

When it does, you become free. You're no longer controlled by the invisible forces of obligation and guilt. You reclaim your power and realize you always have choice. You remember that you are a cause in this world, not an effect. As a cause, you must get clear on what you want, and you must claim what you want with clarity, conviction, and power. Without apology or shame.

<u>YOU MUST CLAIM</u>

"If a man does not become what he understands,
he does not understand it."
- Kierkegaard

This is how the typical process works with clients that are becoming less self-denying and healthier in their self-interest. First, they're completely trapped in the nice-person cage, only vaguely aware of the pain it's causing them. They have the occasional thought of, *I'm too nice,* or *I shouldn't be so nice all the time,* but it passes and they remain in the same patterns.

Then, as we work together and they see how much pain nice is causing, and how rooted it is in fear, guilt, and people-pleasing, they begin to transform their beliefs. They start to acknowledge that it's OK to not be nice all the time, and sometimes you have to put yourself first. So far, so good.

But then they almost always hit this snag. They intellectually get that it's good to act in their self-interest, and that being overly nice isn't working. They "understand" that it's good to ask for what you want and be direct. But...

I still *feel like* it's bad.
I still *feel like* I'm hurting people.
I still *feel like* it's selfish and wrong.
I still *feel like* people will be upset with me.

I'm mentioning this now because there's a good chance that might be happening for you now. First off, whatever follows the phrase "feel like" is never a feeling.

I feel like you're hurting me.
I feel like you don't care about me.
I feel like it's time to do something about it.
I feel like a sandwich.

All of those are ideas or beliefs. Except for the sandwich, that is a thing you can eat. The others are statements of thought. I think you are hurting me. I believe you don't care about me. I think it's time to do something about it. The feelings underneath these statements don't have the word like in them. They are:

I feel hurt.
I feel rejected and unwanted.
I feel frustrated and determined.
I feel hungry.

Do you see the difference? So, when you understand it intellectually, but you still feel like it's bad, guess what? That means you still believe it's bad. It means the nice-person programming is still holding on there, telling you that it's not OK to ask for what you want or put yourself first.

There are two ways to deal with this. The first would be to re-read this chapter from the beginning. Slow down and really let yourself see how painful and damaging the nice patterns can be. If you really understood how much it was hurting you, then you would reach a pain threshold that would help push you to the other side. If needed, you can also go back and re-read Chapter 5 from Part I – "The High Cost of Nice."

Secondly, take a few minutes to write out all your objections. All your "Yeah, buts…" Are you thinking of certain situations where you just couldn't possibly put yourself first? Are you thinking about how your partner, or colleagues, or friends, would get upset with you if you acted in your self-interest more? Is your mind cataloging evidence about why it wouldn't work if you spoke up?

Write all these objections down and see if you can answer each one. Perhaps you'll see that many of them are just fear. They're just your Safety Police holding on even tighter. *If you do that, terrible things will happen! Terrible things, I say! Whatever you do, do NOT open that door! You hear me?!*

In other instances, perhaps you're seeing yourself as helpless or powerless. *He won't let me do it. She gets too emotional if I speak up, so I "have to" keep quiet. It's her fault.*

This is where you must do the inner work. You must be more interested in seeing the truth than defending your old way of being. The truth of what creates happiness, health, and loving relationships. The truth of what actually works in life.

Once you have done this, the key is to claim what you want. Fully and completely, beginning with complete self-interest.

COMPLETE SELF-INTEREST (CSI)

Do you remember Jason's story from just a few pages back? As he agonized over the particulars of exactly how and when to end his relationship, I could hear a major problem. He was not in himself.

No, I don't mean this in some science fiction or astral travel sort of way. Psychologically, his focal point was his partner, not himself. He was imagining all of his actions as they would be interpreted and felt by her. In short, he was missing from the equation.

To bring him back, I re-oriented him to the complete opposite end of the spectrum.

"Just as an experiment, let's say you were going to operate from your own complete self-interest–where every choice was based entirely on what was easiest, most desirable, or best sounding to you, regardless of how she felt–what would you do? What would CSI Jason do?"

He laughed in response to my reference to the cheesy police show on TV. This question gave him permission to go inward and find out what he really wanted. It helped him step out of his old perspective, in which his actions were always guided by what he thought others wanted.

"I would wait three weeks until after the holidays, then I would end the relationship. I wouldn't go on the trip we had planned. I'd rent myself an AirBnB so I could get away after having the breakup conversation. Then I'd come back a week later and start moving all my stuff out."

In that moment, everything shifted. His voice tone was completely different. The hesitancy, uncertainty, and long pauses were gone. His pitch was even deeper. He was reconnected with himself, his desire, and his power. He was back in.

But isn't this bad, selfish, wrong, and inconsiderate? This is what Jason had been telling himself for years. This is what you may be telling yourself every day. Unfortunately, it's a misguided attempt at being a noble, "good" human being. In fact, it's actually rooted in fear and makes you even more selfish. Here's how:

Jason is focused on keeping his partner happy and remaining in the relationship because he does not want her to feel pain, right? In reality, *he* does not want to feel pain. In fact, when she's hurting he feels not only pain, but a particularly intense form of shame. As we explored this more, it turned out his shame was telling him he failed at taking away all her pain and making her feel happy. She had a rough life growing up, and he felt it was his responsibility to show her that the world was a good place, that men could be trusted, and that she could finally feel happy with him. So, when he no longer wants to be with her, he is failing her, and he isn't a good enough man.

If she totally lost it after their breakup and went into a spiral of addiction, his guilt and shame would only intensify. He was scared of those feelings. He was also scared of her being angry at him, and judging him as a bad or selfish man. He was afraid of her friends thinking negatively of him, and them discussing how bad and selfish he is over brunch. Who is all this really about? Her or him? Who is he *really* most focused on?

The truth is he is already causing her pain in the relationship. No matter how much he thinks he's hiding his discontent and playing the role of happy boyfriend, she feels that something is off. In general, women are more perceptive, intuitive, and emotionally aware than men. If something's off, they feel it. Even if they don't think about it consciously. Who knows how much her dissatisfaction in her friendships, job, and life are the result of her partner not really loving her for who she is?

And that's just short-term pain. In the long-term, delaying the breakup is one of the most painful things to do to someone you love. Those two, or three, or ten years that you are just biding your time and planning your escape are years lost for you both. Jason's girlfriend could be building a new relationship with someone who's a better fit. The longer he waits, the more pain is created.

In most cases trying to be nice and pleasing people are just self-focused ways to avoid fear and discomfort. They provide short-term relief for us, but long-term pain in others.

I saw this play out dozens of times in my own dating life. I would be warm, enthusiastic, and totally interested in everything she shared. I would be affirming, positive, and upbeat. I did this because

I wanted her to feel good. Or so I thought. In truth, I also did this so she would like me, and so I could think of myself as a "good person."

Being this way with someone isn't necessarily bad, if it's authentic. But I would portray this energy, even if I didn't fully believe it myself. Because I had to, in order to be a good person and to get her to like me, remember? This would continue for weeks, sometimes months. I was the perfect guy. I made her feel deeply loved, special, and maybe like she was the one.

And then I'd leave. Often quickly and abruptly, with no solid explanation to satisfy her confused mind, let alone her aching heart. I know I caused many of these women great pain. I'm sure many of them asked themselves questions like: *It was so good, what happened? What did I do wrong? Did I not see something?* For some it may have undermined their sense of trust in men—*can I really believe what he is portraying?*

It took me many years to learn what you are learning in this book, to see that becoming clear on what I actually want, and then directly sharing that with others is beneficial. That looking at a situation with Complete Self-Interest helps me know where I stand so I can fully engage in a relationship with someone that is mutually rewarding. Paradoxically, the more you come from this place, the more you are able to freely decide when and how much you want to give. You will end up being more loving, generous, and giving than you ever were as a struggling nice person.

HURTING VERSUS HARMING

Yes, but isn't it bad to hurt people? And when you tell your boyfriend you don't want to be with him anymore, that's hurting him. Or if you change the subject when someone's talking, that's hurting their feelings. They'll feel dismissed and ignored. They'll think you're not interested (which you're not) and then they'll think that they're not an interesting enough person. They'll feel bad, and you did it to them. You hurt them, and that's bad.

As I write this line of thinking, which you've most likely experienced, I am smiling. I can almost see the upset mother or school teacher bending down at the waist, emphasizing the "you're bad" message with an upright index finger. Can you hear the childhood nice person programming?

Don't do X because then you're bad. Anytime you have that thought, it's a glaring light on your dashboard to slow down and check your engine. There's something not right going on under the hood (a.k.a. in your brains). When our minds tell us that something is "bad" we immediately stop, as if it were an electric fence. Or an electric chair. It's not. It's just the pain and shame that you felt while being criticized or shamed by a parent, or teacher, or some other authority when you were young. It may not be accurate, based on your values, or even real.

The fear of hurting someone is an example of childhood nice programming gone awry. The reality is that life is full of pain. Physical and emotional pain cannot be avoided no matter how hard you try. Hurt is nothing more than a word to describe feeling pain. I stubbed my toe and my foot hurt (physical pain). He called me stupid and I felt hurt (emotional pain).

No matter what you do, people around you are going to feel hurt. And much of the time it has nothing to do with what you did or didn't do. It's all about the other person's ideas, beliefs, rules, and past wounds. If Aunt Linda made a lovely meal for you and you said, "gosh, Aunt Linda, what a lovely meal. Thank you." Guess what? She could still be hurt. Because while you thanked her for the meal, you didn't ask for seconds. Instead, she saw you eating some desert later and she thought, "If he was still hungry, why didn't he eat more of my meal? It must have not been that good, he was just saying that. I'm a terrible cook." Is that your responsibility? Are you somehow to know that and fix her distorted beliefs? Should you ask for seconds at every meal served to you from now on, just to be safe?

When Jason breaks up with his girlfriend, she will feel great pain, I'm sure. She will feel hurt. But that is not Jason's job to prevent. He can't prevent all pain in her, or even in himself. His job is to get clear on what he truly wants, and to communicate this with directness, compassion, and love. In fact, the more direct, the better. If he dilutes his message and implies that he's unhappy but maybe they can work it out, she now has false hope that drags out the pain even longer.

People will feel pain, disappointment, and hurt around you. Your beloved spouse and innocent children will feel hurt too. I'm sorry, it is just the way of things on this planet.

This kind of pain, however, is very different than intentional harm. Harm is when someone is feeling pain or anger themselves, and decides to act on an impulse to intentionally cause pain in another. Obvious examples of this are physical violence, verbally attacking someone's character, or abuse. These are forms of harm and are signals for you to leave the situation. If you are the perpetrator of these acts, they are signals that you need help now to heal whatever is going on inside. More common, everyday examples of harming others include saying that biting and critical comment even though you know it's not true, but you just want to get back at someone. It's losing it and yelling at your kid for doing something small that you know isn't a big deal.

These are things that we all might do from time to time, and are indications that we are still growing, healing, and evolving ourselves. They are reminders to continue developing patience, non-reactivity, and our capacity to love more unconditionally.

In short, if you harm someone, do more inner work. If someone around you feels hurt when you clarify what you want and speak your truth, that is a sign for *them* to do their inner work.

FULL PERMISSION

Once you have identified what you truly want and asked for it directly, you might find that you get it. Hurray! Well, maybe. Many recovering nice people, myself included, can have difficulty receiving. Whether it's some time for yourself, going to the restaurant you want, or your partner touching you in that new and exciting way you asked for, it can be hard to relax and enjoy yourself. Instead, your mind might become active with worry, and you may feel guilt or anxiety.

Is this really OK? Do they really want to be here? Are they upset with me right now? Are they enjoying this too, or is it all just for me? These thoughts, and many others can cloud your mind and prevent you from really enjoying the experience. They seem to be a normal part of the Boldness Training process and diminish over time. They are a sign that you have not fully bought into the idea that it's OK to ask for what you want and to act in your healthy self-interest.

They could also be a sign that you don't say no very much, so you assume others don't as well. The more relaxed and capable you become with saying no, the more you trust others will do the same. This helps you know that if they granted your request, it's because they wanted to. If it was because they were scared to say no, that's on them, and they have some inner work to do. We will transform your relationship with "no" in the next chapter so you can easily and calmly decline anything you want.

In the meantime, give yourself full permission to receive and enjoy. While the fear, doubt, and guilt may still pop up, do your best to ignore them. Instead of feeding them with your attention, simply dismiss them as signs of remaining over-niceness leaving your body. Then, bring your attention fully into the present.

If you're spending some cherished time alone, see what sounds delightful to do. Watch that movie that your partner would never want to go see. Go for a run. Eat your favorite kind of food. Speaking of food, if you're at the restaurant and wondering if your friend really wants to be here, or just said yes to please you, bring yourself out of your mind and into the moment. What is the restaurant like? What is the atmosphere, the sounds, the smells? Why do you love this place? Pay attention to your friend. How is she doing? What's going on in her life? And if you're so fortunate as to be receiving that new touch you requested from your partner... tune in to your body, my friend, because you don't want to miss out on that one. What does it feel like? Bring your attention to the physical sensations, sounds, and pleasure of being touched how you like.

You deserve this. It's OK to receive. People love you and want to support you and help you meet your needs. You're not bad. You're beautiful.

> *"You do not have to be good.*
> *You do not have to walk on your knees*
> *For a hundred miles through the desert, repenting.*
> *You only have to let the soft animal of your body*
> *love what it loves."*
> - Mary Oliver

IT WILL BE MESSY

I considered titling this section, "There Will Be Blood" after the epic Daniel Day-Lewis drama about a brutal oil tycoon, but that's taking it a little too far. When you become more selfish, it can be messy, I promise you that. There will be feelings. People around you might have feelings. They may feel upset, angry, or hurt. You may feel upset, angry, or hurt. Or guilty and bad about yourself.

At this point, you might be thinking: *Wow, Aziz. That sounds delightful. Sign me up!*

But it's the only way. The only way out is through. Human relationships are inherently messy. People have all kinds of feelings. These are not signs that we're doing something wrong. In fact, they may be signs that you're doing exactly what you need to do.

Quite recently I had a messy experience taking care of myself and claiming what I needed. Late last summer my family and I traveled down to Monterey, California, for a week-long vacation. It was the first time we'd flown with two little boys, who were ten-months and two-and-a-half-years-old at the time. Chaos. Packing, food prep, rental cars, non-baby proofed rental house with grandparents, the works. Quite far from your sit-on-the-beach-for-hours-and-watch-the-sunset kind of vacation. But it was beautiful and sweet, too. So many magic moments of being on the beach, playing in parks, going to the aquarium, and time with family. It was an exhausting, full, heart-achingly lovely experience.

Within several days of returning home, we needed to decide our plans for Thanksgiving because it involved purchasing plane tickets. In years past, my family gathered in Los Angeles, California. I enjoyed seeing my cousins, aunts, uncles, and having a chance to spend time with my brother and parents. But doing the entire family plane ride trip again, with all the accommodations, food planning, car renting, and all the rest sounded terrible.

So, I asked myself, "What do I want?" Gasp! This is already becoming quite selfish. You can't ask that sort of thing about holidays. But ask I did, and I discovered I didn't want a family trip. Well, part of me did. Moments sounded fun. But a larger part of me wanted to split up the weekend. Spend two days at home with Candace and the boys, then spend two days in Los Angeles with my extended family. Solo.

Using the techniques from the previous chapter, I spoke up for myself and talked about what I wanted. In the moment, Candace agreed quite easily and I purchased the plane ticket. I texted my cousins to get ready for a 2-day binge on *Magic: The Gathering*. I was excited.

Then, about one week before my trip, Candace became more fully aware of what she agreed to. She felt sad about missing out on time with family, and hurt that I didn't want to bring everyone along. She also felt upset about me having two days of care-free gallivanting about, *Magic* cards in hand, whilst she pulled a super long two-day solo-parent shift.

THERE WILL BE BLOOD!! No, but there will be feelings. And my brain and nervous system can react as if something terrible is happening and I need to fix it now, now, now. Candace voiced her upset and was clearly feeling hurt and angry with me. I attempted to empathize with her and not defend my choice or try to talk her out of her feelings. I'd give myself about a "B-" though. Because the moment she expressed her hurt and upset, I was slammed with a wave of guilt and shame. My nice guy programming rushed in hard and fast to tell me what a bad person I was for ditching my poor wife and abandoning my children. Selfish monster!

Then it would pull this little number, which you might be familiar with. It started cycling through all the people I know, and what they would think about the situation. Of course, since this fantasy is just a form of my own guilt and self-criticism projected onto others, they all agree that it's a terrible thing to do. They all shake their heads and cluck their tongues, murmuring amongst each other what a bad husband and father I am.

That wave of guilt and shame made me much less able to be fully present with Candace, tolerate her feelings, and lovingly be with her as she struggled. I tried though, and was sort of able to. Hence the "B-". In any case, it turned into a fight. Not the yelling and screaming kind of fight, we don't ever have those. More like a calm but painful discussion.

Later that day, as I was paying attention to my feelings and working through them, I remembered the men's group I used to be a part of. I slowed down and imagined being in the room where we met each Tuesday night for years, retraining ourselves to be more clear, powerful, loving men. I imagined what each of them would say.

As I did so, my nervous system instantly calmed down. The wisdom of that group infused my body as I began hearing the messages I learned from them. I heard things like:

"Yeah, I hear you. That's a tough call. I wouldn't know what to do. I know most of my life I would just not even question it, go as a family, and then be upset and resentful about it."

"You are an amazing father and husband. You give so much of yourself. You also have to take care of yourself. Sometimes that is really hard to do."

"Whoa, that's intense. That makes me uncomfortable just to think about it. I wouldn't do that personally. Good for you, though."

I could also imagine Elliot, the leader of the group, saying something like this: "Of course she has feelings about it. She loves you. She wants to be with you. And you're not responsible to feel all her feelings for her. You're responsible for you and your feelings. She's not a fragile broken creature. She's a strong and powerful woman, and she can handle it. And... it's a lot to ask. You may need to make it up to her. Help her do things that support her and help her have more of what she wants."

Then, I had clarity. I was able to release the guilt and self-attack and fully give myself permission to take care of myself. I no longer needed to defend my decision or my right to choose something that was for me. It was OK. I was OK.

Now I could give more spacious and relaxed attention to Candace. I could hear about her feelings of sadness and loneliness, which pre-date our relationship and stem from her childhood. I could hear stories, and see her cry. I could hold her and love her in her sadness, pain, and anger. And so, I did.

The next morning after our fight, I greeted her with a big hug and an apology. I told her how much I loved her and how sweet and beautiful and tender she is. How much I wanted to support her and love her no matter what she's feeling. These words were combined with a deep, attentive presence that she instantly felt. Of course, I was promptly ambushed by an insane three-year-old dressed head to toe in a dinosaur-covered tracksuit. It wasn't until later that morning that we could actually have a more in-depth conversation, but by then the energy had shifted and harmony had been restored.

What do you notice in yourself as you read this story? Do you feel envious? Upset? Uncomfortable? Does part of you judge me for doing this? Notice your reactions because they will reveal a great deal about your own experience of taking care of yourself. Maybe part of you longs to be freer to take care of yourself and put yourself first sometimes, but the messiness and internal guilt of it make it feel too daunting to try.

If so, here is one thing that may greatly help you on your path. For many years I continually strove to be some sort of superhuman. The kind of person who was always kind, always loving, always generous. Able to give endlessly, be good-natured, always upbeat, never angry or irritable or sad, or anything else "negative." I demanded that of myself and I attempted to be that way in all my relationships. And guess what? I never made it. I was never able to actually be that perfect person, that saintly figure.

What ended up happening is I would act that way and pretend to be that way, but inside I'd have all kinds of conflicting feelings. I would feel sad, resentful, or burned out. I wouldn't want to do something, but I'd do it anyway. And when I didn't feel happy about it, I'd internally beat the crap out of myself for being a "bad, selfish guy."

As far as I can tell, it doesn't work. It doesn't transform you into some kind of superhuman. It burns you out and wears you down. It makes you tired, anxious, and depressed. And so, I decided some years back that I was not going to do that to myself any more. I am good in many ways, and even great in some, but I'm definitely not perfect. I'm not completely selfless, completely generous, and completely loving all the time. **I stopped trying to be and appear perfect, and started being honest, authentic, and real.**

While it was terrifying at first, because I was convinced I had to be perfect in order to be loved, over time nothing bad happened. In fact, I became a lot less resentful, upset, and full of inner turmoil. Aches, pains, and bodily symptoms started to disappear. Relationships went from feeling like a restrictive cage to something that enhanced the quality of my life. In short, it was good.

To come full circle and conclude the Thanksgiving saga, I want to share one last piece of that story. I went down to L.A. and hung out with my parents, brother, cousins, and extended family. And guess what? It was OK. To be honest, I missed my wife and boys a ton. My heart ached most of my waking hours for the two days that I was there, and I wished I had brought them. Getting what we want doesn't always feel amazing, apparently. But asking for it, and claiming it, keeps us sane.

And now I know. Next year I plan to bring the whole gang with me, rental car, child seats, and all. Or maybe we'll all just stay close to home and keep it simple. All I know is we'll be together, and it will be awesome.

THE SELFISH ALGORITHM (A.K.A. "GOOD PERSON" ALGORITHM)

So far you've learned two breakthrough ideas about selfishness. First, it's in the eye of the beholder–whether something is deemed "selfish" varies based on who's deciding. Second, after years of excessive niceness, your sensors may be a little off. You might not be the best judge of what is selfish, and tend to conclude that any act of self-interest is too much and "bad."

Enter the Selfish Algorithm. (Insert theme music here.)

This is a formula I created after my bloody, err, messy Thanksgiving experience. It is a series of questions you can ask yourself to determine if something is self-denying, in your healthy self-interest, or indeed too much to ask for. Think of it as a re-calibration process to go through until you return to your natural sense of healthy self-interest.

Simply ask yourself the series of questions below to determine if something is too selfish or not. First, we'll just go through the questions, then I'll give you some examples so you can see exactly how it works. Then you can try it using a situation in your life.

1. What Do I Want?

Pretty standard, you are quite familiar with this question by now. Yet it is the place we must always start from. What exactly do you want? If you were operating from complete self-interest, what would it be? Do not water it down or compromise yet. Start with what you truly want.

2. How much do I want this?

On a scale of 1-10, rate how strongly you want this. How important is it to you? How strong is the desire? 1 being minimal and 10 being strong.

3. What needs of mine am I trying to meet?

Remember the six human needs? Certainty, variety, significance, love/connection, growth, and contribution. Which of these needs are you trying to meet? If you notice that trying to please others or avoiding conflict is driving you (a.k.a. certainty/safety, trying to preserve connection), make a note of that.

4. How will this impact the other person?

Determine what the other person might feel and experience as a result of your actions. Then on a scale of 1-10, rate how strong the impact will be, 1 being minimal impact, 10 being high impact with burden or cost associated to it.

5. How can other people meet their needs and get support?

Get creative and think of other ways that the people you're impacting can get the help or support they need. How else could they meet their needs if you don't do it for them?

6. Are there any other ways to meet my needs?

Similarly, get creative about how else you might meet your needs. Are there other ways to do it beyond what you came up with in question 1?

Let's take the Thanksgiving example to illustrate how to use the Selfish Algorithm.

1. What Do I Want?

I want to spend time with cousins, my brother, and other extended family. I don't want the effort of flying with and managing kids, and I want some adult time.

2. How much do I want this?

I really want this, and the need feels strong, so I give it an 8 out of 10.

3. What needs of mine am I trying to meet?

Variety - time away from kids, playing games with cousins and Tariq (my brother).

Love/Connection - spend quality time with Tariq, connection with extended family.

4. What will be the impact on the other person?

Candace feels lonely and left out. She also experiences several days of solo parenting and increased demand. Impact is 8 out of 10.

Here are a few tips on answering questions 1-4. First, don't water down number 2. If you have a habit of discounting your own desires and only letting them be strong if you are certain everyone would support you, pay attention. Notice how much you want this, and how important it is to you. Set aside judgment or what you "should" want.

Similarly, when it comes to question 4, pay close attention. Old patterns of niceness may make you imagine negative impacts where none exist. You might create a fantasy of how someone will react, without actually finding out the true impact. In addition, it's easy to exaggerate the size of the impact, imagining your friend will be utterly crushed if you decide to not attend their dinner party, for example.

In short, slow down and be aware as you do this exercise. The purpose is to examine years of conditioned thinking and see clearly what is really happening.

Also, note that if your desire is higher and the impact on others is lower, then in most cases it would be optimal for you to take action to go after what you want. This is healthy self-interest. Habitually denying this will lead to passivity and resentment while frequently acting on your desire will bring energy, power, freedom, and a more loving and generous disposition. Let's continue on now to look at questions 5-6.

5. How can other people meet their needs and get support?

When I travel for work, I ask myself this question about Candace and our boys. There are often other ways she can get some help with parenting, ranging from my parents being in town to a nanny, so she can have a few breaks, take a shower, and otherwise be an autonomous human. In the Thanksgiving situation, because it was a holiday weekend, no help was available and friends were all busy.

6. Are there any other ways to meet my needs?

One of my major draws to fly down to L.A. was to spend time with my brother. Another possible way to meet the need for connection would be to schedule an extended phone call with him. I was also craving some sort of variety. Other ways I could meet this need overall in my life would be to challenge myself, grow, get crazy with my kids, and take risks in life.

So, what's the verdict? To go or not to go? After running it through the Selfish Algorithm, my decision would be to not go. Or to change my plans and fly down as a family. This is primarily because my desire to go and the impact on Candace were the same level of intensity. That, in addition to the fact that she didn't have support while I was gone, and I could meet one of my core needs of connection with my brother in a different way.

Now it's your turn. What is a situation where you struggle to make a decision? Perhaps a situation where you judge yourself as selfish and don't even examine what you want, let alone ask for it. Practice going through the Selfish Algorithm now to see what insights you have about your current situation, and how you decide things for yourself in general. Over time you will start to ask yourself these questions without having to sit down and formally go through this process. Your ability to discover your own healthy self-interest and act on it while supporting and respecting others will grow, as will your trust in yourself that what you are doing is truly beneficial for all.

X-RAY VISION

One of the biggest obstacles to acting in our healthy self-interest is simply the discomfort of doing so. Most nice people, I've discovered, tend to be sensitive humans. I myself am very sensitive, a term I used to find mildly offensive as a man. Early in our relationship, my wife would occasionally comment on my sensitivity and I'd take it as an insult. She had to clarify, on several occasions, that she was actually complimenting me. Unconvinced, I looked the word up and found it simply means being more responsive to the environment, which definitely describes me. It may describe you as well.

This means you have the capacity to see into others, hence the title of this section. While a less sensitive person may speak with someone and move on, oblivious to that person's emotional state, you might be the opposite. You may be able to see someone is sad as you speak with them, even if they're trying to hide it. You can also pick up on anxiety, anger, hurt, and other feelings in others.

What you notice in others might impact your own emotional state. If you can see the sadness in someone else, you may start to *feel* their sadness. This is what some people refer to as being an "empath" or "highly sensitive person."[5]

Thus, being a sensitive person can make acting in your self-interest challenging, especially if someone else feels disappointed or sad as a result. You feel their disappointment so strongly that it can be hard to stay aware of yourself and what you need. The boundaries between you and them start to blur.

But boundaries are exactly what you need to help you in this situation. You can start by using what you learned in the boundaries chapter, especially around letting go of over-responsibility. In addition, be sure to practice the Peace Process and Energy Bubble meditations. These can help you create space between you and other people.

And, most importantly, do not stop. Just because the other person feels pain, or you feel discomfort, does not mean something has gone wrong. It does not even mean you should change your mind and do whatever you need to in order to smooth things over. Stay the course. Set your sights for healthy self-interest and take small strides towards your target. If you experience a wave of empathic suffering or guilt, return to this book and use it as an affirming guide to keep you on the path. Trust me, it does get easier.

Even though I'm still a sensitive person, I have more choice around how to use those abilities now. I can use it to tune into the emotions of clients, my wife, children, and those I connect with to serve them more powerfully. I can also wave my hand, say "Whatever, they'll be fine," and dismiss a guilty thought or impulse to take responsibility for others. And this often helps me let go and move on. Except when it doesn't. Then I have more inner work to do as I head due north towards healthier self-interest.

---

5. To read more about this topic, I highly recommend the author Judith Orloff, MD. Her book The Empath's Suvrival Guide is full of practical tools to help manage sensitivity.

DEATH OR JUST DISCOMFORT?

A big part of the intense guilt and uneasiness that occurs when we're putting ourselves first is the fear that it is going to lead to the death of the relationship. Our nice programming taught us this little chain of logic: If you put yourself first (and others have negative feelings about it), then you're selfish. If you're selfish, then you're bad. If you're bad, then you're not worthy of love and belonging until you "shape up" and "do the right thing" (i.e. become less selfish and put others first).

When we act against these dictates, a young part of our minds activates with fear and anxiety. Remember our brief discussion about attachment styles earlier in this book? Basically, part of us fears we're going to lose connection with other people and end up being isolated and alone. Thus, acting in our self-interest will lead to the death of the relationship.

But is this really true? Will it lead to death, or just discomfort? Most of the time we never test it to find out what actually happens. As with most things in life, our fear and anticipation of terrible things is worse than what really occurs when we face fear and take action. Perhaps another person does get upset at something you say or do. Maybe they even get fired up and say something critical, or storm out of the room in a huff.

This is the moment of truth. This is when your mind will want to race at 300 miles per hour, predicting the end of the world and life as you know it. You're fired, dumped, friendless, penniless, and on death's door. Panic. Freeze. Run after them and say whatever you need in order to make their upset (and your discomfort) go away.

Or, pause. Breathe slowly in and slowly out. Notice the fear, panic, and restless energy in your body. Notice the dramatic stories and wild predictions of terrible futures. Stay right here in this moment. It's just discomfort.

Your capacity to tolerate discomfort is one of the most valuable muscles you could ever develop. It will not only break you out of the cage of niceness into freedom, authenticity, and confidence, it will also help you get anything you want in life. Any skill, any level of career success, and even the best relationship of your life—it all comes back to your ability to tolerate discomfort. This is such a liberating insight, we'll speak more about it in the next part of this book.

But first we must highlight one last area where more selfishness is good—sex. Oh, yes. About time we got a little spice up in here. While I can't promise you a graphic romance novel-style sex scene, I can show you how healthy self-interest will actually lead to more sex and better sex for the rest of your life. Ready? I'm sure you are.

SELFISHNESS AND SEXUAL ATTRACTION

"Women want to be pleased, but they don't want a pleaser."
- Tony Robbins

Nothing reduces attraction more than too much niceness. When one person in a relationship sacrifices themselves, doesn't speak up or ask for what they want, and feels guilt and fear about being themselves, it doesn't go well. It's even worse if both people are doing it. Because as you've seen in this book (and perhaps your own life), doing so kills confidence and builds resentment. And low confidence and high resentment doesn't exactly put people in the mood for romance.

Conversely, being more direct, bold, outspoken, and authentic does put people in the mood for romance. These behaviors create powerful attraction that draws people together and lasting passion that sustains relationships for a lifetime. In fact, the original subtitle for this book was: *Why Saying No and Being More Selfish Makes You More Sought After, Sexier, and Highly Successful In Life.* Let's take a look now at some of the key reasons for why this is.

THE PLEASER'S PLIGHT

My entire teenage years and into my early twenties could be called a "dateless drought." Well, that's not entirely true, because I did have two women in that decade who pursued me. And I did start working up the courage in my early twenties to ask women out on dates, although usually it lead to a polite "no" or just one date. I guess like any drought, it rained occasionally. But it was so infrequent, so unsatisfying, and so mysteriously unsustainable, that I naturally concluded there was something deeply, terribly wrong with me.

I simply did not realize that I was experiencing the subtle rejection that a pleaser gets while attempting to date. As a pleaser–if you're good at it–no one harshly rejects you, tells you to buzz off, or gets upset at you. They just feel "meh" towards you and politely distance themselves, don't return you calls, or say "no, thank you" to a second date.

Have you experienced this? It goes both ways, always. Men dating women, women dating men, men dating men, women dating women, and transgender dating too… in all scenarios, being a pleaser doesn't produce the best results.

Of course, this doesn't mean it never works. I know many nice people who end up in long-term relationships as pleasers. Usually, however, there is some sort of suffering in this relationship–they feel inadequate, there's no sex life or passion, their partner frequently criticizes them, they feel tons of (mostly unconscious) resentment, or the two of them never fight and live completely peacefully… as roommates who live separate lives. These are just a few of the scenarios that I and many of my recovering nice-people clients have found ourselves in.

This suffering occurs because people-pleasing and niceness do not work in romantic relationships. As Tony Robbins points out, "women want to be pleased, but they don't want a pleaser." I think this is true for everybody, not just women. Why is this the case? If we all want to be pleased, why doesn't someone who's eager to please us turn us on?

After reading through this beast of a book up until this point, why do you think? What's your guess? You probably have some keen insights and powerful awareness after having made such a deep study over these last days and weeks. Because if I share my ideas, it can be helpful. But if you decide for yourself, it will be instantly transformative.

People pleasing isn't attractive because it's not authentic. We're not being who we really are. When we're looking to please, our focus is on how to say and do what we think the other person wants, regardless of what is true for us. This disconnect from our true selves immediately reduces our attractiveness. Then, to make matters worse, we're operating from a place of fear. Fear of upsetting the other person, fear of saying the wrong thing, fear of looking foolish, fear of being judged, and even fear of our own guilt. All this fear is another layer of attractiveness repellent that we spray on ourselves when we're being nice.

We think that a polished, polite image is what's going to win the hearts of those we desire. But actually, it's your true shape, rough edges, and unrefined energy that is going to attract your beloved. Those are powerful, compelling, and highly desirable. The way you just say what you think, express what you feel, and laugh at what's funny to you. The way you scrunch your nose up in disgust at oysters and other things you don't like. Your ability to be right there with the other person, making real contact with each other. That is what creates the charge.

When I went on many of those first dates I didn't know all this. I felt deflated, confused, frustrated, and inferior after those women didn't want to date me again. I had overcome my shyness enough to ask them out; I was warm, outgoing, curious, and engaging on the date, and yet they didn't seem to want more. It made no sense to me.

But now that I understand the opposite of nice, it's clear to me. Without consciously knowing it, I was hiding that rough stone with the unpolished edges, hiding my authentic self. I smoothed it over so many times that what I revealed was a soft, watered-down version of myself. This smoothing most likely showed up in smiling more than I normally do, being too quick to laugh, agreeing too much with everything, and not showing any dislike or preferences about anything. Everything is great. Let me put on this nice show for you.

This comes from a deep fear that if I was to simply reveal who I really am, rough edges and all, that others would be repelled. The niceness created an invisible barrier between me and these women that blocks true connection, and thus attraction. I did this to avoid rejection and stay safe. Safe and alone.

(NOT) HOLDING BACK

The way out of niceness-induced rejection-land is to stop holding back. Everything you read in the previous chapters will naturally prepare you to do this. You're already well on your way, and perhaps have already noticed being more bold and direct with those you are attracted to. This section serves as a reminder to keep doing so, and encouragement that it is especially important in your romantic life.

Holding back prevents attraction from ever forming. If we're scared to make strong, direct contact with someone, then we have pretty much lost from the beginning. Even if we can talk with them, and even if we somehow exchange numbers and set up a date. It's unlikely it will carry on for long because without strong contact, there's no charge, not enough energy for both people to want to continue.

Do you have a clear sense of what I mean when I say "strong contact"? If you're applying what you learned in the previous chapters, you're already doing it. I'll highlight a few of the key qualities as it relates to sexual attraction and romantic connection. It begins with your inner stance, which then determines how you stand, move, and look at others, and finally creates your words and actions.

The stance: I'm here. I'm aware of my body and I inhabit my body. I am solid and grounded and I know who I am. I know what I am after. I know what I like and what I don't like. I'm OK with myself, and I like who I am. I'm not the best, and I don't need to be the best. I'm me.

From this grounded place, we turn our attention to another. Who are you? I'm curious. What are you like? What are you *really* like? What's beneath the persona or the mask?

When you come from this place, you tend to stand taller yet more relaxed. Your head is level instead of looking downwards. You make eye contact with people in general, and strong eye contact with those you're speaking to. You can hold their gaze in a relaxed, steady manner. Your body moves in a more fluid, graceful, and natural way.

Your inner stance directs you away from looking to please and garner approval from whoever you're with. Instead, you're there to share who you are, enjoy yourself, and discover who this person in front of you is. This comes across non-verbally and in your energy. It also comes out directly in what you say and do. You're better able to share what you actually think and feel. You can share what's in your mind and heart. You ask what you really want to ask. You make comments, jokes, or silly responses. You're expressive.

Here are some examples of what you might say to someone when making strong contact. I also include a brief description of how you might say it.

"Wow, you look amazing. I love the way your hair falls against your shoulders. It gives you this timeless beauty."

(Looking straight into their eyes with a slight smile on your face, appreciating the beauty you see. Your tone is slow, measured, and not rushed at all. You are sharing something profound and letting it be so.)

"What? No way. Get outta here! There's no way they're going to win. You have no idea what you're talking about."

(Loud, playful, boisterous. You are giving someone a hard time about their opinion, about their prediction. Your tone is light and invites discussion.)

"Wait, what happened when you got there? Did you just smile and pretend that everything was normal?"

(Interrupting their story to insert a question that deepens things. This shows curiosity and helps you get to know the person behind the mask. Your tone is open, curious, nonjudgmental.)

There are countless examples of how you might do this, and for each person it's slightly different. Because it's you being you. Fully and directly.

If you're afraid of doing so, worried that the other person will not like you, then you have two options. You can choose to hold back, play nice, and try to be everything you think they want you to be. Or you can choose to step up, be real, and share who you really are. The first option is safety-and-comfort-zone-city and, in my experience, leads to pain and isolation. The second can feel like a risk because you might get rejected. In fact, you will get rejected at times along the way. But you'll also be accepted, and deeply loved by the people you're meant to connect with. You're not looking for every man, or every woman to like you. You are looking for your man, or your woman. You are looking for your people. Remember: "I'm not for everybody."

NOT NICE SEX

If there's ever a time to not be nice, it's during sex. Because nice sex is the worst. Well, maybe not the worst. I'm sure it can get much worse than nice. But nice sex is certainly not fun, engaging, hot, passionate, or memorable. It's "nice, I guess."

The fundamental misconception of nice that we've been unraveling this entire book comes back hard and strong when it

For example:

"Hang on one second. I notice I'm feeling anxious and distracted and it's pulling me out of the moment."

"I feel self-conscious about the way my face looks as I get close to orgasm, I imagine it's not relaxed or feminine enough."

If you imagine doing that, how do you feel? Does that seem easy or hard? Is it terrifying? If so, why? Do you imagine your partner would roll their eyes in disgust and impatience, urging you to get over it and get on with it so they can just get off already? Is that really what they'd do? Because if so, that is important information. That doesn't indicate a very high level of maturity and generosity.

Sex is not about having an orgasm and being done with it. It' about connection. Physical, emotional, and deep spiritual connection. And if you're struggling with something and trying to hide it, all of these forms of connection are blocked.

My wife and I have an understanding that it's OK to talk about anything during sex. And, if we feel like the other person isn't fully present, we can ask, "What's happening for you?" I like to tease my wife because she will sometimes try to push something aside and not talk about. She thinks it's "too heavy" or "not very sexy" to talk about while making love. However, the second she pushes aside the discomfort, I instantly feel it. Her body becomes tenser and her movements more mechanical. Her energy and life force are less permeable. She's closed off, even if she's trying to be present. In that moment I will ask, "What's happening sweetie?" And after she tells me and we talk, everything opens back up and our energy is flowing freely once again.

Tip 2: Men: Do. Take. Own.

This tip is for the partner that embodies more masculine energy. In most relationships that's the man, however in some cases this will be a woman (lesbian relationships, transgendered relationships, and some heterosexual couples as well). For the sake of ease, I will simply refer to this person as the man.

Do. Take. Own. While it's good to ask what your partner likes and have conversations about sex, you must take this information and act on it. You must lead. Instead of pausing after each move to see if it was well received, and waiting for approval, just do. Take her. Own her. Deep down this is what she wants, this is what she craves.

I stopped myself from doing this for many years. I had the fear that this was bad, wrong, too forceful, unwanted, and aggressive. And so, I held back. But if you're connected with her, you don't have to worry about that. You're in, you have permission, it's OK. In fact, many women have a secret fantasy about "being taken" by a powerful man who loves and respects her. Let your primal animal emerge. Let the force that has propelled life for billions of years move through you. Grab her. Take her. Own her.

This un-self-conscious immersion in the experience transports both of you to a different place. It has nothing to do with ideas about what's OK or not OK, what's right or wrong. It's just passion, energy, and raw power. It's hot. Do it.

Tip 3: Women: Open. Release. Let Go.

On the flip side of the equation, women (or the more feminine partner) must open, release, and let go. This means letting go of worry, doubt, and fear. Letting go of any old story that you're not good enough, or don't look right. Letting go of the toxic notion that your breasts, or belly, or butt has to look a certain way to be worthy and attractive. These are poisonous images that we have taken in from toxic aspects of our culture. Don't buy into them.

Your beauty comes from within. The freer and more open you are to express all of yourself, the more magnetically attractive you become. A woman who is free, flowing, full of emotion, feeling, and heart, fully exuding feminine energy will turn heads, no matter what her dress size is.

The more you can relax, let go of old stories and fears, and free yourself to be exactly as you are in the moment, the better sex you'll enjoy. This may require taking action on Tip 1 and having some conversations during or after sex. It may involve doing some inner work to fully love and accept your body, just as it is, replacing judgment with gratitude. It may involve creating a deeper connection and better relationship so that you feel fully safe and free to open up.

Tip 4: Revel in The Beauty

Let yourself enjoy whatever you enjoy in your partner. As a man, I greatly enjoyed the physical beauty of the women I made love with. I loved their eyes and cheeks. The way their hair cascaded down their neck and back. The smoothness of their neck and shoulders. The shape of their waist and the groove in their low back. Their breasts and belly. I could go on...

And yet, I noticed I didn't let myself fully enjoy this visual and sensual pleasure. I feared they would think I was objectifying them. Or that they may be self-conscious about a certain feature and feel uncomfortable if I were to look at it. And so, I would cast brief glances at their bodies while maintaining all my focus on their faces and eyes.

It wasn't until I was with my wife Candace that I shared this insecurity. She was surprised and said it felt exciting when I looked at her and enjoyed her beauty. She said it made her feel sexy and turned her on. Go figure. Another inaccurate story that limited me for a decade.

CHAPTER 11:

SAY NO

"My biggest challenge with being nice is that people tend to take advantage of me. It seems like I'm doing everyone's job at work because I'm too damn nice and can't bring myself to say NO to anyone."

\- F.V.

What is your relationship with the word "no"? It may seem like an unusual question, but we all have an emotional love (or hate) relationship with the word. Some people like it and use it all the time. Other people think it's the worst and avoid using it at all costs. And still others don't like saying it and dislike hearing it even more. For them, "no" is a bad word. How about you?

Your answer to that question has a surprisingly large impact on your life. As you will see in this chapter, your ability to freely and skillfully say no when you want and need to has a wide variety of benefits in your life, from career to friendships to your love life. In short, "no" is your friend. "No" is where it's at. "No" is good.

In many situations, saying "no" can be uncomfortable. We don't like disappointing people. And yet, doing so is essential to break free from the life-restricting cage of niceness that strangles true happiness and fulfilling relationships.

So, we are left with a choice. One that is going to be familiar to you by now, as it is repeated with each of these Pillars of Not Nice: You can choose to start saying no when you want to and need to, and face the initial discomfort, or you can continue to avoid saying no, and continue to play nice to avoid the disapproval of others.

If you choose the first option—to begin saying no when needed (and I suspect you will)—you are going to build yet another form of strength, another muscle. Building this muscle allows you to choose what's most important in your life, and how to prioritize your time, activities, and every aspect of your life.

In short, being able to say no gives you power. Power in this context refers to personal power—your ability to choose to do something and act on it. By saying no when you need to, you are automatically saying "yes" to what you really want. This creates a sense of choice, autonomy, and freedom. It makes you feel like you are the captain of your ship and the master of your destiny, rather than a rudderless raft floating at sea.

Are you ready to start building your NO muscle? Fortunately, life is the gym for building this muscle, so you will find an endless number of places to practice. Let's begin by seeing just how powerful the word "no" really is.

THE POWER OF NO

*"The level of your commitment is measured not
by what you say 'yes' to, but what you say 'no' to."*
- Rich Litvin

Being able to say no when you want to can set you free in all areas of your life. In your business and work life, saying no allows you to stay on track and not get swept away by other people's agendas. There are so many competing demands for your time and attention that you could spend your entire day, week, month, or year simply doing what everyone else wants you to do. In fact, if someone has an inability to say no, other people in an organization may discover this and take advantage of it for their benefit, placing more and more of their work onto that nice person's plate.

Saying no allows you to preserve your own agenda, direction, and goals. Imagine a ship sailing north to get to a specific island. If it sailed due north each day, it would get there within three weeks. But what if each day it went different directions: west for a little bit, then east, then some north. The next day it started out going north, then went east, then even south for a bit, then back to north. How long would it take to get to that island, if it ever even made it?

Without the ability to say no, we are that boat, bouncing all over the place. You want this done now? Sure thing. You need me to do this over here? OK, you got it. Other people's requests become demands. Other people's urgency becomes our own emergency. The extreme example of this is when someone says to jump, and you say "how high?" This is insanity. It's people-pleasing at its worst and it makes us feel our worst. Yet, the compulsion to continue out of fear and niceness can be strong, so we stay the course: nice and meandering.

Saying no in your business and work life ends the insanity. It clears away the confusion and declutters your day. It helps you be more productive, achieve more, and best of all, feel more happy and free. It keeps you connected to your bigger purpose and mission so you can do what you're here to do.

The importance of saying no doesn't stop at your workplace. It's an essential ability in your personal life as well because what you say yes to and what you say no to determines what you do with your time and your life. If you are invited somewhere and you say yes, that's what you're doing for the next few hours (or more). Which is great, *if* you wanted to go... It can also make you feel trapped, bored, restless, unhappy, and resentful.

Being able to say no to invitations, offers, and suggestions from friends, family, and loved ones helps you guide your ship in your personal life as well. While you may not have the exact same goal-driven direction as you do in your business life, you still generally know what you want and don't want. (Since you've been asking yourself that question all the time since you read Chapter 7 on boundaries, right?)

Being able to say no operates in an even subtler way than where you go and what you do. It even includes moment to moment interactions, including what you talk about and how long you speak with someone because saying no doesn't literally mean using the word "no." You can say no by interrupting someone's extended story at a party and telling them you need to go somewhere else. You can say no by changing the subject in a conversation, or asking a new question. This subtle use of no adds to your sense of complete freedom.

That is the goal of this chapter, and this entire book: to give you a sense of freedom to be you in the world. Saying no is a big piece of that puzzle. Without no you are not free at all. You are trapped, obligated, stuck, and living in a world of "I have to."

Is this where you live now? Doing things you don't really want to do, but feel you have to? Being driven more than you'd like by obligation? Feeling trapped in conversations, in meetings, or in situations that are not making you feel most free and alive?

If so, it's time for no. You just might need to go on a NO Rampage. Later in this chapter we'll talk about how to do that skillfully and successfully, so it enhances your life and those around you. First, let's dismantle our fear of no. Let's see why we used to hate using that word, and how to befriend it so it can become a liberating tool on a daily basis.

CREEPING DREAD

If no is so great, how come we don't use it all the time, whenever we want? In fact, I may be preaching to the choir. You may already know that it's good to say no and have been wanting to do so more. And yet, something stops you. What is it? The only thing that ever really stops any of us: fear.

At its core, the main obstacle is simply fear of what will happen if we say no. We have dozens of predictions about what might happen and how people could react. They will be upset, turned off, angry, frustrated, hurt, disappointed, and unhappy. This will lead to break-ups, firing, loss of clients and customers, and death and ruin.

Fun side note: After studying fear so much these last fifteen years, I was fascinated by how if you follow the fear down to its root, it leads you to intense isolation, pain, death, and loss of everything we love, hence the phrase death and ruin. To snap myself out of worry and fear-based thinking, I will often playfully call out, "DEATH AND RUIN!" in my mind. For example, if my mind starts worrying, "did I do that intervention right? That client is probably disappoint-ed and upset with me–DEATH AND RUIN!" This always makes me smile and helps me keep perspective. Use that as you will, or don't. And now back to our regularly scheduled programming...

We are scared of saying no. We think bad things will happen. In fact, we even accumulate evidence of bad things happening after we did say no at different times in our lives. People *did* get upset. We *did* get in trouble at work. It *was* bad, see? This selective evidence gathering keeps the anti-no propaganda campaign going, so we never use the word.

While bad and undesirable outcomes might happen, this is actu-ally very unlikely because for significant loss to occur, such as the loss of a job or relationship, many things have to be going wrong. If you are an amazing team member and continually produce outstanding results, and then you say no to some things you don't want to do, no one is going to fire you. If you are a loving spouse who is deeply connected with your partner, they're not going to leave you if so say no to some invitations. So, these outcomes are actually very unlikely.

What we're really scared of is the emotional discomfort around saying no. We're afraid of that tension that can occur when our desires differ from someone else's, that feeling of discomfort and unease in your chest and stomach when someone is upset with us. Why is this so emotionally upsetting, even if rationally we know that it's OK to say no and speak up for what we want?

What are your biggest fears about saying no? Take a moment to think about that now. The more specific you can be, the freer you will become.

Here are the most common fears about saying no:

• Fear of confrontation
• Fear of upset
• Fear of loss
• Fear of our own judgment of being a bad, selfish person

While all of these contribute to the fear we feel about saying no, there is one that is underneath them all. It feeds many of them and is responsible for the strongest resistance and avoidance. At its root, the fear of saying no comes from insecure attachment.

Remember way back when in Chapter 2 we talked about relationships sometimes feeling like walking on a tightrope? If we are securely attached, we know that we can be ourselves, make mistakes, and generally live our lives and people close to us will love us for who we are. They aren't going anywhere. When we are insecurely attached, we can feel like we have to earn love and continually keep people close to us by not making mistakes, never upsetting, and otherwise being "good."

In short, saying no makes us feel unsafe. It can trigger a fear of being abandoned in emotional centers in our brain. When people are sad, disappointed, or angry, they tend to be less warm and available. This withdrawal can trigger that insecure feeling, which is uncomfortable. Most people will react to this feeling by trying to hastily apologize. Have you ever had that urge after saying no or being assertive? Lord knows I have.

But insight leads to liberation, if it's coupled with action. When you step up and take the risk to say no, it might not be pretty, and it might not be comfortable. After you do it, your stomach may lurch and your brain may kick into hyper-worry mode. If you know, however, that your discomfort, no matter how intense, is due to an internal fear that long predates your current situation, you are much better equipped to deal with it. Instead of going outward to fix the situation, you'll turn inward to feel. You can soothe that frightened part and see how to calm yourself so you feel safer and grounded in your body. Doing so is the pathway to freely and easily say no without guilt, and is what you're going to learn later in this chapter. First, let's explore what most people do with the creeping dread–avoid it.

OBLIGATION-BASED RELATIONSHIPS

"How often do you two speak?" I asked.

"About once a month or so," she replied.

"Do you enjoy those conversations?"

"Eh… Sort of. Not really. I feel anxious ahead of time. It feels like there's so much to catch up on," she said.

"I see. Not beforehand…What about during the conversation, or afterwards? Do you feel energized? Lighter, happier, excited?" I said.

"Ehhh… No, not really," she said.

"Why do you do it?" I asked.

"After a few weeks goes by the pressure starts to build up. I feel like we're due for a call. Then I wait a week or so more and it becomes so intense I reach out to him. Or if he reaches out to me and leaves a message, I feel like I have to get back to him."

Sounds like fun. This is a brief snippet of a conversation I had with a client who was trapped in a web of obligation-based relationships. Pretty much all of her relationships were strongly dictated by obligation: what she should do in order to do what others wanted and thus be a good person.

These kinds of relationships are born from avoidance of the word "no." In order to avoid the tension, discomfort, guilt, or fear of loss, we simply say yes. Yes to spend time with someone, yes to talk on the phone, yes to do what they want. This, like all avoidance, provides short-term relief from uncomfortable feelings. But it generates greater pain in the long-term. The extended phone calls, coffee hangouts, lunches, dinner parties, or other unwanted encounters tend to be unpleasant and agitating. In addition, your own sense of strength and personal power is diminished, leaving you with less ability to boldly be yourself in the world, which creates another layer of pain. And then, while you're doing all this stuff you don't really want to do with people you don't really want to be with, your life is passing you by. You could be filling that time with people you love, doing things that bring you energy, vitality, and joy. Missing out on this is the next layer of pain that comes from avoiding the discomfort of "no" in the short term. As always, avoidance equals pain.

We often have belief systems we've adopted that support our need to sustain obligation-based friendships: It's good to be a team player. It's important to sustain friendships for a lifetime. You can't leave friends. Friends don't just leave each other. Friends are forever. If you don't nurture these relationships, you'll be all alone when you're older. You have to be there for family—always and no matter what.

These, and many more, are a mish-mash of ideas we've heard, things parents told us, and our own values. They merge together into all-or-nothing rules that have very little nuance for the complexity of life.

Friends are forever? But what if I don't enjoy spending time with a certain friend anymore? What if our connection was based on the fact that we worked together and could talk about our co-workers?

What if I've grown a lot and they are still similar to when we first became friends ten years ago? What if they tell long stories that I don't enjoy and don't ever seem interested in my life?

The same goes for our obligation-based relationships with family. I should be there for my parents (or brother, sister, uncle, etc.). This could be a core value of yours—to support and be there for family. But what does that mean? In all cases, no matter what? Does that mean everything from being at the hospital bed to picking up their laundry? Does that mean you can't say no to flying out of state to attend your uncle's 60th birthday party?

I understand that family relationships are complex and sometimes involve doing things we are not excited about. This is because we value the connection and understand that doing something for others is part of sustaining a long-lasting relationship. The key, however, is to determine to what extent you will go. You just might find that you can say no to a lot more of the small stuff, while still saying yes to the big stuff.

One client in my Mastermind program was struggling with an obligation-based relationship with her mother. Her father had passed away several years earlier, and she was the child who got along best with her mom. She would go over to her house regularly to help her garden, attend church with her on Sundays, and call her frequently. She was struggling, however, because she didn't like going to the church and she hated gardening. She was frustrated and wished her siblings would help out more, although attempts to push them into doing so had been unsuccessful.

In the group call we explored her options. I started by having her explore her CSI (complete self-interest) desires. That's where you ask yourself what you really want in a situation, if you knew the other people involved would be completely fine with your decision. In this case it was: "If you could choose anything you wanted and you knew your mother would be fine and feel great about it, what would it be?"

It turned out to be way less contact, and different activities entirely. Did she really need to garden with her mom? Could they do something else together? Did she have to attend church with her? How often did she want to call her? What did she actually want to talk about on the phone? These are the kinds of questions that freed her up to choose a way to connect with and support her mother that were more engaging, nourishing, and fun for her as well.

In many cases, our strong internal dictate of "be there for others 100%," which sounds like a noble virtue, is actually a clever form of avoiding saying no. We are scared to do something and feel guilty for doing it, so we take control by saying it's part of our values. This keeps us locked into behaving this way, no matter what it actually feels like inside. Is it working for you? How would you know?

To discover what's really true, slow down and pay attention, especially when you agree to do something with someone, or after you've spend time with them. Do you feel energized after the activity? Do you feel lighter, happier, and more optimistic? These are the signals of positive, beneficial connection that is nourishing you. Even if you don't love the activity, like the gardening for example, perhaps spending time with someone you love feels good in a deep way. Knowing you brightened your mom's day warms your heart.

Or do you feel drained afterwards? When you slow down and pay attention, and honestly check in with yourself, do you feel resistant, upset, negative, frustrated, or resentful? Do you drive home pissed off at your brother because he never does gardening and he should, dammit? Do you have an urge to call him up and chew him out for not doing enough with Mom? Do you feel tense in your body? Does your back hurt when you wake up in the morning before gardening day? *(Must have slept on it wrong...)* These are signs to pay attention to. These are indicators on your dashboard that you are out of alignment.

The way out of obligation-based relationships is to begin with asking yourself the million-dollar question—what do I want? When you do, go out as far as possible on the selfish spectrum. For just a moment, let go of what you "should do," or what is acceptable, or what the other person would think. Just try it on. You don't have to buy it. Just see what that feels like to tune into your heart and see what you really want, deep down. Then, and only then, you can work your way back to the nuances of the situation to see how to steer it. What can you shift? What can you change?

A number of years ago I learned how to do this when my parents or brother would visit me. In the past I would be 100% available, planning on just hanging out from Friday afternoon to Sunday evening. That would mean dinner on Friday, breakfast on Saturday, followed by all day hanging out together, non-stop. Then repeat that again for round two on Sunday. And if my folks came in on a Thursday, well I'll have dinner with them on Thursday before we kick off the weekend immersion.

By the end of the weekend, without my typical alone time, self-care, and things I did for fun, I would feel burnt-out, sensitive, and irritable. Then I would conclude I felt this was because I was a bad son, or brother, or perhaps just a bad human being.

When I brought up this pattern in my men's group, the leader asked me, "What would your ideal visit look like?" Simple question, and one I had surprisingly never thought about. I had been making the assumption for years that what my parents or brother wanted was me all day, every day. After all, they lived in different states and we didn't see each other all the time. So, I asked myself what I really wanted, feeling quite uncomfortable in just the asking of the question.

"Well," I paused, hesitating, "I guess dinner Friday would be nice when they come in. Then I'd have the morning to myself to read, make breakfast, and work out. Then I could meet up with them in the early afternoon. I'd love to take them for a hike out in the Gorge; that would be fun. Maybe have some time with Dad to get his ideas on investing. Instead of going out on Saturday, I'd love to eat one of Mom's meals. Maybe I could help her cook. Then Sunday I'd like to have the morning on my own again, then meet up in the afternoon for a movie and some hanging out. Then have the evening to myself and relax before the week begins."

As I write it now, it sounds so fun and I feel love for my parents. As I spoke it then, I felt tension, fear, and guilt. How could I be such a bad son? They've come all this way and I don't even want to see them in the mornings? For shame!

But at this point in my life, I knew I had to do what scared me if I wanted to grow and create the life I wanted. I also had a growing clarity that acting in my healthy self-interest and having boundaries allowed me to truly love others and deeply connect with them.

Despite some spasms of guilt as I carried it out over the next several visits, they went well. My parents seemed delighted by me saying what I wanted more and were game to do what I wanted. In fact, they were looking to me to suggest what we could do. The space in between periods together helped me recharge and take care of myself, so I felt more energized and engaged.

It went so well that I actually decided a number of years ago that I am only going to spend time in relationships that energize me and enhance my life. My time here is finite and there are so many people I like and love, I do not want to spend time with anyone that drains me. I slowly moved away from and ended relationships that did not serve me, including ones with drama, chaos, or frequent negativity. Over time, my energy rose higher and higher. Now I am surrounded by supportive, inspiring, intelligent, and loving people. I spend time with those that bring out the best in me and inspire me to grow even more.

I only work with clients I like. Those who I feel love and connection for and who inspire and excite me with their motivation, openness, and heart. I only spend time with friends who are bright lights, who are intelligent, motivated, self-aware, loving, and amazing people. I only spend time with family members who I deeply love and connect with, like my brother, dad, mom, and some aunts, uncles, and cousins.

Sure, I still see other family members at weddings, funerals, and other events, but I don't have ongoing contact with them. I ended friendships that didn't serve me. I concluded with clients who weren't at level 4 or 5 of motivation.

Life without obligation-based relationships is full of so much more love, appreciation, energy, freedom, and fun. I highly recommend you take the actions you need to create your own path to more choice in your relationships. In fact, let's see what that would actually look like for you, so you can start acting on that more and more.

HELL YES OR HELL NO

"Anything less than a hell yes is a hell no."
- Rich Litvin

The choice is yours. You can choose to avoid the Creeping Dread and carry out a series of obligation-based relationships, all the while feeling more drained, dissatisfied, and resentful. Or, you can choose to give yourself permission to say no. Not because it was allowed, or because everyone else would agree, but simply because you wanted to.

One of my teachers who've I'm mentioned before, Rich Litvin, taught me about the idea of "hell yes" or "hell no." He was sharing this when it came to working with clients. He wanted both his clients and himself to be a "hell yes" on working together. If they felt ambivalent about it, or if he didn't feel fully on board, then it wasn't a hell yes, and so he would not work with them.

I instantly loved this concept and began expanding it to all areas of life. What if you only did things that were a "hell yes"? *Impossible! Outrageous! Offensive!* I get it, it's not the typically nice way of being in the world. In fact, it might even seem selfish. But is it really?

Is spending time with someone out of obligation enjoyable for them? If you agree to go somewhere you don't really want to be, are you that fun to be around? Perhaps you're the world's greatest actor, but most people can't fully hide their displeasure. It might not be obvious, but most likely your energy is lower, you are a little tighter in your body, and shorter with your words. In other words, you're probably less fun to be around.

Let's do a little experiment to see what your life would be like if you only did your "hell yes(ses)." Take out a sheet of paper, or open up a file on your phone or computer, and make a list. Write down all the things you do on a regular basis in both your professional and personal life. For example:

> Write book
> Go to gym
> Time with boys
> Make breakfast
> Make smoothies
> Team meeting with Jenee
> Emails
> Prepare materials for live event
> Plan schedule for live event
> Record podcasts
> Record videos
> Lunch date with Candace
> Session with 1-on-1 client
> Session with potential client
> Session with 1-on-1 client

This is just a sample. Your list would be longer than this, most likely. Be sure to include all of the activities you do regularly at work and in your personal life. Go ahead and do that now, before reading any further.

Welcome back. Did you get everything? Now, go through and rank each item on your list. Yes, every single one. Put a "Y" next to the ones that are a "hell yes" for you, and an "N" next to the ones that are a "hell no" for you. Remember, anything less than a "hell yes" is a "hell no," so if you're hesitating and hovering, trying to decide, it's probably a "hell no." Do this now.

So, what did you notice? Is your life filled with more Y's or N's? Did this surprise you? Or does it make sense? Typically, if our lives are filled with a majority of "hell no(s)" that we're doing anyway because we feel like we have to, we feel worse. If it's full of "hell yes(ses)" that we have chosen, we feel better.

As you look at your list, do you want to change anything? Are there any hell noes you could let go of? Stop doing entirely? Delegate to someone else? Take a few minutes to really ponder this. It might not be all of them, all at once, but what if you could just start with one, or a few. How would that impact how you feel?

I like to do this process every three months or so, for both my business and personal life. My goal in my business is to do only what I love. That doesn't mean only what's easy. There are things that I don't quite love because they're challenging, or uncomfortable, or stir up fear and feelings of rejection. Those are still a "hell yes" for me because my life is not about avoiding discomfort, it's about doing what scares me in the service of something greater. It's about being a force for good and a warrior of the light.

But there are many things that I didn't enjoy doing that were not a hell yes. So, they were a hell no and I found a way to stop doing them. These include editing my own videos and podcasts, uploading and posting them, managing social media posts, coordinating the logistics of live events, and dozens of other tasks in my business. This allows me to focus on working with clients, running groups, creating, writing, recording, reading, teaching, and all the other stuff that I love doing.

The same goes for my personal life. I don't know about you, but I love cleaning up dishes in the sink and putting them in the dishwasher. Perhaps because it's such a simple task and it's relatively easy and quick. Perhaps because it is so tangible and I get to see the results of my efforts instantaneously. I don't know exactly why, but it's a hell yes for me. Cleaning my toilet? Not so much. Deep cleaning on the stove under the burners? Ew. So, we hired someone to come for three hours per week to do that sort of cleaning. One more hell no off my list.

Of course, when it comes to life with small children, I do end up doing things that are not a hell yes for me. When it's dinner time and my son loudly proclaims he has to poop and wants me to read a story to him while he does so, that's not necessarily a hell yes for me. Sometimes, I will find it in me to make it a hell yes. I'll get playful, find perspective, and see the sweetness of his desire for some alone time with me (even though it's in the bathroom), or even bring the rest of my dinner in there to tell him a story while I eat. Yes, it's as glamorous as it sounds.

Sometimes, when I really don't want to, I'll say, "How about I get you started and then I'll come back out and eat." Offering this shows me if he really needs to go or if he just wants some story time with daddy. I then offer this: "I can tell you a story while we eat at the table. Do you want to do that?" And if I don't feel like telling a story, I offer to read a book.

Even within the realm of being a child-centric parent who values giving to your kids, there's room to find the hell yes for you. This is essential or you will go insane.

My point here is even when we feel like we can't say no to something, we still have wiggle room. We still have the choice of how we want to do it, and alternatives we can offer. Once we're no longer terrified of their reaction to our alternatives, we can get a lot more creative.

It's also helpful to realize that you always have a choice. Everything you do is a choice. This is one of the core realizations that helps you be an owner of your life instead of a victim. I'm choosing how I want to parent based on my values. You are choosing where you want to work, and what kind of work you want to do. You're choosing how to respond to your spouse, boss, coworkers, friends, parents, and everyone else.

As your niceness decreases and your authenticity and power grow, you will see that no one is "making" you do something. In truth, the only thing that creates that perception is the fear and guilt we feel if we imagine saying no. It's not them, it's us. We are "making" ourselves do it. With our own internal demands, our own need to have strict adherence to being a "good" son, daughter, father, mother, employee, spouse, or friend.

This can all shift once you start to decide what is a hell yes and what is a hell no for you, and to stick to it. It's uncomfortable at first, and then becomes much easier, much more a part of who you are and what you do. In fact, let's look at an example of this in action right now.

IT WILL BE MESSY (PART DEUX)

In my reality, I don't do things I don't want to do.

That's a statement I remind myself of often. It's another way of bringing me back to hell yes, hell no, and my power of choice. In some places it's harder than others. And in some areas of life, I have to dig deeper to see that I really do want to do what I'm doing. For example, changing a poopy diaper is generally not on my preferred list of activities. So, in a sense, I don't want to change the diaper. However, I do want children, I want to take care of them, I want them to feel nurtured, loved, and safe. I want to help Candace and create a home that is filled with love and harmony. So, it looks like I want to change that poopy diaper after all. Now, if you'll excuse me for just one moment...

One place that I'm very clear about what I want and don't want is in my social time. With two small children, a wife who I can't get enough of, and a mission that I'm passionate about, my time for hanging out

How do you feel as you read this? Uncomfortable? Upset? Are you judging him or me? Pay attention, because it will reveal your own stance on saying no.

Let's take a moment to break this down, because it can help liberate you to have full permission to follow your own inner guidance. He clearly wants to spend time with me, and is making a direct request for it. In your rulebook, is it OK to say "no" to that? Is it sometimes OK? Never OK?

Does your preference matter in this situation? If you want to spend time together, it's a no-brainer. But what if you *don't*? What if you feel a sense of resistance or aversion in your heart to the idea? Does your mind come in and try to convince you? Does it start to tell you that you're wrong for saying no, that this person "needs you," or that you're someone selfish or bad?

Most of us learned in our early days of nice-programing that our preferences are secondary. That it is our duty to meet other people's requests, regardless of how we feel about it. And if we don't feel like it, our feelings are wrong and must be overridden.

I used to operate from this rule book too. And it led to a great deal of anxiety, pain, and frustration. In fact, being too nice is what led me into the men's group where I met Eric in the first place!

Several years ago I would have been unable to have this kind of exchange with Eric. I most likely would have simply agreed to see him to avoid the discomfort. The fear and guilt I'd experience around saying no would have been so intense that it wouldn't have felt worth it to me.

But, I've been flexing my NO muscle all these years. I've had hundreds of opportunities to practice as my business has grown and I've begun to interact with thousands of people through the internet. To say yes to everything that everyone asks me for and wants me to do would be impossible. And so, I've learned how to say no.

What I found most surprising about this exchange was how little guilt I felt. It was clear to myself that I wasn't available in the way he wanted me to be, and I didn't feel a sense of guilt or obligation as if I "should" be.

The more you say no, the easier it gets. You become more clear, direct, and relaxed with doing what you want to do, and not doing what you don't want to do. This creates a much greater sense of choice in your life, which generates feelings of freedom, happiness, and enjoyment.

Let's turn now to the specifics of exactly how to do it. Below you'll discover how to say no in a way that is clear, respectful, and loving, while still maintaining your boundaries.

HOW TO SAY NO

Step one: start doing it. That's the biggest and most important step in the whole process. Because much of our need to know exactly how to say no is really just fear. When we say we don't know how to do it, it implies that we need to go learn how to do it before we can take action. This creates some sweet, sweet relief through some temporary avoidance. It gives us some breathing room so we can start saying no "later."

But to really gain the freedom to say no when you want to, you must start doing it. Now. The more you do it, the better you get, and the more skillful you become. In fact, there seem to be three levels to the process of saying no.

THE 3 LEVELS OF NO

Level 1 - Internal

In this level, you learn how to determine whether you are a "yes" or a "no" internally. As in, "do I actually want to do this?" This might

sound simple, but it actually takes quite a bit of practice. After decades of nice-person programming, we can find it quite difficult to
determine what we really want. We might agree to something instantaneously without even pausing to see if we really want to participate.
Or, the other person wants it, so we just agree because we don't want
to hurt or offend them.

The goal of level one is to slow down and make a practice of
checking in with yourself. It's an extension of the MVP question of
this book—what do I want? Because you can't say no to something if
you don't even know what you want.

For the next few weeks, make a practice of checking if you actually want to do something or not. It's OK if you find out it's a no,
but you're already along for the ride. That will probably happen a
number of times, as you build awareness. Heck, it still happens to me
sometimes, even after all this work on being less nice. My wife and
I might have made plans during the week to do something during
our Sunday afternoon date. Then, when Sunday comes around, and
we're out doing whatever we planned, I'll notice that I don't want
to be doing it. Why didn't I mention this at the start of our date so
we could change our plans, or at least discuss alternatives? Because I
didn't slow down and ask myself these questions.

As you make a practice of checking in with yourself, you'll become more skilled at discovering what your mind, heart, and body
really want. Then you can start doing more of level two.

Level 2 - Get It Out

The next level of no is simply to say no. To get it out of your head
and into the world, no matter how it comes out. We all want to be
smooth operators who skillfully say no in such a way that everyone
is completely pleased, happy, and content. But this requires a lot of
practice, and even then is not always possible. Sometimes needs and
desires differ and people feel upset. That's part of being human. Relationships are messy.

To practice step two, begin saying no more. I highly recommend setting a goal for yourself. Pick a time frame and a number of noes that you want to say. When I first did this, I decided I would say two noes in one week.

You can apply the techniques you'll learn in a moment so that you are more tactful and graceful, but it's not always smooth. Often times when we start saying no, we have lots of feelings about it. We feel guilty, or afraid, or have a backlog of resentment from not saying no for years. We feel tense in our bodies, worried about how they'll respond, and ready for their push back. All this inner turmoil makes smooth execution challenging. And it energetically sends a message to the other person that can bring about more weirdness in their response. They feel our tension and interpret it as shortness or rudeness, for example.

But don't worry about it. See it as a process and a skill you are developing. Your first noes can be a little rough. When I decided with firm conviction that I would say my two noes, I was working as a resident at the Portland State University counseling center. I had just finished reading a chapter in a book about assertiveness and declared to myself, "That's it! I'm going to start saying no. Starting right now!"

A few seconds later, I opened my office door to head to the bathroom. At the very same moment, my fellow resident and good friend, Banjo, was coming out of his office.

"Hey, Aziz!" he said, smiling.

"Hey man," I said.

"Can you get to the group early today to set up the room? I know it's my turn to set up this week, but I have an assessment that's due tomorrow and I want to try to finish it today," he said.

"No."

"Uh. Oh, OK," he said, looking a little confused.

I continued on my way down the hall towards the bathroom, freaking out inside. *Good Lord, that was so uncomfortable!* I didn't even mind getting to the room early to set it up. I normally would have said yes. I was so set on getting my two noes I just took the opportunity. I had a panicky urge to turn around, run back down the hall to his office and tell him that I'd be happy to set up the room. But I didn't. I slowed my breathing, calmed my body, and reminded myself that I had a right to say no without justifying or explaining myself.

It wasn't smooth and it wasn't pretty, but I got it out and was well on my way to saying no more freely and easily. Let yourself be messy during this stage. It's OK. And often times it's the only way. There's a lot of fear, guilt, discomfort, and everything else preventing you from casually saying no. The only way to work through all of that is to change your beliefs about niceness, which you're doing with this book, and then just do it until it becomes relaxed and natural.

Level 3 - Refined Communication

Once you've practiced the first two levels a number of times, you'll discover that you can be quite good at saying no. In your core, you're a natural. We all are. Because saying no is the most natural social interaction in the world. We say yes to what we want and no to what we don't want. It is only after years of conditioning that we learned this is wrong.

This third level involves saying no in a less guarded, more relaxed way. We are no longer tense or aggressive from feeling scared that we're doing something wrong. And we're no longer overly submissive from guilt. Instead, we can simply say no in a calm and loving way when we don't want to do something. It's no big deal. It flows out of you like asking for a drink, or for someone to pass the salt.

Even in instances of higher stakes, such as dating, business, and social situations where people are more emotionally attached, you'll discover that you can speak clearly and directly, saying no and offering alternatives whenever needed. If the stakes are high for you, of course you may feel nervous or anxious. But your capacity to have all your wits about you and still say what you want to say will still be there. In short, you'll be a badass.

I want to stress that for virtually all recovering nice people, this comes over time. We want to get there instantly and skip levels one and two—especially level two. That one sucks. But there is no other way to get better at something than to do it messily at first. When we wait to somehow magically leapfrog to level three, we generally take less action and slow down our progress.

Below you are going to learn some smooth-move ninja tactics that naturally emerge when you're at level three. These can help accelerate your progress and make you better at saying no than most people. Following these tips tends to create less friction and make your experiences more rewarding, so you'll want to say no again. Still, give yourself time and space. Let yourself swim around in the first few levels for a while. Because the real secret to being at level three is not what you say, it's being calm and collected in the face of potential upset and friction. And guess how we develop that capacity?

5 TIPS FOR SAYING NO LIKE A NO-MASTER

In my glory days, I played my fair share of *Warcraft* computer games. If you're not familiar with them, they involve maneuvering orcs, wizards, night elves and other fantasy creatures around a cartoonish world so that they can build armies and slay each other. It's one part strategy, one part creativity, and one part frantic clicking.

I loved these games and I played all the solo missions and thoroughly beat the computer. I was the best. And then I decided to try my hand at online combat, playing against some anonymous dude (or dudette) somewhere on the other side of the country or the world.

I logged into the online combat mode, and awaited my opponent in the arena. Several seconds later, I had been matched! Warcraw43. I like it. Sounded like a nice chap.

and hitting a biker—that's worth an apology. Saying no to an invitation or an offer? I don't see anything wrong with that. You are simply stating your preference.

"I'm sorry, I like yellow socks." Would you apologize for that?

Notice how in the example above, the No-Noob apologizes twice in one simple message. The No-Master does no such thing. She does say "unfortunately," which conveys that she is disappointed to not join in because it sounds like fun. But this does not convey that she is at fault for saying no.

3. Make It About You

Sometimes, further information or an explanation is needed. For example, if a friend invites you to do something, and you know that you don't want to do that activity, it can be helpful to let them know. Otherwise, they will keep asking you to do it, and you will keep saying no, which can create a sense of rejection. But the truth is you like that person, you just don't like the activity they are suggesting.

One of my clients had a group of several girlfriends who loved to spend an entire weekend together. They would go up to some house in the hills and hang out all day, go out in the evening, and sleep over at the house. They would wake up, make breakfast, and hang out again the next day, lounging on the deck and soaking up some sun.

That sounds delightful to me, assuming I really liked that group of friends, but my client didn't like it. She was more introverted and really needed alone time in between being with people. She had gone once and found the experience both fun and exhausting.

Since then, her friend would invite her each time the group was getting together. My client had avoided going several times by providing excuses as to why she couldn't make it. Her friend had asked her yet again about an upcoming weekend when we spoke about it in our session.

We began by exploring what she really wanted. Did she want to go at all? What if she could go for part of the time? Or if she could go and then also step out from group activities for several hours each day? These were completely new options for her, because in the past she would have immediately dismissed them as inappropriate and offensive things to ask for.

She decided on going for just one day. She'd join the group Saturday morning, then drive home Saturday night to sleep in her own bed. She liked the chance to spend time with friends, and the idea of having all day Sunday by herself. It was a win-win. There was only one problem. How on earth could she say that to her friends without offending them?

One of my mentors in graduate school, Matt May, told me this phrase which I'll never forget: "You can say anything, if you say it in the right way." I use that as a reminder when I want to say no, or ask for what I want, and I feel like it's "wrong" or "inappropriate."

In this instance, the choice to attend less about her, instead of about them, is a much more skillful way to communicate her desire. Instead of saying, "I don't want to spend the entire weekend with you guys, it drives me nuts," she might opt for something focused more on herself that is more vulnerable and real. She could say "Thanks for the invite! I love spending time with you and the others. I noticed the last time I went that I really need more alone time on the weekends to recharge. So, here's what I'd like to do. I'd like to come up there Saturday morning, spend the day with you all, and then drive back Saturday evening, instead of spending the night."

Notice how this is about her, and her preferences and needs. Also, notice how she doesn't check at the end, "Is that OK with you?" She could do that, and there's nothing wrong with doing so. I just question why she would need to. She's not doing something wrong. She's not asking to borrow someone's car. She's simply stating her desired plan for the weekend.

After we came up with this way of phrasing her "no" to the whole weekend hangout, she had a concern, which you might share with her.

"But, how will my friend respond? Won't she be upset and feel rejected? Won't she try to convince me?" she asked, sounding alarmed.

"Maybe," I said. "We could play that out and see how you might handle it."

"OK," she said.

"OK, you say what you're going to say, and I'll be hurt and offended and try to convince you to spend the entire weekend," I said.

"Hi, Jessica…" she began, hesitating a little, "I'm looking forward to seeing you this coming weekend. Thanks for inviting me. I wanted to tell you ahead of time that I plan on just coming for Saturday. I love spending time with you all, but I find that I get filled up socially quickly. I really need my alone time to recharge on the weekend, so I can do that on Sunday. How does that sound?"

"What?" I replied, with a little mock drama. "You don't want to hang out with us both days? Didn't you have fun last time?"

"I did. I really enjoyed our conversations about dating out on the deck. I just feel like I need a little less time with everybody is all."

"OK…" I inserted a long pause, just to intensify the guilt and discomfort—this is exposure after all. "Well, if that's what you want to do. I'll let everyone know you don't want to stay the whole weekend."

We concluded the role play and I checked in with my client. "How was that?" I asked.

"So painful!" she said. "So awkward. I don't know if I could do that."

"What makes it so painful? What do you feel as you practice saying no to what you don't want and stating what you'd prefer?" I asked.

"I feel so guilty. She's hurt and disappointed. I can't stand doing that to her," she said.

"Doing that to her," I said. "That's strong language. As if you are actively hurting her…" I paused for a moment, thinking of what to say next. I knew the way out was to take less responsibility for others, for my client to finally give herself permission to honor her own desires, and to trust that she could still have love, connection, and friendships, even when she said no. The way out was through.

"Let's slow down for a minute. Breathe and feel your body. Where do you feel that guilt and discomfort?" I asked.

"In my chest," she said.

"Good, let's slow down even more. Bring all of your attention right to that place in your chest, and just breathe. No need to make it go away or run from it. Just meet it with curiosity, patience, and love."

We sat in silence for several minutes, both paying attention. I could feel her energy shifting from fear and flight to being more centered, clearer.

"What if it were safe for you to say what you wanted?" I asked. "What if others temporarily felt disappointed, but loved you anyways?"

She sat in silence for a few moments pondering these questions. I knew the answer that she spoke wouldn't matter as much because the question had already gotten in. Her mind was already processing the possibility that it is OK to speak up for herself and say no.

And the same is true for you.

4. Warmth & Appreciation

This approach helps you stay connected with the other person as you say no. Many people, just like my client above, feel uncomfortable saying no. We imagine all kinds of negative feelings and reactions from the other people involved. And so, to combat this, we marshal our inner warrior and gear up for a fight. This makes our no come out more harshly than needed, which often brings about the reactions we are most afraid of. In the words of the wise Taoist master Oogway, "One often meets his destiny on the road he takes to avoid it."

Instead, you can convey warmth and appreciation as you say no. This starts with fully realizing that you are not doing anything wrong and that you have complete permission to say no. It also requires that you let go of over-responsibility for the feelings of others. Yes, they might feel sad or disappointed, and that's OK. You can witness that and even support them, just as you might if their upset had come from something else in their life.

Warmth is communicated in your voice tone, facial expressions, and body language. Appreciation is communicated verbally by thanking them for the offer.

Here's an example from just last night. We were having dinner with my parents, who were visiting from Las Vegas. My wife, children, and I are planning on flying out to Las Vegas for four days in the spring to visit my folks and have some fun in the sun. It will be the first time we've flown our kids out there. As we ate dinner, my dad began.

"How long are you planning on visiting?" he said.

"Four days," I said.

"That's it?" he said.

"Yeah," I said. My voice tone was upbeat and friendly. Note the lack of apology or explanation here. I had done nothing wrong.

"Well, you guys could come for longer," he said. "You had mentioned wanting to rent an RV for a week in the summer. You could start your RV trip out in Vegas and make a road trip home."

"Thanks for the invite, Dad, I appreciate how much you love having us out there. I think we'll pass on the RV idea, but I'm really looking forward to bringing the boys out there. I think they'll love your pool."

Warmth was conveyed in my voice and sharing the aspects of the trip I'm looking forward to. I also directly thanked him and said that I appreciated his offer. This is a simple yet masterful way to stay connected with someone when you're saying no. This allows you to still be kind, without having to say yes to something that you don't really want to do.

Side Note: Beware using the word "but" when appreciating someone. But is a contradicting phrase that tends to negate whatever you said before it.

For example let's say you ask a friend how a recent baseball game was, and they replied "Watching the game was fun, but it was way too hot." It was fun, BUT it was too hot. The heat tends to overshadow the fun.

In terms of saying no, notice how you respond to this: "Thanks for offering, I really enjoy spending time with you, but I'm busy that weekend." It's subtle, but people often hear the first part of that sentence as just a platitude or you being nice. They don't buy that you really feel that way.

One simple solution is to avoid using the word but in those situations. You can either use the word "and" or just make it two statements.

"Thanks for offering, I really enjoy spending time with you, and unfortunately I'm busy that weekend."

"Thanks for offering, I really enjoy spending time with you. I'm busy that weekend, so I won't be able to join."

Both of these allow your warmth and appreciation to be received more fully, and make it less likely that they will be seen as something you are just saying to make the other person feel better.

5. Say No Early

Do it. Rip off the Band-Aid and just say it now. Because in so many instances, you already know that you want to say no. You know you don't want to attend that event, or that you don't feel like going out with that friend that evening. But instead of saying no right away, because that might seem offensive or dismissive, and it's your job to take care of everyone's feelings after all, you say, "Hmm, maybe. Let me check my calendar and get back to you."

Now you have this future no hanging over you. It becomes a bigger deal, and something uncomfortable you want to avoid. In addition, it leaves the other people involved hanging with a loose end, unsure where you stand. It's not good for you or them.

Instead, say no early. Say no instantly.

"Hey, do you want to go see that new Captain America movie?"

"Ehh, I'm not a big fan of the comic book movies. Let's do something else."

"The three of us are getting together after the conference to get a bite to eat. I'd love to catch up with you. Want to join us?"

"Oh, thanks. Catching up sounds really good, and I'd love to do that. This evening won't work though, I'm planning on running and then having some down time. Want to do breakfast on Sunday?"

(If you don't want to catch up with this person, just leave off that last question. Do not offer this out of politeness!)

Rather than offending others, saying no early is actually refreshing and very appealing. People know that you will say what you want and don't want, and they will trust you more as a result.

Here we are, at the end of part II. You've now discovered the five pillars of bold assertion and have clarity on how to shed your niceness and build your authenticity.

I want to honor you for joining me this far in the journey. Breaking out of nice programming and being who you really are in the world is not an easy feat. It requires deep commitment and courage. You making it this far demonstrates that you have both.

Well, it demonstrates you are committed. As for courage, that can only be demonstrated by one thing—action. Will you take action on what you are learning? Are you applying your insights and taking risks in your life to be more boldly you?

If so, then your freedom and success are inevitable. It's only a matter of time. The more you practice being authentic instead of being nice, the more doors will open in your life. Your energy will increase because you are not wasting it on worry, fear, and guilt. You become more and more powerful and are able to pursue what you want, create what inspires you and live life on your terms.

This is exactly what the next part of this book is all about: living life on your terms. It will help you shed any remaining fears, doubts, rules, and inner criticisms that keep you from fully being who you are in this life.

The final part of this book is focused on helping you create a road map to put everything you've learned into practice. Because if you aren't taking action by the end of this book, then I haven't done my job.

PART III:

LIFE ON YOUR TERMS

CHAPTER 12:

INCREASE YOUR DISCOMFORT TOLERANCE

As you're reading this book, you've discovered many of the reasons you used to hold back and be nice. You've uncovered all the psychology behind this pattern of people pleasing and learned why you do what you do.

Despite all the nuance and complexity, we can sum up your need to be nice in just one word: comfort. Being nice, pleasing, and polite is more comfortable than doing otherwise. Sure, it creates pain and suffering in the long run, leading you to feel held back, restricted, anxious, and depressed. But in the short term, it's a heck of a lot more comfortable.

Speaking up, being direct, having conflict, expressing what you really want, saying no—all of these can be quite uncomfortable. And so, staying nice is a great way to stay comfortable.

But if you want to be more you, then there is only one pathway to get there—discomfort. Yes, I'm afraid it's true. There's no way to intellectually solve this entire situation from the safety of your cozy armchair. The only way out is through.

Saying no, taking risks, making mistakes, being messy, and learning and growing is the only way. Of course, understanding your old beliefs, upgrading your map of relationships, and all the other mindset shifts from this book are helpful. They're liberating. But only if they lead to direct action, which will be uncomfortable, no matter how many affirmations you say today.

I've known this to be true for many years. In fact, that's why I included a warning in my previous book that said "comfort is killing you." I wanted people to act so they could take control of their lives and their destinies.

But it was only recently that I became fascinated with discomfort. I was thinking about it one day during a long run on a wet spring morning in Portland, Oregon. As I'm known to do, I will often speak out loud to myself while running, just to seem slightly insane to the people I pass. Good old embarrassment inoculation.

"If the desire for comfort is what keeps us stuck, then willing to be uncomfortable is what sets us free," I said to myself.

"So, discomfort equals freedom... It equals results and success. Really?" It seemed strange since so much of what people are pursuing is more comfort.

But the story checked out.

Meeting people and expanding your social life? Requires discomfort.

Finding love and then creating a deeply fulfilling, life-magnifying relationship? Big time discomfort.

Growing a business, pursuing your dream career, or rising to the highest levels in a company? Mega discomfort.

"If that's the case, then **the more discomfort I can handle, the faster I'll grow, the more I'll achieve my dreams, and the better my life will be.**"

It may sound crazy, but it's true. The main obstacles that stop you from having the life you want are not external. They're internal. It's your fears, doubts, unwillingness to fail, insecurities, and so forth.

And all of these are simply painful emotions that we experience in our bodies. So, if we can build our discomfort tolerance muscle, then we can handle all of these inevitable discomforts more easily, and not shy away from them.

This still seemed a little strange to me, but I decided to test it out. What if I actively made myself uncomfortable, on purpose, to strengthen my discomfort tolerance muscle? What would the results be? And, how could I give myself some discomfort?

SEEKING OUT DISCOMFORT

The body isn't used to the 9th, 10th, 11th and 12th rep with a certain weight. That's what makes the body grow: going through this pain barrier. Experiencing pain and aching in your muscles and then just going on and on and on… That's what divides one who is a champion from someone who's not a champion. If you can go through this pain barrier you can become a champion. If you can't, then forget it. That's what most people lack — the guts. The guts to go through and say, I don't care what happens. I might fall down. I have no fear of fainting in the gym. I know it could happen. I threw up many times while working out, but it doesn't matter. It's all worth it.

\- Arnold Schwarzenegger, 7-Time Mr. Olympia Winner, 1977, Pumping Iron

Ice showers. This was the first thing I thought of as I began intentionally seeking out discomfort. I'd heard about taking cold showers for a long time, and had never really done it more than a handful of times, always finding it miserable. Miserable you say? I'm in!

So, I made a commitment to take a one-minute cold shower every day. I ended up on a routine of one minute hot, one minute as cold as our water would go (which is pretty cold, especially in the winter), one minute hot, one minute cold.

The first day, I noticed I felt nervous before the shower. I anticipated the discomfort and was dreading it. My son Zaim heard me mention taking an "ice shower" and had come into the bathroom to witness the spectacle.

"I'm scared!" I said to him, right before hopping in the shower.

"Why?" he asked.

Good question, little Yoda. Why was I scared? I actually had to pause and think about that one. *Because it's going to be so uncomfortable!* my mind said.

But why is that so scary? I wasn't in any physical danger. As far as I knew, sixty seconds of cold water never killed anybody or permanently damaged them. In fact, research on the subject by Scott Carney, author of *What Doesn't Kill Us*, suggested cold showers actually strengthening our bodies and immune systems. I didn't have a good answer, so I just said the truth:

"I don't know."

I got in and began with my minute of sweet, sweet hot water. Delightful. Except for the impending doom. After about fifty seconds, as I reached towards the faucet to turn the dial from the far left to the far right, my heart began to pound. My body was getting geared up for fight or flight. I was fascinated by the level of fear pumping through my veins. And then... ICE.

The freezing cold water shocked my skin. I involuntarily gasped and began breathing rapidly. My body wanted to pull out of the stream of frigid water, but that would defeat the purpose. Then, my clever brain offered an alternative form of escape, which would be to have the water just hit my back, not my chest, armpits, or head, which was more uncomfortable. But discomfort was the name of the game, so I turned around, raised my arms, and let the water hit my warm, tender armpits.

The minute of ice-cold water seemed to take longer than the minute of relaxing hot water. Shocking! But eventually the minute passed and I turned the faucet back to max heat. Sweet relief. I repeated the process once more and the second blast was not as bad as the first. Then, I got out of the shower, feeling wide-awake, energized, and victorious. Who needs coffee?

My original commitment was to do the cold shower once per day for thirty days. Within two days, my body stopped responding with rapid heartbeat and fear. Within two weeks, the cold blasts felt normal and I actually liked the intensity of the experience, and the energy I felt afterward.

My son Zaim even started taking his own ice showers. Like me, he was scared at first.

"I want to do the warm water first," he said.

"Start with warm water?" I said. "Sounds good."

"Then do cold for really short. Cold for four minutes," he said. He held up four fingers as he said this, showing his newfound power to make number symbols with his hands.

"Four minutes?" I exclaimed. "That's kind of a long time. Do you mean four seconds?"

"Yeah."

So, we did cold for four seconds his first time. Within several days he was going back and forth between hot and cold for longer and longer. In one shower he actually had it on cold for more of the time than he had it on hot. Beast.

Based upon this simple little experiment, I started to ask life-changing questions. **Is it possible that we get used to discomfort and then tolerate more of it? Can we actually build our discomfort tolerance muscle?**

And, most importantly, is discomfort tolerance transferable from one thing to another? As in, does being able to withstand icy water increase my capacity to resist unhealthy foods, take risks in business, or be more bold and authentic while sharing? There was only one way to find out: more discomfort.

For my next feat of masochism, I decided to bring discomfort-building to my diet. I had been working out in earnest for about six months and had noticed increased strength, energy, and sexiness (everybody says so). I was speaking with my personal trainer about how to enhance my body composition, build muscle, and reduce body fat. He gave me a specific ratio of carbohydrates, fat, and protein and had me reduce my total intake by 600 calories per day.

"Let's try this for two weeks and see how your body responds," he said casually.

Sounded simple enough. Except it involved greatly reducing the amounts of the delicious healthy fats I was using to make my meals tasty, like guacamole, almond butter, and olive oil.

In addition, 600 hundred calories is uncomfortable. I was hungry much of the day. Hungry, fewer yummy fats, more vegetables, and tons of beans. If the ice shower was a five-pound weight for my discomfort tolerance muscle, these new changes were a twenty-pound weight.

I began to study discomfort even more closely over the next few weeks. What was the sensation of hunger? Where did I feel that discomfort in my body? When I ate simple foods like beans and vegetables, how was that uncomfortable? Where did I feel that discomfort? In my mouth? Elsewhere in my body? In my heart? In my mind?

Even more fascinating, I began to see how discomfort has two elements:

1. The actual uncomfortable sensations in the body.
2. Mentally labeling something as "discomfort" and then resisting it.

The first one can involve many different feelings, depending on the discomfort. It can also be localized, in that I can feel discomfort in one part of my body, and be totally comfortable in another part.

The mental label of discomfort, on the other hand, was global and more static. My mind would say: *I'm uncomfortable. I don't like this. This is bad and it should stop now.* This would create frustration, unhappiness, and suffering. It would also imply that the experience was wrong and somehow shouldn't exist. *Everything* is uncomfortable right now, and it's terrible.

My journey into discomfort tolerance continued and still continues to this day, including things like sprinting and extended meditations. I find the entire thing utterly fascinating and see tremendous growth from being willing to intentionally take on things that are uncomfortable. It's the secret gateway to glory, to achieving anything we want in any area of life.

What about you? What's your relationship to discomfort? When do you avoid it? Do you do so habitually, automatically, without even considering it? Are there times when you seek it out? As you reflect on these questions, let's look at how increasing your discomfort tolerance will serve you specifically in this process of being less nice and pleasing, and more bold, authentic, and expressive. Let's explore how being willing to be uncomfortable is the secret to freedom and power.

HANDLING UNCOMFORTABLE FEELINGS

As you've seen throughout this book, the core force keeping us stuck in niceness is fear. But fear of what specifically? While we can have a long list of different scenarios, it really comes down to just two things: We are afraid of feelings that upset others, and uncomfortable feelings in ourselves.

We are afraid that, due to our actions, other people will feel hurt, sad, disappointed, angry, frustrated, ignored, unloved, or inferior. When other people experience those feelings, this creates discomfort in us, especially if we have a habit of being overly responsible for the feelings of others. We feel responsible, guilty, offensive, bad, selfish, and then hurt, sad, disappointed, angry, frustrated, ignored, unloved, or inferior. Feeling soup.

This interplay between our feelings and theirs can be so murky, and so uncomfortable, that we choose to avoid the whole mess by suppressing our feelings, desires, and most of ourselves. This avoids the messy feeling soup, but it creates other things that are problematic, which we discussed earlier in this book: resentment, anxiety, depression, physical pain, and other life-draining experiences.

So, in a sense, you really only have two options:

Discomfort A: Expressing the real you and dealing with the uncomfortable feelings that arise as you do so; Or,

Discomfort B: Stuffing the real you and dealing with different kinds of uncomfortable feelings.

On the plus side, Discomfort A is temporary and, when you do it consistently, leads to greater and greater levels of power, ease, and freedom. Discomfort B, on the other hand, only compounds. The feelings don't discharge, and suffering continues to mount. There is no end to this kind of pain, unless you choose to switch over to Discomfort A.

I'll just assume you are on board for trying out Discomfort A, since that is the whole point of this book. If you're still not ready, take a quick tour back through Chapter 5 about the costs of nice. I think it will inspire you to try something new and to do what it takes to liberate yourself.

UPSET IN OTHERS

Do you spend a great deal of time worried that someone might get upset with you? Does it cause background anxiety when you're on your way to work, or going to the gym? Is your body subtly braced for impact, just waiting for that moment that someone might criticize you, voice disappointment, or otherwise show upset?

Or, it might be less pervasive and arise in specific situations. Perhaps you feel that fear only when having a conversation about money or sex with your partner. Or when you negotiate your rates for your business or services. Or when you speak your opinion firmly in a meeting. The list of potential places is endless, but the underlying fear is the same—someone might be upset with me.

Let's handle this right now. It's time to stop living in fear of this generally infrequent, non-threatening event. This fear is a remnant of our evolutionary past, when our brains needed to scan the environment for threats to our lives. Currently, few of us have daily threats to our lives, yet our brain is designed to run that scan all day, every day. Given the absence of predators or physical danger, "someone being upset with me" has moved up the hierarchy of danger.

That's OK, because that's just our two-million-year-old brain doing what it's designed to do. The issue is when we respond to the danger messages as if they're entirely real and life-threatening. **The truth is, someone being upset with us is just a trigger for a series of uncomfortable feelings in our body. That's it.** So, if you can manage those uncomfortable feelings, you're fine. No puncture wounds from teeth, no skulls cracked, no being ostracized from the tribe to starve in the wilderness, and no death. Just discomfort.

Let's look at three specific techniques you can use today to handle the discomfort of someone being upset with you. These tools will give you confidence that you can deal with the situation when it arises, and help you let go of the chronic fear of it happening in the future.

DISARM

Knowing that you can disarm someone who is upset with you is one of the most valuable skills in the world. I learned a great deal about this technique, and the acceptance paradox, from one of my teachers, Dr. David Burns. If you want to go deeper with these, I highly recommend his books, including *Feeling Good, Intimate Connections*, and *When Panic Attacks*.

There are two elements to disarming someone who's upset: empathy and agreeing with them. Now before you cringe at how nice this sounds, hear me out. It actually allows you to connect with them without taking responsibility for their feelings, saying things you don't mean, or letting them walk all over you just to make the problem go away. This is different from being nice.

First, when someone is upset, they want to be heard. They want to be seen, acknowledged, and validated. They don't want to be argued with, told they're stupid or wrong, or ignored. Unfortunately, out of fear of conflict, this is often exactly what we do. Even when we're trying to be nice. Let me demonstrate with an example.

Let's say your spouse's parents are in town for the weekend. You plan on hosting them, taking them out to dinner, and otherwise being a great son or daughter-in-law. At the same time, you have an opportunity to spend some time with your friends on Saturday, which you decided to do. Your spouse has feelings about this. Perhaps they come out immediately. Or perhaps it starts with some huffy sounds and a lack of eye contact. Maybe their responses are a little terse, or they ask you why you bought so many damn green crackers that are clogging up the pantry. (That one is totally hypothetical. I've never done that.)

You notice the clues, so you ask your partner how they're doing, and if they're upset about something. Then this comes out:

THEM: I'm sad about you not being with us today. I feel hurt that you'd rather spend time with your friends than be with me and Mom and Dad. It's so rare that they come into town.

YOU: SHUT UP! *(run crying out of the kitchen)*

No, that's probably unlikely. But, the impulse here is to defend yourself, isn't it?

YOU: It's only for this afternoon. We went out to dinner last night and then I'll be spending the day with everyone on Sunday.

This response seems perfectly reasonable, and it is. But it doesn't actually do anything to handle the underlying feelings. If anything, it will intensify the other person's upset, because they won't feel heard, acknowledged, or validated. Thus, they might come back with more intensity to convey their point, which in turn creates more defensiveness. Then the rest of the weekend sucks for everybody.

Instead, you can disarm them. This involves simply acknowledging what they are feeling, and then finding the grain of truth in what they are saying. Your spouse in this example is actually doing a great job of specifically voicing their feelings. Sometimes people don't actually do this, and instead they speak in code. You have to infer what their underlying feelings are. Once you do, you simply acknowledge that they're feeling that way.

THEM: I'm sad about you not being with us today. I feel hurt that you'd rather spend time with your friends than be with me and Mom and Dad. It's so rare that they come into town.

YOU: I'm sorry you're feeling sad, sweetie. I get it. You were hoping that we'd all spend the afternoon together, and you're feeling hurt that I'm choosing to spend time with Landon and Ben. It feels like I'm choosing them over you.

That's it. No apology, no defense. Just a simple reflection of what they must be feeling like, described with empathy and love. You know you're doing it right when as soon as you finish speaking, the other person wants to share more. "Yes! And…" That's a good sign. If your tone is dismissive or subtly mocking them for having so many feelings, then it won't work very well, and they'll most likely shut down, or defend their feelings.

The key here is to really empathize with their situation. This only becomes possible when you're not overwhelmed with guilt and pain every time you act in your own healthy self-interest. If you haven't worked through that, then it will be almost impossible to not defend yourself, because on some level you feel shame and as if you've done something wrong.

Another element of disarming someone is to find something to agree with in what they're saying.

YOU: I know Mom and Dad come into town only once in a while; it's true.

YOU: I get it. I imagine I would feel upset if it were the other way around. I'd want you to want nothing more than to just spend the entire day with us. It's so much more fun when you're there.

If you combine this kind of agreement with empathy, you will rapidly resolve conflict. Typically, upset people just want to be seen and heard, and if you can do so, their upset will often pass quickly.

Then, it's possible to go deeper and explore what's really going on. Not to defend yourself, but to get closer to your spouse, and have them gain self-awareness. Why are they so upset about you taking some time for yourself? Do they have any feelings about their parents visiting? This can often stimulate a lot of feelings in people, ranging from longing for a connection they never quite get, to memories from childhood, to sadness about the awareness of their parents' eventual death. There's so much you two could be talking about and using to share a deep connection.

This technique is so powerful because it gives you a tool to handle conflict when it arises. Take a moment to think about someone in your life that you sometimes fear might be upset with you. It could be a specific person, such as your supervisor or spouse, or a category of people, such as clients or employees. Regardless, take a moment to think about who would make you most anxious if they were upset. Instead of briefly touching on the fear, and then scrambling to make sure it never happens, slow down. Breathe. Move towards the fear instead of avoiding it. Lean into the discomfort.

What are you afraid they would be upset with you about? Be as specific as possible. What would they say? What are they *really* thinking, but would never say? Then write it out and actually have a dialogue with them on paper. Go back and forth, in the dialogue, approaching that imaginary upset person with empathy and curiosity.

The Acceptance Paradox

The most powerful way to handle any upset or criticism is to simply accept a piece of it as true. This is often the last thing we want to do because when someone is upset they might be stating or implying that we're bad, hurtful, selfish, or otherwise no good. Even if they don't think this, we might start to feel that way, and then need to defend ourselves.

And yet, if we can agree with some aspect of the criticism, without agreeing that we're a bad person, we neutralize the conflict and boost our self-esteem. We acknowledge that we're human, and let go of the need to be perfect. As humans, sometimes we say the wrong thing, are insensitive, focus too much on ourselves, harbor angry or resentful thoughts, and so much more. It's a huge relief when we can stop pretending that none of that is happening.

To gain skill with this technique, I recommend you write out some of the criticisms you fear. Then, practice simply accepting a piece of each one. Let me demonstrate. Here are a few criticisms that come to my mind. The first three I've received from others. The last one has come solely from my own inner critic.

Criticism: You don't really care about helping people. You are greedy and just want to take their money. *(I get this one about once per month, usually from someone I've never met via email).*

Response: It's true, sometimes I don't care about helping people. Sometimes I'm focused on myself and not really thinking about all the people in the world who are suffering in different ways and need help.

Criticism: Your *YouTube* videos are too focused on helping men, you don't care about women.

Response: Yeah, a lot of my videos, especially my early ones, were geared specifically towards men. I didn't directly address women in those videos.

Criticism: Your books are total garbage. Long-winded, no value in them at all.

Response: Ha, they definitely are long! I have a lot to share. My books are not for everybody. Some people really don't like them.

Criticism: Your clients don't actually improve. You don't really help anybody. You suck as a coach.

Response: I have had clients who didn't make that much progress. That has happened.

Even in doing this exercise, my impulse here is to defend myself. And, to be clear, that's not necessarily a bad thing. But if we can embrace the acceptance paradox and not need to clarify, justify, or make ourselves look better immediately, we gain a tremendous freedom.

Because even though we're afraid of these criticisms coming from the outside, what we're *really* afraid of is these criticisms coming from the *inside*. It's our own critic that we're most scared of.

The only kind of criticism that really gets to us, that cuts right to our hearts and then lingers in our minds for weeks afterwards, is one that already aligns with a criticism we have of ourselves. Let me demonstrate. If I were to meet you and then tell you, "you have weird hands. Your hands are stupid looking," what would happen next? (Other than you thinking I'm a jerk). Would you be hurt about it for days? Would you feel terrible and ashamed of your hands? Most likely not.

What are you talking about? They're hands. They seem normal enough to me...

Unless, of course, you have some ongoing criticism of your hands. If so, replace the word "hands" in this example with "elbows." I'd imagine very few people receive self-criticism about their elbows.

The point here is criticism only gets in when your inner critic has already paved the way. And when you're doing these kinds of exercises, like the acceptance paradox, you're mainly dealing with your own inner critic. You can argue with and defend yourself against your critic all day, and usually not make it very far. But if you simply accept the grain of truth, without taking on the implication that you're bad, you can feel a deep sense of freedom and relief.

The Peace Process

We discussed the peace process earlier in the chapter about boundaries. It's an extremely valuable tool, and one that I use every day. It's especially valuable in helping resolve feelings of fear and anger about others being upset with us.

There are many ways to access the feelings you have about others being upset with you. Sometimes, it's easy because there is actually someone upset with you. If that's not happening, you can imagine doing something you learned in this book, such as asking for what you want or saying no to someone. When you imagine doing that, you may start to fear someone being upset. I've found that behind almost all of our surface fears, there's a deeper fear of the pain that comes with someone being upset with us, judging us, or otherwise disapproving of us.

Once you've accessed the feeling, simply bring all of your attention right to the sensation in your body. Stay out of your mind – no need to make sense of the feeling, justify it, or challenge it. It doesn't need to make sense or be rational. Drop beneath your mind and go down, down to the center of the feeling in your throat, chest, stomach, or anywhere else you feel it in your body.

And then, just breathe. Be with it. Meet it with curiosity, acceptance, patience, and love. This is a form of self-soothing that is often much more healing than trying to think your way out of it. As you tune in even deeper to the subtle sensations in your body, you can gently repeat in your mind the following phrase, "It's OK. You're OK."

If you want to significantly become less afraid of others being upset with you, I recommend doing this exercise for twenty minutes each day. Sometimes the feelings will dissolve and you will feel completely relaxed. Other times you will feel them for twenty minutes, and you'll still feel fear or pain about someone being upset. That's fine. Each time you do this, you're providing a level of love and healing to yourself that you may have never received before. It's like working out or eating vegetables: even if it doesn't immediately feel good every single time, it's extremely helpful overall. Trust that each time you do it, you're healing, releasing fear, and becoming more powerful, confident, and free to be you.

Just a reminder, you can go through the peace process with me by visiting the website for the book and listening to the Peace Process audio there: NotNiceBook.com.

HIGH QUALITY DISCOMFORT

As you build your capacity to tolerate discomfort, more and more possibilities will open up in your life. In fact, the pathway out of Extra Niceville and into being your most powerful, authentic self *requires* discomfort tolerance. Here are just a few of the things we've discussed in this book along that pathway:

Saying no
Asking directly for what you want
Being assertive
Having disagreement or conflict with another (and approaching it directly)

Speaking up for yourself

Taking care of yourself

Acting in your healthy self-interest (instead of self-sacrificing)

If you've been nice for years, virtually every single one of these will be uncomfortable when you first start doing them. Hell, some of them are uncomfortable for me even after doing them for years. But I do them anyway because I know they will greatly enhance my life and help me do what I'm here to do. The discomfort is not totally gone, I'm just more powerful in the face of it. And the same will be true for you.

CHOOSE IT

Discomfort is inevitable in life. No matter how safe, predictable and small we might try to keep our lives, we can't escape. Even if you avoid all of the items from the list above, play it extra nice, and avoid all risks, you'll still get uncomfortable.

You will become stagnant, stuck, and bored with your life. You'll feel the pain and discomfort of life passing you by, and living on the sidelines. You'll also feel the discomfort of living a fearful, sedentary life—low energy, weight gain, fewer deep connections, and a lack of love in your life.

On the other hand, you can avoid these kinds of discomforts by choosing another kind. **You can experience the discomfort of taking healthy risks, moving towards what you want, being authentic, and taking life on.** That brings a whole new set of discomforts with it – fear, doubt, guilt, uncertainty. But unlike the first kind, these discomforts are like working out: uncomfortable in the short term, but liberating in the long term. When you voluntarily confront discomfort, you become stronger, more resilient, and powerful.

In fact, some part of you knows it's right to face discomfort. It can actually feel good as well as uncomfortable when you say no, speak up for yourself, or ask for what you want. That's the entire point. To be able to take action, and do what you want, in spite of fear or others' feelings. This is freedom.

Many people I speak with have this as their goal: I want to feel comfortable speaking in groups, or getting closer with others, or sharing myself more freely, or approaching someone I find attractive. I think these are great goals, but I always tell them that comfort is the last result.

Action comes first. It usually goes something like this: Let's say your goal is to be more comfortable speaking in groups. First, you speak up in groups, and it's uncomfortable. You feel nervous, and maybe a little clunky or awkward. Then, eventually, when you speak up it becomes smoother, but you still feel nervous inside. Then, finally, you speak up in groups *and* it's smooth *and* you feel relaxed. Comfort is a long way off, I'm afraid. And if comfort is a prerequisite for action, then you will never take action.

The same is true for every single one of the Not Nice Pillars. Each one will be awkward and uncomfortable, then externally smooth but internally uncomfortable, then externally smooth and internally relaxed. There is no magic way around this process. Of course, by doing inner work, changing your beliefs, using the peace process and other tools from this book, you can lessen the discomfort and increase your capacity to take healthy action. But instant and complete comfort from the get-go is not an option.

RELISH THE DISCOMFORT

Since discomfort is inevitable, and moving into it by choice actually makes us more powerful and free, we might as well enjoy it. Now, I know that might sound crazy, but let's see how that could actually become a reality.

Imagine you're in a conversation with someone and there's a moment of silence. In that moment, you aren't sure what to say. It looks like they aren't either. You start to feel awkward, with a growing sense of pressure to come up with something else to say. In other words, discomfort.

Our typical response to these kinds of situations is to react with an internal: *Blegh! Make it stop! Make it go away!* We generally perceive it as a bad thing that is somehow harmful or damaging to us. But what if you turned towards it. What if you said to yourself, "Yes! This is so awkward! Bring it on!"

How on earth could you do such an insane thing? Because you know it's actually good for you. It's just like lifting weights or working out in any other fashion. When you're in that moment of pushing through a challenging set, or hitting a wall on the fifth mile of your run, you have two choices. You can start fighting it: *Ugh! This is too hard. It's too hot out. I can't do this. I hate this exercise. When am I going to be done?*

Or...

You can lean into it. You push harder and feel the burn because you know that leaning into the edge of your capacity will make you grow. If you can lift that weight now, you'll be able to lift more later. If you pump those legs and feel that burn in your chest as you run, and you keep going, then you'll be able to run further and faster in the future. You move towards the discomfort because you know it's making you stronger.

What if you started seeing emotional discomfort that way? What if you approached awkwardness, embarrassment, fear, challenge, conflict, and all the other things you used to be scared of in the same way? You just might find that you start to enjoy it.

After doing years of a technique called Embarrassment Inoculation, I've found I actually relish the experience of embarrassment. Embarrassment Inoculation is a method of eliminating your fear of what other people think of you by intentionally doing things that embarrass you. These might include lying down on a busy sidewalk, dancing on a street corner, or trying to order a pizza at Baskin Robbins ice cream shop. You do things that *will* draw attention, and *will* draw judgment. On purpose. And by doing so, you discover that it's no big deal and you can handle whatever happens.

It's a profoundly liberating experience and I have everyone at my live weekend events get a chance to practice doing this. Reading about it is one thing, but actually doing it repeatedly over the course of three days is entirely different, and life-transforming.

Having done these types of exercises myself for years, I've essentially burnt out my embarrassment circuit. As in, it's very difficult for to do something that makes me feel embarrassed.

Just recently I was with a client in a 1-on-1 VIP day, and we were out in the streets of Portland on a beautiful, sunny spring day. We were playing a game where we took turns telling the other person who to walk up to and what to say. He told me to chase down a delivery man pulling a cart of soda cans and snacks and ask him if I could pull his cart for a minute. I did, and the guy put his head down, walked faster, and didn't look at me. Perhaps he thought I was trying to hijack his palette of soda.

Then my client told me to walk over to a woman on her cell phone and ask her what she was talking about. Done and done.

"Excuse me," I said, leaning my head forward to get into her peripheral vision.

"I'm on the phone," she said, sternly.

"I know," I said, nodding. "Who are you talking to?" I asked in a loud whisper.

"A friend," she said, furrowing her brow.

Awkward city. I could feel her resistance to me talking with her. And yet the challenge was to find out what she was talking about, so my job wasn't done.

"I gotcha. What are you guys talking about?" I said.

"That's none of your business," she said firmly.

"Fair enough," I said, cheerily, and walked off.

I would never have been able to have this sort of thing years ago. I would have been too terrified, too mortified, or both. The embarrassment would have destroyed me. And now, I felt no embarrassment whatsoever. I found the entire exchange fascinating and amusing. I liked her boundaries and her use of the phrase, "that's none of your business."

Now, asking strangers random and strange questions could be a cool party trick, but is not likely your ultimate goal. But what doors could it open up? I remember one instance in graduate school when I was out to dinner with a group of friends. Two women in the group were discussing a couple at a nearby table, and playfully debating over what date the couple was on. Was it their first date, fifth date, or were they a long-term couple? Each one was offering her opinion, based on cleverly deduced clues. At some point the debate petered out and they seemed to be done.

"Do you guys want to find out who was right?" I asked.

"How would you do that?" One of my friends asked me.

"By asking them," I said, slightly amused at her question.

"No!" One of them exclaimed. As if doing so was somehow wrong or dangerous.

I smiled. She needed to read my future book.

"I'll be right back," I said.

I walked over towards the couple and with a smile said, "Excuse me." They looked up, curious.

"A few of my friends couldn't help but notice you from over there," I said as I gestured towards my group of friends. The two women who'd been discussing the couple smiled sheepishly. Well, one of them smiled. The one who'd exclaimed "No!" at the idea of me approaching the couple directly looked more like she was grimacing. Good. The benefits of Embarrassment Inoculation are partially transferable, even if you're just observing the experience.

"You guys are a beautiful couple. Have you been together a long time, or just recently started dating?" I asked.

They both smiled and lit up. "We've been together about three months," the woman said.

"Wow, that's great," I said. "How did you two meet?"

We ended up having a ten-minute conversation about their relationship. They were so sweet and open, and excited to share. When you approach people with boldness, curiosity, and positive energy, the world is a friendly place.

What could open up for you in your life if you leaned into discomfort? If you no longer recoiled or fled, but instead moved towards the very thing that scared you, what would you find on the other side?

You may have an intuitive sense, or some guesses. There's only one way to really find out for sure. Start getting into that ice shower.

"Sometimes you have to get past your fear to see
the beauty on the other side."
- Papa from *The Good Dinosaur*

CHAPTER 13:

CHOOSE YOUR RULES

Why don't we frankly say to children, "How do you do? Welcome to the human race! We're playing a game and we're playing by the following rules. We want to tell you what the rules are so that you know your way around, and when you understand what rules we're playing by, when you get older, you may be able to invent better ones..."
- Alan Watts, *Playing the Game of Life*

How do you determine what is allowed? How do you come up with your rules?

Of course, there are the Big Rules — the laws of your state and country. Most people follow most of those, most of the time. But most of our day-to-day lives and choices are not determined by laws.

How you speak and engage with people, the actions you take, the ways you approach and interact with your fellow humans... all of these are determined by your own internal set of rules.

Some of these are situation specific. For example, you may be more quiet and soft spoken at a funeral, wearing simple, formal clothes. Other rule sets are not situation specific at all. In fact, you may be carrying them with you wherever you go.

As I emerged from my cloud of niceness and began to be bolder and authentic, I realized I had no idea how to behave. For most of my life my choices were based on what I thought other people wanted or would approve of. The topics I would share in conversations, the jokes I would make, even my clothes and hairstyle were all chosen to conform to what other people would want.

I've seen this again and again in clients recovering from excessive niceness. From years without use, they've lost touch with their own internal compass. The only determining factor for their rules was: *Will someone have a negative response to this?* If the answer could be a yes, then they would avoid that thing. They've spent years, or decades, orienting themselves to what other people think is "right."

To make matters worse, the rulemaking process is cumulative. Each time we learn someone doesn't like something, we add it to the list of never-do's. To take a trivial example, let's look at socks. When I was a little kid I didn't give a second thought about my socks. Zero percent of my young childhood memories are of sock choices, preferences, or who wore what kinds of socks. And then I got to middle school.

On the first day of my new middle school, I instantly realized I had made a huge mistake. I had worn white knee-high socks with two red bands encircling the top. It was my standard attire. I don't think I'd even chosen them myself. Perhaps my mom did, or they may have been a hand-me-down from my brother. I didn't know and I didn't care, because I didn't have any rules about socks.

But from that day forward, I did have a rule because every single boy in my class had short white socks that only went up a few inches from their shoes. In an attempt to not stand out as some sort of mutant, I hastily pushed my giant knee-highs as far down as they could go. This created a strange thick puddle of red and white around the tops of my shoes. Fail.

So, from that day forward I learned your socks have to be short. As soon as possible, I enrolled my mom into a trip to the department store to get me some new socks so I could fit in. For years I wore that exact kind of sock, which got me all the way through high school. Then, when I was in college, I happened to be wearing short *black* socks with shorts. Gasp!

I'll never forget when I learned the second rule about socks. I was standing in line with several friends at the Coachella music festival. It was early afternoon, and blisteringly hot. I could hear the band playing on the main stage and the distant thumping of the electronic music tent, which was always my primary destination.

Being in an upbeat, energized mood, I turned to two women in line next to us. I don't remember exactly what I said, but it was a simple question asking their opinion on something trivial or silly. Instead of answering that question, however, one of the women instantly fired back, "Well it doesn't matter what you do with those black socks on."

My memory of the exact wording is fuzzy, but the emotional charge is not. Her tone was harsh and dismissive, and I felt rejected. I didn't know I'd broken another rule, and I felt a wave of shame in that moment. *Oh no! All this time, black socks are not allowed either?*

Flash forward to this day, decades after the first incident, and I still have rules in my head about socks. If I'm wearing longer black socks with shorts in the summer time, and we meet up with friends, some part of my mind says, "I wonder if they think that looks ridiculous."

Seem crazy? It is. Yet we're all doing it. We're all accumulating rule after rule about what's ok. And each person that we get disapproval from adds to our list of rules until our band of acceptable behavior has narrowed down to the thinnest strip of bland nicery.

FOLLOWING ALL THE RULES

Remember that list of rules of you came up with way back in Chapter 3? Your list of shoulds? Take a moment now to find that list. And if you didn't make it at the time... SHAME. SHAME. SHAME.

You've just broken a terrible rule. That's OK though, because you can always flip back to Chapter 3, review that section (called "The List"), and create it right now.

Take a few minutes to read through your list. Do you still believe all of these rules? Perhaps your reaction to some of them has changed since reading through this book and coming up with your bill of rights. If so, and you're feeling more liberated, that is fantastic. Because ultimately, if we're trying to live by fifty oppressive rules, life is generally miserable.

As you look at your list, I want to ask you some questions. Where did these come from? Where did you learn them? Did *any* of them *really* come from you?

In Chapter 3 I had you mark the ones that caused the most problems in your life with an unhappy face. And if you didn't do that part, no worries, just do it now. Go through and mark each rule that causes you to feel bad about yourself on a regular basis with an unhappy face.

For each rule marked in this way, ask yourself, "Where did I learn this?" The answer might come right away, or it may be something you recall later, when you're not even actively thinking about it. You can reflect on what you learned from your parents, since this is a major source of many of our rules. As you do so, think about what they told you directly, but also what you saw them do.

For example, let's say one of your old rules is, "I should never do anything that hurts anybody's feelings." Maybe your parents didn't sit you down and say to you, "Don't ever hurt anybody's feelings. Ever." (Although some people's parents do pretty much exactly this.) Instead, you may have seen the disapproval and upset they expressed when you did do something that upset someone else. Or you may have witnessed how worried they were about upsetting others, and how timidly they moved through the world. This modeling is one of the most influential ways we learned from our parents.

You don't need to pinpoint an exact source. In fact, even doing so, might not instantly free you from that rule. But just engaging in the process of examining, "Where did I learn this rule anyway?" already begins to shift something in your mind.

It shows that you did indeed learn this rule. It isn't some objective truth passed down from the beginning of time through all humans everywhere. It's made up. Maybe by your mom, or her mom, or her mom's mom. Maybe it's been unconsciously passed down for generations, completely unexamined. Maybe you learned it from some kids in school when you were small. They were following the rule because their parents did. Who knows?

The liberation here comes from seeing that anything that was learned can be unlearned. It can be changed. And changing your rules is exactly what we're here to do.

IF ONLY I WERE GOOD

"Yes, I'm doing that," she said.

I was about twenty minutes into a session with a client and I had just pointed out that she was being expressive and authentic around one group of people (certain doctors and nurses in the hospital), but not around another group of people (senior consultants and doctors who she viewed as "more senior" than herself).

"Why?" I asked.

"Because I'm afraid they won't like me. They'll think it's inappropriate if I treat them like this," she said.

"So to avoid that potential judgment, you're showing up differently. How do you act around them?" I said.

"I'm very respectful, polite. I keep it very professional, just talk about the cases, no chitchat. I don't smile or make jokes as much. I'm very serious and much nicer," she said.

"I see. So the plan is that if you're serious, professional, and nice, then you'll be seen as appropriate and they will then like you," I said.

"Yes."

"Is it working?" I asked.

"No!" she said quickly. "It's not. They don't get upset with me, but I don't think they really like me either. And I feel anxious inside. I'm not being my real self around them. I'm not showing by best self. I can be way more assertive, warm, and funny. I think if they saw these things they would like me more…" She paused for a moment, then continued, "it's like I'm following all the rules, but I'm miserable."

Indeed she was. As was I, for many years. I played by all the rules that I had in my mind, that I assumed everyone in the world agreed upon. I believed that if I pushed myself hard enough, if I were just "good" enough, then I would get love and respect from others, relationships, success, and finally be able to love myself.

Unfortunately, it never happened. Partly because my rules were so numerous and often conflicting. If one rule says, "Don't ever hurt anyone's feelings, ever," you're already screwed. It's completely unobtainable, because if you're interacting with humans, at some point, someone is going to have some hurt feelings around you. Even if you never intentionally did this, and took extra care to avoid it, it will happen. I promise you.

You can cause pain in another person by giving them a compliment. Seriously. Just recently, a man in my mastermind program brought up this exact point. He was at a party with his wife and he was having a great time. He was making great strides in his social confidence progress and was really enjoying himself, mingling with the people there (which is something he would have avoided like the plague in the past). Instead, he was starting conversations, flowing freely, and lacking self-consciousness. He was on cloud nine.

Then, just as he and his wife were getting their coats on and about to leave, the hostess approached them.

"I just have to say," she said, "that you two are the cutest couple here."

My client instantly felt uncomfortable and became flustered. "Uh, mm, thanks," he said, awkwardly. According to his report in the mastermind, he then proceeded to just keep talking, not even aware of what he was saying. It triggered so much anxiety and discomfort that he talked and talked.

After he left he felt self-conscious and embarrassed. He criticized himself on the way home about how foolish he looked, and how he should have just said "thank you" and left it at that.

In short, that compliment produced way more pain than it did pleasure. Therefore, that hostess was a bad person. At least according the The Rules.

So not only is the "Don't hurt anyone's feelings ever" an unobtainable rule, but what if you have another rule that says, "I should be honest and assertive with people all the time." This leads to all kinds of confusing experiences where your two rules send opposite commands: *Say it, no don't say it, but you have to say it, but I'm bad if I say it...* It's like a robot that has two conflicting commands, working itself up into a tizzy until its circuits fry.

And that's pretty much what happens. You feel anxious, self-critical, and depressed. It also makes relationships, friendships, and all sorts of interactions feel restricting and painful. You feel trapped. And you think it's the other people, you think it's your workplace, or your boss, or your girlfriend, or husband, or parents, or someone. But it's you. **The rules are inside of you. You are the one writing them, then following them.**

And it's time to break free.

BREAKING THE RULES

What if there were no rules? What if you could do whatever you wanted?

Now, before you dismiss that question and say, "Come on, Aziz, obviously there are rules, so this is pointless. Besides, without rules, people would pillage, rape, and murder each other. It would be chaos."

This kind of dismissive response is actually the nice-person programming speaking, not you. It's what you would call a straw man argument, and it's a favorite among debaters and politicians all over the world. It's when you put forth an extreme example and then discredit it.

For example:

BOB: I think we should stop giving money to group A and instead give it to groups B and C.

ALLEN: Do you want people in group A to die in the street?

Now, most likely, Bob does not want anyone to die in the street. But this extreme example makes shifting the money allocation around look bad. After all, doing so would lead to people dying in the street.

This is exactly what your nice-person programming does when you start looking beyond life in your cage of rules. Instead of simply dismissing the idea though, what if you really considered it? If there were no rules on what you could say or do, what would you do?

If your mind keeps going to bank robberies and stolen G6's, then we can put this qualifier on the thought experiment. Assuming there are still laws in place, and this isn't The Purge, what would you do? So you can't rob banks or prowl the streets of downtown LA with a chainsaw, but you can say anything you want, relate to others however you want, ask for whatever you want, and say no to anything. What would you do with no rules?

Interesting to imagine, huh?

And if you could change, or completely let go of three of your most restrictive rules, what would that be like? How would you feel? What would you do in your life?

Look back at your list of shoulds and select the three worst offenders. Which are the ones that have caused you the most pain, frustration, restriction, and self-hatred? Which ones are the electric fence that confine you or the hammer that bludgeons you?

Take a moment now to find your three.

For me, currently, I'd say these are the ones that cause the most pressure, anxiety, or self-judgment:

I should be able to help anyone become completely and permanently confident, instantly.

I should reach more people, serve them more, and earn more, now.

I should always want to play with my kids.

So, to break these rules, I can simply forget helping people, forget my mission in the world, and forget my kids. Done and done!

As you might find with your top three, it's more complicated than that. Usually our biggest rules are related to what we value and how we want to live in the world, so we can't just throw them out entirely. For example, perhaps you had a rule that is from this list:

I should be more outgoing and charming.
I should be able to speak up in a group and command the room.
I should eat healthier.
I should lose weight.
I should spend more time with my spouse.
I should never hurt anyone's feelings.
I should never say no to someone in need.
I should give more than I do.

That's just a short list of potentials. Notice how each one reflects an underlying value. Can you spot it?

"I should be more outgoing and charming" highlights a desire to connect with others. This person values making friends, finding love, growing in their business, or being a leader. Maybe they also value freedom, expressiveness, and authenticity. Those are all great things!

If someone's rule is "I should lose weight," what do they value? Health, vitality, aesthetic beauty. Perhaps there's also a value for love and connection if they perceive that being in better shape will help them receive more love from others.

The same is true for your top three rules as well. Each one reflects your values. For each one, write down what it shows you value. Just a few sentences or bullet points is all we're talking about here, nothing fancy. And don't try to make it sound good either. If you want to lose weight because you want to get laid, then write that down. Sex, connection, companionship, love, or whatever else you imagine it will bring you. No one is going to see this list and no one's going to judge you. This is about you liberating yourself, not trying to look good to imaginary people. Write those out now, then keep reading.

What did you discover?

How was it to do this exercise? I noticed it really stirred things up in me, creating some feelings of anxiety and sadness. It also brought up some existential questions, like the purpose of life and how we want to live. Maybe it wasn't so deep for you, but it might have kicked up some feelings. If so, that's good. Because **the rules are designed to control behavior without allowing you to fully feel.** But feeling in your heart, discomfort and all, is the only way to truly discover the answer to your deepest questions. How do I want to live? What really matters to me? What is my life about?

Here's what emerged as I did this exercise:

I should be able to help anyone become completely and permanently confident, instantly.

This shows that I want to help people. I want to alleviate suffering and create liberation. I want people to love themselves and be able to love others, feel powerful, worthy, and free.

This shows that I value freedom, love, contribution, and mastery.

I should reach more people, serve them more, and earn more, now.

This shows I have a big mission and a desire to positively impact the world. It also shows me I still have a piece of my self-worth determined by how many people I help, and how much money I earn.

This shows I value contribution and significance.

I should always want to play with my kids.

This shows that I love my kids. I value love, being with them, bringing them joy, and deeply connecting with them at their level.

Doing this exercise, I realized how much I value love and contribution. I also see how I value significance, and how doing so can trip me up. Especially if I have the game setup to make it very hard to earn that significance. I can see how there's an element of "I'll be worthy when…" in some of my rules. I'll be worthy when I can help people better. I'll be worthy when I've reached enough people. I'll be worthy when I've made enough money.

These are dangerous requirements for significance because in my experience they're never enough. The more you hit your target, the farther out the goal becomes. This is the standard MO of the high achiever and the perfectionist, both of which I identify with (even though I don't like the sound of the second one).

What did you see about yourself? Did it stir up any feelings in you?

We're going to do something else with these rules to help you break free of them, but first let's address any feelings that came up. Take a few minutes to just feel what's happening in your heart, your stomach, and anywhere else in your body. Slow down. Feel it, fully. It's ok. You're safe, and you can handle this. There's nothing wrong, with you, or these feelings.

Just breathe and feel.

Meet any sensation in your body with curiosity, acceptance, and love. Let it know it's safe for it to be here, and you're allowing it fully. Gently repeat in your mind, as you focus right on the feelings in your body, "It's OK. You're OK."

You're doing awesome by the way. This rule stuff is no joke. There's a reason you've obeyed them for years or decades.

Let's see if we can soften the grip even more, and keep the healthy aspect of the rule, while releasing the extreme nature of it that causes us so much pain. Look at the first rule on your list. Can you see the beauty in that rule? Can you see the heartfelt desire underneath? Can you see the nobility in it? Can you love that part of you that wants it so badly?

To see this even more clearly, replace the word "should" with "really want to." If some of your rules have a "should never," as in "I should never hurt anyone's feelings," you can rewrite this part to reflect what you really want. For example, if you don't want to hurt others' feelings, perhaps you want others to feel accepted, loved, and safe around you. In that case, you would write: I really want others to feel accepted, loved, and safe. Here are some more examples:

I really want be more outgoing and charming.
I really want be able to speak up in a group and command the room.
I really want to eat healthier.
I really want to lose weight.
I really want to spend more time with my spouse.
I really want to treat people with kindness and respect.
I really want to help people in need.
I really want to give more than I do.

As you see your rule in this way, can you feel that desire in your heart? Let yourself breathe fully and deeply, and just experience that ache. As you do this, think less and feel more. You don't need to understand everything that's happening. As best as you can, just stay with the feelings in your body as you re-read your rules with this new language. If you feel like crying, let yourself cry. This is good. This is healing.

Now, let's take it one step further. In response to each of your top three rules, written out with "I really want to…" you're going to write a response. This response is you speaking to yourself, as if you were your own best friend, a loving spouse, or loving parent. Someone who sees the beauty of that desire and deeply appreciates you for it. For example:

I really want to be able to help anyone become completely and permanently confident, instantly.

Of course you do! How amazing would that be? What a beautiful desire that fuels you to learn more and more, take risks, and pursue mastery for your entire life. What a powerful driving force. This is amazing. I'm so proud of you, son.

I really want to reach more people, serve them more, and earn more, now.

I know. And that's more of that mission, that purpose. It's a beautiful thing, my man. I really admire that. And I feel grateful that you found that purpose, because it gives you an energy and passion for life that is really inspiring. I love you so much, Aziz.

I really want to play with my kids.

Of course you do. They're beautiful and amazing. They're so sweet, funny, and delightful. I'm grateful you have them in your life. They give an even deeper purpose that goes beyond your bigger mission in the world. It's amazing to have them in your life.

Go ahead and write your responses now. Be as loving, expressive, and warm as you can be, even if you've never spoken to yourself like this before. There's a first time for everything, my friend.

Then, read this to yourself. Read it over and over, fifty times if needed. Write it on your phone and read it each day in the morning and night. Slow down, and let it in. Be sure to use your name as you do it, because that has a powerful impact on your subconscious mind.

I love you Aziz.
You're enough.
You don't have to do anything more to earn my love.
I love you no matter what.
You are amazing just as you are.
I can see how big your heart is, and it's beautiful.
I love you.

Once you've done this process with your top three rules, you can experiment with doing it with other rules that cause you pain. As you go about your day, notice when you're feeling anxious, guilty, or self-critical. See if you can uncover which rule you've broken and write it down.

Then, set aside just a few minutes to go through this process:

1. Identify the exact rule, and write it down: "I should…"
2. See what you really value underneath.
3. Replace "should" with "really want to."
4. Appreciate yourself for wanting this.
5. Read your love letter.

Going through this process repeatedly, with different rules, or with the same rule a number of times, will help soften these in your mind. Instead of being a baton that you beat yourself with, they become preferences and desires that guide you in life.

MAKING THE RULES

So, how do you make new rules? How do you consciously choose and create the rules you want to live by. Not your mom's rules, or your dad's rules, or even many of the rules you grew up with in your society. YOUR rules.

Guess what? You already did! Whew, finally, a break.

The good news is you already did all the heavy lifting back in Chapter 6 with your personal Bill of Rights. Remember that exercise? Take a moment to find what you wrote now.

Once you have this list, you simply tweak the wording ever so slightly on your list by changing "I have a right to" to "I am allowed to." For example:

Bill of Rights

I have the right to approach anyone I want to start a conversation with them.

I have the right to change the subject or end the conversation whenever I would like.

I have the right to say "no" to anything I don't want to do, for any reason, without needing to justify it or give an excuse.

I have the right to ask for what I want.

Aziz's Rules

I am allowed to approach anyone I want to start a conversation.

I am allowed to change the subject or end the conversation whenever I would like.

I am allowed to say "no" to anything I don't want to do, for any reason, without needing to justify it or give an excuse.

I am allowed to ask for what I want.

And so on, all the way down your entire list. Take a moment now to write out your new list in this way, giving it the title "_____'s Rules," using your own name. If your list is digital and on your phone or computer, you may be tempted to use copy and paste. I would actually encourage you to type it out again, or even better yet, write it another time by hand. The more you drill these rules into your mind, the more powerful and free you become.

tion. Most people have a knee-jerk reaction to guilt that causes them to feel bad because the unconscious logic goes like this: *If I feel guilty, then I must have done something wrong.*

The way out of guilt is to slow down and examine it. When you notice you're feeling guilty, identify it out loud. "Ahh, this is guilt." Then pay close attention. Slow down, bring your awareness to your mind and your body. Because the feelings of guilt can be painful, your impulse might be to stay in motion, distract yourself, or compulsively apologize. Instead of reacting to guilt, examine it.

What do you say to yourself when you're feeling guilty? What does that internal, chastising part of you say about you? This is the "voice of guilt" and it's very important to notice how it's speaking to you. Is it calm and loving? Is it angry and critical? Is it like a raging parent who's lost it?

What do you feel in your body? Do you feel tightness in your chest or a squeezing in your belly? Do you feel scared, uneasy, or heavy inside? Become intimately familiar with the patterns of guilt inside of you. Study how you "do guilt."

Then, ask yourself the most valuable question you can ask yourself whenever you feel guilty: *What rule did I break?* This is the first step in neutralizing guilt because it will give you valuable information about what's happening and how to deal with it. You need to determine if this is healthy guilt or unhealthy guilt, if this is something pointing you towards being your best self, or just another sneaky pattern of perfectionism and self-hatred.

To determine what rule you broke, simply listen to the voice of guilt in your head. It's going to tell you clearly what you should do, or should not do. What you should have done, or shouldn't have done. Those shoulds are the rules.

Here are some examples:

You shouldn't have eaten that hamburger, fries, and a milkshake. And so much of it! What's wrong with you? You're going to lose everything you've been working towards. You're going to get fat. That was terrible. You should have more self-control.

The Rules:
I should not eat fast food.
I should not eat to the point of being overly full.
I should have more self-control.

You should've said "yes" to John's invitation. He really wanted you to come, but you didn't. That was very selfish of you. You could've just gone for an hour. That wouldn't have been a big deal. He's going to be so disappointed. And maybe he won't want to hang out with you later because you hurt him so much.

The Rules:
I shouldn't say no to a friend's invitation.
I shouldn't do anything that disappoints others.

Are you getting a sense of how this works? Try it out in a scenario in your life that used to make you feel guilty in the past. Notice what the voice of guilt says to you, and then practice identifying the underlying rules. Once you are able to do this, you are well on your way to neutralizing guilt and feeling happier, freer, and loving with yourself and others.

THE WAY OUT

In Chapter 3, we discussed two kinds of guilt: Healthy Guilt and Unhealthy Guilt. Do you remember the difference?

Healthy Guilt is a feeling that arises when you've broken a rule that you actually do value and aspire to live by. This guilt is guiding you to get on track and be the kind of person you want to be in the world. It reminds you of what matters most, and inspires you to live in alignment with your values. It's a positive force for change and is rooted in love.

Unhealthy Guilt is a form of punishment and self-attack. We believe we've done wrong and must be punished for our sins. If we punish ourselves enough, and suffer sufficiently for our badness, then we'll have atoned for our transgression. This is a distorted form of logic that is not connected to your values, does not positively influence behavior, and is rooted in fear.

So how do you determine which is which? That becomes much easier once you notice the underlying rules that you broke. Look at your list of broken rules and ask yourself: *Do I want to live by these rules? Do they reflect my values? Are they realistic? Do they take into account variations in the environment and the fact that I'm a human?*

If your answer to these questions is yes, then there is a message in your guilt that is trying to serve you. However — and this is *extremely* important to understand — if you don't receive the message in the right way, you will get stuck in unhealthy guilt. Let me illustrate with an example.

A few nights ago, it was bedtime in the Gazipura household, and everyone was tired. When an adult gets tired, they want to lie down, relax, and welcome restful slumber. When a little kid gets tired, they draw upon the chaotic energy of the universe, lose all impulse control, and go wackyballs.

On this particular night, Zaim was pushing his younger brother over, refusing to let me brush his teeth, and generally unleashing the beast. I wasn't handling it well. My patience tank was empty and I went into control mode. My tone became exasperated. My energy became harsh. He wanted to put the cinnamon toothpaste on himself, but I wouldn't let him because last time he squeezed out a huge wad of toothpaste all over the floor. Then he started crying about not being able to put the toothpaste on and I stood there impatiently waiting for him to finish. Patience tank empty. Compassion tank empty too.

We finally get everyone in to bed and I'm reading him stories to help him fall asleep. He wants a different book that's not in the bedroom. He wants almond milk. He doesn't want to be quiet and wants to keep his brother up. My voice becomes sharper as I respond to each of these demands. I don't yell at him, because I decided long ago that I was never going to yell at my children, but I couldn't contain my resentment in that moment. Even though I wasn't saying, "You're being bad for staying awake and not doing what I said," out loud, my body language and tone of voice was sending this message loud and clear.

Then he fell asleep. Thank God. Sweet relief. I passed out next to him on his little toddler bed, as I listened to the sweet sound of his breathing.

I awoke the next morning with a pang in my heart. Good morning, guilt. My mind began reflecting on moments from the previous night's bedtime, seeing all the ways I was being critical and unloving with him. I felt upset with myself, sad about being disconnected from him, and pain in my heart.

Is this Healthy Guilt or Unhealthy Guilt? It all depends on how I receive the message.

The rules I broke were pretty clear. I want to be patient with my sons. I want to be non-reactive to their wild behaviors, and come from a place of connection and love when attempting to influence them. I don't want to convey the message that they're bad for being awake, or doing something else that they have little control over.

Yep, these are all values I aspire to. So far, so good.

But when I tuned into the voice of guilt more closely, I heard this message:

This is totally unacceptable. How could you do this to your kids? You're a bad father.

Whoa. That's intense. And that's how even healthy guilt can go wrong. Even if you break a rule that you actually aspire to, if you treat yourself with anger, harsh judgment, or self-hate, then you will miss the true message. You will miss the gift in the guilt.

The truth is you cannot beat yourself into being a better person. Attacking, judging, punishing, and criticizing yourself will *not* lead to improvement. This is an antiquated and unexamined pattern that many of us run, despite it clearly not working.

Instead of buying into that self-attack message, I simply brought my awareness to my body and heart. I felt the pain and ache of being angry at and disconnected from Zaim. I felt his pain. I felt my pain. I felt the burning in my heart. And I sent it love. I sent myself love and forgiveness. I sent Zaim love and forgiveness. What a sweet boy doing the best he can. What a sweet dad doing the best he can.

This is how you let healthy guilt transform you in positive ways. Get out of your head and into your heart. Feel whatever is there and keep meeting it with love and forgiveness, even if your mind tells you that it's unforgiveable. It's not. Everything is, because forgiveness is infinite and always accessible.

Sometimes we feel a need to internally proclaim: *I will never, ever do this again. From this day forward, I will be perfect!* We think this is required in order for forgiveness to occur. But we forget that we actually access forgiveness. It's already available and there, right in this very moment. Our mind just holds the keys and says: *You must do A, B, and C before I open this door.* And one of those requirements is that we have complete and total certainty that we'll never, ever do it again (whatever your "it" is — getting upset, yelling, overeating or eating junk food, avoiding a scary situation, procrastinating, and a million and one other things that you might attack yourself for).

But here's the thing. You *might* do it again. In fact, you probably will. Can you forgive yourself anyway? What if your mind has it all wrong, and everything works completely opposite than you think? What if forgiving yourself made it way more likely that you wouldn't repeat the behavior? And what if attacking yourself and withholding love made you much more likely to repeat the behavior? Guess what, it does!

So, no matter what the rule, and how many times you've broken it, focus on your heart, feel your body, and meet whatever you find with love and forgiveness.

Love the unlovable.

From this place, you may be able to make new choices, or create a powerful new commitment. Not the, "I promise I'll never do this again!" mental proclamation. That is a desperate attempt to bargain away the guilt. I mean a decision in your core to do something differently, and then resolving to create a ritual that helps you actually make that change.

For example, fully feeling the guilt after getting upset with one of my children lead to a deep commitment in me to become less reactive, more patient and more loving. I'm sure every parent alive has made that decision again and again, only to find themselves repeating the same patterns of anger forty-seven minutes later. I'd done this myself many times.

But one day I reached a threshold and I decided to create a powerful commitment. I decided I was going to wake up even earlier and meditate for one hour per day, for the rest of my life. Extreme? Perhaps. Badass? You know it. And so that is what I did, and that is what I have done for the last eight months. Never missed a morning, never missed a day.

Sure enough, as I meditated more, my reactivity, irritability, and crankiness reduced radically. My capacity to remain connected and unconditionally love my boys, no matter what their behavior, grew exponentially. And the depth of love and joy that I feel in spending time with them is so much greater that I am shocked at how much I was actually suffering before.

Willpower is not the answer. Commitment is. If you slow down, feel, forgive yourself, and listen for the message in your healthy guilt, it will tell you what you need to do. You'll see the values you hold dear, and exactly how you want to be in the world. Then, use your willpower, drive, and desire to be your best and create a small habit or ritual that you will do every day. That is the secret to changing all behavior, and putting something in place that guarantees lasting transformation and success. What will your new ritual be?

PERFECTIONISM AND INSANE RULES

To recap the Guilt-Neutralizing process so far, it goes something like this:

1. Notice when you are feeling guilty and identify it.
2. Slow down and study the experience of guilt: what does it feel like in your body, what thoughts do you notice in your mind?
3. Ask yourself this question: *What rule have I broken?*
4. If it's a rule that's realistic and reflects your values, then feel your heart, forgive yourself, and receive the message.

However, there is another major source of guilt that is very different than the one we've been focusing on. This is what we've been calling Unhealthy Guilt. This is guilt that comes from rules that you've broken that aren't based on your personal core values.

Instead, they are based on completely unrealistic standards for human behavior, emotions, and relationships. They are rigid, all-or-nothing, demanding, and generally impossible to adhere to.

These include rules like:

I should never feel angry.
I should never feel anxious.
I should never make a mistake.
I should always know what to say.
I should never hurt anyone's feelings.
I should never upset anybody.
I should always have total self-control.
I should be able to predict all outcomes.

I should foresee all problems and avoid them.

I should obtain _____ *now*. (Insert any result you are striving towards)

When you're feeling guilty and you slow down to pay attention, you'll hear these kinds of rules running through your mind. Sometimes it's direct, such as, "I should be able to predict all outcomes." More commonly, you'll just hear that voice in your head chastising you with comments like: *I should have known! Why did I do that? So stupid!*

These kinds of commands are driving you to go harder, perform better, be more, achieve more, and do it all faster. Reach your goals by yesterday. You're taking too long. Why aren't you there already? You should be making faster progress. You should have achieved everything you wanted by now.

Underneath all of these commands is one central theme: *What's wrong with you?* The more you listen to them and follow them unquestioningly, the worse you feel about yourself. The more insufficient, inadequate, unlovable and unworthy you think you are, regardless of external achievement or how much others love you.

These are insane rules. When you identify one of these rules, the answer is not to take the message to strive harder and set up more rituals or commitments. **The response in these situations is to slow down, and let go of the demand on yourself to be superhuman.** Let go of this insane rule that is driving you so hard and creating so much suffering.

This rule is not your friend. It might seem like it's your inner coach, pushing you to succeed and "be your best," but actually it's the voice of self-hatred. It's coming from a mindset of: I'm not complete or whole as I am. I am inadequate, insufficient, lacking. I am not good enough. I am not fully lovable as I am. I must do this, achieve this, live by this crazy rule. *Then*, I'll be enough. Then I'll be somebody. Then I'll be worthy.

four times per day. We had him count during the next week, just to find out. Guess how many? Ten times per day. One day he noticed he apologized twenty-four times.

And trust me, this guy wasn't walking around pushing down old ladies and taking kids' candy money. He wasn't doing anything that was highly offensive or worth apology. He was just existing.

That's what I've found with the excessive apologizing. It's almost as if we're apologizing for our existence. It's as if we're saying to the world, "I'm sorry for being here. Sorry for bothering you. Sorry for imposing on you with my existence." Yuck.

You have a right to be here. You belong. You matter. Why? Just because. You exist on this planet and you have a right to be here just as much as anyone else.

To help my client break this habit, I had him go on an apology fast. If you notice that you have a habit of saying sorry all the time, I would suggest the same activity for you. Here's how it works.

For the next three to four days, simply count how many times you say sorry per day. It may be high like my client, or it may be much lower, in the one to three range. Whatever it is, just notice it, without judging yourself.

Then, commit to go on a 10-day apology fast. That means you don't apologize unnecessarily for ten days. The only time you apologize is in a specific instance where you've really reflected on it, and decided that you were out of line. Perhaps you were harsh with your spouse or cranky with your kids. In that case, you can go back to them and say, "I'm sorry I was cranky with you yesterday. You didn't do anything wrong, I was just irritable."

Aside from those apologies, for the next ten days, eliminate all others. These include favorites such as:

Sorry to bother you…
I'm sorry, what was that again?
Sorry?

Oh, sorry.

I'm sorry, you go ahead.

It may be difficult at first. In fact, an apology might tumble out of your mouth before you realize it. That's OK, it's part of the process.

My client came back after a week of doing this and shared his report.

"How did it go?" I asked.

"Well, it was really hard. I did OK, but not that great," he said.

"Oh yeah? What happened?" I said.

"I got down to about three or four per day. Those ones just came out before I knew it. It's almost like I couldn't control it."

"From ten to three or four! That's a seventy percent decrease in just seven days," I pointed out.

I see this pattern all the time in my clients. They do something big in a short period of time, and then find a way to discount it, as if it were no big deal. I like to point this out and tease people about it, helping them start to own their progress and make them laugh at themselves a bit.

"That's not good enough, Steve. Seventy percent in seven days. What the hell is that?" I said, smiling.

"I know," he said, laughing. "I'm just amazed at how strong the habit is."

So, he continued the fast for another several weeks, and soon he was down to zero unnecessary apologies per day. He told me that he was amazed by how much this simple exercise increased his confidence.

"I feel more powerful walking around in the world," he said. "I can look people in the eye and stand up taller. I never realized how afraid I was of upsetting people, and how that was affecting me."

Give it a go. Decide to do it for ten days, then decide if you want to do another ten. Enroll a friend to play the game with you, if you'd like. You just might find that it transforms your sense of confidence, strengthens your internal core, and gives you the power you need to live life fully on your terms.

CHAPTER 14:

100% YOU

As we've gone on this journey together, you've seen how being nice and pleasing is not who you are. You've grown in your assertiveness, social power, and ability to speak up and say what you need to. You've been letting go of guilt and fear as motivators, and are moving into more powerful sources of fuel, like inspiration, excitement, passion, purpose, love, contribution, fun, or anything else you value.

In a sense, you are becoming more you. More and more of who you really are, who you're meant to be. Let's see if we can turn that dial up even more, into the realm of **Bold Authenticity: Complete freedom and permission to be who you want to be without shame, guilt, fear, or self-condemnation.** Powerfully, freely, delightfully you.

After working with thousands of people over the years, I've seen one simple pattern. Regardless of the focus of our sessions — work and business, romantic relationships, friendships, confidence and self-esteem — this pattern was the same for everyone. It didn't matter whether they were married or single, rich or poor, old or young, it always came down to this:

If someone feels like they cannot be themselves, they suffer. Period.

It doesn't matter how many people love them or admire them, how famous they are, or how much money they're making. If they aren't being themselves, stuffing instead of speaking freely, or acting a role that is not congruent with their essence, there will be pain. They may try to push this pain down or ignore it because they don't want to disturb the status quo, or the relationship. They tell themselves, *How could I leave this job when it's so stable and I get paid so well?*

But that pain doesn't go away. It just goes underground. It comes back as physical symptoms or "injuries" in our bodies. It manifests as apathy, anxiety, depression, negativity, dissatisfaction, or restlessness. All of these might feel uncomfortable or terrible, but they are actually beautiful. They are evidence that the human spirit will not settle for anything other than complete freedom. That you will not settle for anything less than authenticity and the freedom to express yourself in the ways you are meant to.

Let's explore together how you can be more you. 100% you in fact.

BOLD AUTHENTICITY

Let's take a moment to discover what you being 100% you actually means. I've found for myself that simply thinking about the words "one hundred percent me" starts to impact my thoughts and actions. But let's give it more clarity.

To start, let me ask you, what do you think 100% you is? If you gave yourself complete permission to be the real you in all settings — work, with family, as a parent, as a son or daughter, when meeting new people, with friends, by yourself in the woods — what would you do? How would you act? How would you be?

What are the first words, phrases, or images that pop into your mind? Do you see certain scenes at work or with your spouse playing out in your mind? Take a few minutes and watch and hear anything that comes out of your mind and heart when you ask these questions. These messages just might be your long-lost, buried, authentic self.

GROW UP (OR DON'T?)

Did anyone ever tell you when you were a kid to "grow up"? Or maybe you heard it as a teenager, or even last week. Grow up. Be more mature, more responsible. Depending on the context this often really means: *stop what you're doing and obey me, or, don't focus on what you want, focus on my needs right now.*

In any case, "growing up" just might be part of the problem. Because when you were a kid you had absolutely no problems being fully yourself. When you were three, four or five, if you wanted to talk to someone, you did. Even if they were a stranger or a homeless person that adults avoided. When you wanted to say something, you did. You shared things and told stories, assuming everyone would be interested, because your stories were awesome. If the other person wasn't paying attention, you'd shout, "Hey! Listen to me!"

If you felt shy or didn't want to talk to someone, you'd turn away, or retreat. You wouldn't answer questions they asked you. You might have even simply said, "I don't like you."

If you wanted to dance, you danced. Crazy, wonky, uncoordinated, unbridled, joyful, wacky dance moves. All over the place. To the joy, amusement, and delight of all adults around. They smiled as their spirit longed to be able to move so freely, without self-consciousness or regard for others' opinions.

If you observe young children, you'll see all this and more. I'll never forget one fascinating interaction between two young girls at my wife's extended family's house. We were out in the dry desert landscape of Eastern Washington in the late spring. The sky was bright blue and my (future) wife Candace and I were sitting on a blanket, reveling in the warm sunshine.

Around us was a gaggle of little kids. The young boys were running around the property, engaged in extended and elaborate Nerf warfare. The little girls were closer to the blanket, playing with various dolls, tea party sets, and whatnot.

Here was the interaction I'll never forget. One little girl kept putting a doll in another girl's face so the doll could dance around and tell her something. Eventually the girl got sick of a doll in her face and yelled, "Stop putting that doll in my face!"

Without missing a beat, the first girl responded, "If you don't like the doll in your face, move your face then!"

It's the kind of thing that could happen hundreds of times in a play session between small children. It's the kind of thing that most people wouldn't even notice or think twice about. But to me, someone who has spent years studying how to be more assertive and helping others do the same, I was in awe.

So much uninhibited, simple expressiveness. One girl is doing what she wants to do, and the other one doesn't like it and tells her so, right away. No stuffing, no guilt, no questioning and hesitating and ruminating about the "best" way to say it. She just blurts it out. In response, the second girl fires back. She says whatever comes to her mind. No guilt, no feeling terrible because she did something that another person didn't like, no self-loathing, social anxiety, or fear of losing the relationship.

Obviously, as we get older and more mature, we need to learn some measure of restraint. We don't say *everything* that comes to our minds, and we find more tactful and skillful ways to assert ourselves. However, in the vast majority of recovering nice people (myself included), we can spend *way* too much energy on saying things "just right." We have so many ideas about whether it's OK to speak up at all, how we should say something if we do choose to speak up, and how the other person should not have any negative reaction to us. We have that initial impulse to blurt something out and it travels through this complex mental algorithm of what's right, what's "nice," and either nothing comes out at all, or it's some heavily manipulated communication designed to be polite and acceptable to all. What comes out is often not us. And, as you remember, feeling like we cannot be ourselves is one of the greatest forms of human suffering.

So what am I suggesting? That we should chuck all our filters and just go back to being like little kids? Saying whatever we want, doing whatever we want, all the time? This notion was captured brilliantly in one of the early episodes of *The Simpsons*, in which a popular psychologist visits the town of Springfield to do a seminar. During the seminar, he is repeatedly interrupted by the unfiltered comments of Bart Simpson, much to Homer and Marge's embarrassment. Instead of being upset, however, the psychologist praises Bart for his boldness and uses him as an example. He gets everyone in the audience chanting, "Be like the boy!", encouraging them to run free, follow their impulses, and release the shackles of repression and restraint. The town is invigorated and everyone starts having more fun. However, within a short period of time, people stop going to work, carrying out their responsibilities, and the entire town falls apart.

No, you don't need to "Be like the boy!" We don't need to throw away all of our conditioning and what we learned to be self-aware, kind, attentive, and empathic people. But we may want to fiddle with the knobs a bit. We may want to turn down the filter knob from the "excessive" or "extreme" range towards "thoughtful" or "reasonable."

We may want to turn up the bold authenticity knob from "totally stuffed down" to "I say what needs to be said" or "I can dance if I wanna."

BOLD AUTHENTICITY KNOB

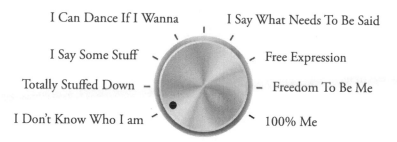

I Can Dance If I Wanna

I Say What Needs To Be Said

I Say Some Stuff

Free Expression

Totally Stuffed Down

Freedom To Be Me

I Don't Know Who I am

100% Me

FILTERS KNOB

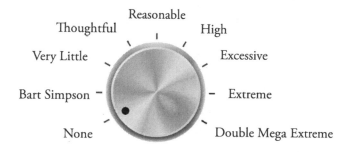

Reasonable

Thoughtful

High

Very Little

Excessive

Bart Simpson

Extreme

None

Double Mega Extreme

What dial are each of these knobs set to for you currently? Have the settings changed at all since you started reading this book? Obviously, you can change out the words and phrases on these dials for ones that speak to you. The key here is to give yourself permission to be you. To turn down the filters that hold you back, and to turn up the bold, free, expression of who you are. As you do this, you will experience an increase in self-esteem, happiness, and freedom. This is because you will be aligning with the real you, that version of yourself that was there when you were six years old, and that gives you energy and power. You being fully you, with complete permission and enjoyment, is as good as it gets.

BE YOU

Has anyone ever told you to "just be yourself"? Perhaps you were nervous or worried about a meeting, a job interview, or meeting your new girlfriend's parents. A well-meaning friend says, in an attempt to reassure you, "Relax, you'll be fine. Just be yourself." It's probably sage advice, if we were to follow it. But often, what is our internal reaction to this is advice? To get a little annoyed, right?

When people used to tell me that, I would smile and say thanks. Inside I would fume to myself: *What the hell does that even mean? Just be yourself. That doesn't help me at all!*

Well, this section is all about just that. Being yourself. Let's break it down and clarify exactly what that means for you, at this stage of your life, in this moment right now.

One of the best ways to do this is to see where you think you should be something other than you are. Take a moment to read that last sentence again. It's a doozy. Where do you think you should be more like someone else? Heck, in some ways do you tell yourself you should literally *be* somebody else?

No, that's crazy, right? We would never do anything that crazy, would we?

When I was seven years old my parents bought me one of those miniature basketball hoops. It stood about five feet high, with a solid backboard and realistic looking rim. Just like a real basketball hoop, only smaller. It was amazing. I spent hours playing with that thing – taking three pointers, slam dunking it like crazy, and imagining myself as the hero of the championship game by scoring the most points and, of course, making the game winning shot at the buzzer. It was glorious. Only it wasn't me.

Aziz was not making all the points and winning the championship game and the love of the imaginary crowds. Andrew McCallister was. Who? Andrew McCallister. This was the name I made up, specifically for this purpose. I didn't use it anywhere else and I've never told anyone about it, until now. But anytime I played sports by myself and imagined an epic victory, it was Andrew.

I would do the voices of the announcers who were calling the play by play of the game. "Andrew McCallister pulls up for another three pointer... and he sinks it. He's on fire!" (Yes, my play by play was heavily influenced by the video game *NBA Jam*).

Why did I do this? I had no idea at the time, it just felt right. In some ways, it's who I wanted to be. I had many different experiences in my life where I was teased heavily or ostracized from a group simply because of my name. "Aziz the disease" one group of kids called me as they turned away to do something that didn't involve me. I learned that having a "weird" name like Aziz wasn't cool. It wasn't what crowds cheered for. It wasn't the kind of name that won championships and love. So, I changed it. I became someone else. Or at least pretended to be someone else.

Oh, little kids are so silly, you may be thinking. I wish it were just little kids. We can do this very thing as adults. We have stories about what makes us lovable, valuable, desirable, and significant in the eyes of others. Wealth, cars, a big house, career success, a certain appearance, thinner arms, longer legs, chiseled abs, and on and on. The options for how you "should be" are endless. Then we find someone who represents those qualities and we subtly pressure ourselves to be more like them. An actor, a model, a sports figure, or even a colleague or friend you look up to. I should be more like him or her. In a subconscious way, part of us actually wants to be him or her.

Lil' Tony

I didn't know it, but I was unconsciously wanting to be someone else for literally ten years of my life. When I was twenty-four years old I attended my first Tony Robbins seminar, and I was blown away. I had been studying clinical psychology at Stanford and Palo Alto Universities for two years. It was a prestigious institution and the best psychologists and psychiatrists were training me to help people. Yet, in four days at Tony's event I had learned more applicable, exciting, and valuable tools than I had in a year of that program.

Tony was confident, certain in himself, and commanded the room. He was certain he could help anyone overcome anything, and he was highly skilled at doing so. He was also willing to demonstrate this to the audience by coaching people live in front of the entire group. It was a life-changing experience and in that moment I knew I wasn't going to be a clinical psychologist, I was going to be a coach, like Tony. I was going to work with groups of people and help more people, like Tony. I was going to be a leader and a powerful force for good in the world, like Tony. In fact, I decided in that moment (unconsciously) that I was going to *be* Tony.

So, for the next ten years, he became the gold standard in my head. While it was inspiring and set me on a course that is my destiny, it also had some negative consequences. Because, as you may very well know, I am not Tony Robbins. But I had this underlying pressure to be more, do more, and help people more, in the way that I imagine he could. This led me to frequently feel inadequate after a counseling or coaching session. Even though most of my clients were engaged in our work together and made powerful leaps and bounds in their confidence and lives, part of me wasn't satisfied. I would think to myself: *Tony could have one conversation with this person and everything would transform instantly, forever. They should leave the session out-of-their-mind-excited, elated, and on fire. And I should feel and be that way all the time too.*

This pressure I placed on myself was generally not front row, center in my conscious awareness. It was in the background, like a hiss of static or the whir of an air conditioner. Even though I wasn't fully aware of it, it prevented me from feeling fully satisfied, fulfilled, and happy after sessions. There was always a lingering feeling of anxiety, being unsettled, or that I didn't quite do it right.

It became much more obvious when I started leading live events. As people flew in from all over the country, and the world, I felt an incredible pressure. I really have to Tony it up now! Every single person here has to have the most, the best, face-melting, earth shattering, permanent-breakthrough-confidence-explosion of all time... all before lunch on the first day.

This strange demand to literally be someone else created excessive expectations, high pressure, and greatly diminished my enjoyment, freedom, and power. In December of 2016, after attending another Tony Robbins event, I was able to see this pattern that had been operating for almost a decade. I saw him very differently than I had ten years ago. Instead of seeing a virtual demigod, I saw him as a human. I appreciated his passion and endless energy to serve humanity. It inspired and motivated me to do more of the same. I also saw him as just another person, making an impact in the world. The need to be exactly like him, and do exactly what he did, in the way he did it, was gone.

I came home with a renewed sense of power and freedom. I don't have to be any certain way. I don't have to be anyone other than who I am. I felt happy, joyful, and above all, free. I was able to see my own gifts, my own strengths, and the unique value that I brought. I trusted in myself more and stopped doubting whether I was doing good enough. This radically increased my enjoyment and sense of purpose in sessions and made me more playful, direct, and powerful. I could call things out more honestly and ask challenging questions. I held nothing back.

As you've been reading this story, I wonder if you're seeing anyone that you've unconsciously been trying to be? Who might you have thought you should be more like? Your brother? Your sister? That popular kid in your high school? That leader in your company or in your field? Who do you constantly compare yourself too, even if you've never met them?

Take a few minutes now to reflect on that. Perhaps it will come to you over the next few days, or in a moment when you are walking from one place to another. Or, you might know exactly who it is right now.

Whenever you identify it, and whoever it is... can you let that go? Can you give yourself full permission to be you? No need to pressure, force, drive, or cajole yourself into being just like that person. That pattern might seem like it drives you to be better, but it actually limits you and drains your power over time. Because your ultimate power, influence, ability to impact and love, all come out strongest when you are most aligned with your inner core. The more you are being fully, 100% you, the easier everything becomes.

As you let go of the need to be someone else, ask yourself these powerful questions: *What about me — what do I bring to the world? What are my unique qualities?* Let yourself fully see, feel, and know the gifts you bring to the world.

As you do this, you fully step into being who you really are, which is a great gift to yourself, and the world. There are two keys to being able to do this effectively, which are: being the authority and letting yourself be known. Let's explore those now.

BE THE AUTHORITY

In order to let go of trying to be someone else, and to boldly be yourself without apology, you must become the authority in your own life. This is a subtle shift away from looking to others to tell us what to do, what to say, how to be, and to look inward and trust our own guidance, our own decisions.

This can be scary at first. We often look to others because we don't feel like the authority. We are unsure, we don't know enough yet, we don't know how, and we're afraid of doing it wrong and messing things up. When we turn to someone else as the authority, and they seem certain about what they're saying, it can be very relieving. *Ah, they have the answers; I'll just do what they say. Whew!*

This can be beneficial at first. If you keep having the same fight with your partner, and you two always get stuck, it can be helpful to get some outside input. Maybe you consult with a couple's counselor, or read a book about how to communicate better with each other.[6] If you apply what you learn, your communication can improve and your relationship gets better. Huzzah!

The same goes for learning about how to build a business, get in better shape, improve your mood, or learn a new skill. Learning from others, modeling, and finding new approaches and solutions is the fast track to rapid growth, and success.

However, learning from others involves trusting in others and seeing them as an authority on the subject. And that can slowly lead to trusting others as a *higher* authority than yourself in your own life. That's where it becomes a problem. That's where you lose connection with yourself and lose your power.

Instead, we must reclaim our power and our sense of internal authority. We may consider what we have learned and weigh what different teachers might suggest, and then decide for ourselves what the best course of action is. Then stand in that decision firmly, clearly, and confidently. As in: I said it, I meant it. That just happened.

LACK OF INNER AUTHORITY

If you're experiencing a lack of inner authority in any area of your life, then you know what it feels like. It involves uncertainty about how to respond to a specific situation, what to say, or how to behave. You may even be unsure of how you "should" think and feel. You might be imagining different people in your life, or different books you've read, considering what each of them might say to you.

You also have the sense that there is a "right" way to handle the situation that someone else knows. But you don't know the right way and whatever was your way wasn't quite as good as it should be. Sometimes this feeling is very strong and obvious and you're filled

---

6. Dan Wile's *After The Honeymoon* is the best on this subject in my opinion.

with uncertainty, anxiety, seconding guessing, and self-doubt. Sometimes it's subtler; it's just a feeling of not being certain, fully strong in yourself, or slightly timid.

You might then look to others too much, hoping they have the answers you need. And, for better or worse, you can definitely find people who have all the certainty in the world. Whether it's a book, your brother, or your colleague at work, there are many places you can find someone speaking with complete certainty and authority. Because they sound so sure of themselves, and you secretly feel unsure inside, it can be natural to conclude that they have it all figured out and you don't. So, it would be best to simply follow their advice. Do what they say.

But certainty does not correlate with accuracy. In other words, someone could be certain about something and completely wrong. Their advice could be terrible. But their certainty is so dang convincing, isn't it?

Only when we're not giving ourselves permission to be the authority in our own lives. Because deep down, you are just as certain. **There is a part of you in your core, in your heart, that always knows the next best move for you.** It knows how to respond, what to say, and what to do. There's just so much mental noise and old programming telling you not to trust yourself. That noise tells you: *Trust in your teacher, your parents, those people with more experience, those people who can talk a better game and sound more confident. Don't trust in yourself. Who are you to know anything?*

Unfortunately, many of us received this message growing up so much that we bought into it and now believe it to be true. But it's not. You are the authority in your life. You know what's best for you. Your heart, when you slow down, tune into it, breath and listen, can guide you forward. You can be you. It's OK. It's safe. The world will not end, friends will not disappear, and you will not end up alone and miserable for the rest of your life. Quite the opposite actually!

Your energy will return and magnify tenfold. Lightness, joy, and your natural sense of humor will come out more and more. Decisions will be easier and doubt will dissolve as you just choose and take action. Once you stop thinking there's someone who can tell you what to do who knows more than you, all your power returns. Then you are a force of nature. Look out.

TRUST YOUR INTUITION

The key to being your own authority is to first give yourself that permission. It might sound simple, but affirming to yourself: *I am choosing to be the authority in my life* is a powerful decision that will significantly impact what you say, think, feel, and do.

Of course, like any decision, in order for it to have a lasting effect it must be an ongoing commitment. Something you do consistently, something you live by. And the best way to do that is to strengthen your sense of intuition, trust in yourself, and trust in something bigger than yourself.

Intuition is a sense of inner knowing that comes from somewhere other than our scared, self-absorbed minds. It is not our survival-based programming that thinks everyone is watching and judging us, and that we need to scramble just to survive. Instead, it's a much deeper intelligence that is accessed through our bodies, and taps into something much greater than what we think of as ourselves.

We all have intuition. You have a sense about something. You get the feeling it's best to go here instead of there. Your gut tells you it's a bad move to work with a certain person, and so you decline an offer. These are different ways we perceive beyond our conscious, analytic left-brain.

The key to being the authority in your life is to start paying attention to your intuition. Instead of dismissing it as untrustworthy and dangerous, start embracing it as a superior form of guidance, one that is vastly superior to your conscious mind.

Our standard way of operating in the world is generally through our ego, or small self. This part of us is obsessed with how we appear to others, if we're "getting ahead" and "becoming somebody" and generally doing everything we should be doing so that we survive. This part of our mind thinks it needs to control everything in order to be secure. It's constantly planning and mentally manipulating the environment, deciding what the best course of action is so that we get what we want, just the way we want it.

What do I need to say or do to make her want to go out with me? What do I need to do to make him ask me to marry him? How should I do this presentation to make these people agree to my proposal? With these questions as fuel, our minds get to work, weighing variables, calculating all factors, and attempting to control the external world.

There is a better way. A way that feels relieving, and gives you a greater sense of authority in your life. And that is to surrender. To trust more and fear less. To float more and steer less.

This capacity is so incredibly valuable, I am actually writing an entire book that will explore it in greater depth. For now, simply begin by tuning into your intuition. Listen to it more, and act on it more, starting now. The more you do this, the more you trust it, and the stronger it becomes. You will start to feel more relaxed self-confidence and trust that emerges from a feeling of being guided in your life. You start to experience the sense of life living through you.

BEING LIKED VERSUS BEING KNOWN

As you've seen throughout this book, being the nice person is driven by the need for approval from others. This need can influence how we approach all people, in all interactions, and make our primary intent to be liked. This leads to a phenomenon known as impression management, where you're monitoring how you come across, and adjusting what you say or do to mold others' perceptions of you. This habit creates tension, social anxiety, and stress.

As you step out of fear-based niceness and into bold authenticity, you need a new goal. If your primary purpose isn't to make sure everyone likes you, then what is it?

To be known.

If you're spending time with someone, and your goal is to get them to like you, then you will avoid certain topics, smile politely, and do a dozen others things from the nice-person playbook. But if your primary goal is simply to get to know the other person, and let them know you, what would you do?

And what does that even mean, to get to know someone? Is it learning all the information about their past? Where they went to school, who they dated, how many jobs they've had and where? While that's certainly part of getting to know someone, it's only a small piece of the equation. You can know all that information and feel no connection with someone whatsoever. Or, you can just meet someone and feel like you've known them a lifetime, and yet know very little about their past.

So, what actually creates that sense of knowing someone?

Knowing someone comes from sharing what is really happening inside, transparently and vulnerably. It requires authentic expression of what we're experiencing in the moment. This includes what we're thinking, feeling, noticing, and perceiving. What we want and don't want, like and don't like. Not some watered-down, heavily filtered version of this, but what's actually happening inside of us. What's actually true.

When two people are doing this, the conversation becomes engaging. Even if they don't agree on all topics, there is a strong connection because both people are fully present, fully there in the moment.

In contrast, when we come from a place of wanting to be liked, we are not fully there. We are hiding large parts of ourselves, and much of our attention is in our heads, filtering what we'll say next to get the person to see us in a certain way. This lack of presence is instantly felt subconsciously by others, and they become less engaged and less interested, even if we're being friendly and asking all the "right" questions. Energy trumps content every time.

So what if you decided, right now, that from now on your goal in being with others was not to be liked, but to be known? To share who you are, and find out who they are. Or, as one of my clients put it in his words: "To connect and have fun."

When you make this choice, and act upon it, you will discover another paradox of niceness. When you stop trying to be liked, and your intention is just to share who you are, as you are, guess what happens? That's right – people like you way more. They are naturally drawn to you, and there is an ease and effortlessness about how you attract them.

You, as you are, right now, are enough. You can share yourself. Be yourself. Reveal yourself. You don't have to wait until you're better, or you have it all sorted out, or you don't have negative feelings. You don't have to read eighteen more self-development books on how to share and communicate better. You can be you. It's OK. It's safe. I promise.

However, me telling you that, and you knowing that, might be two different things. Which actually brings us to the final section of this book, which is all about what matters most: Action.

PART IV:

ACTION

CHAPTER 15:

YOUR BTB 30-DAY ACTION PLAN

Welcome to Boldness Training Bootcamp! It seems highly likely to me that you have already begun to take some action on what you are learning in this book. To make it this far, and not have done anything different indicates a strong pattern of discomfort avoidance. If so, not to worry, we have a clear set path of specific actions for you to take, starting today.

If you have been trying new things, testing out saying no, asking for what you want, and being more expressive, then you're in good shape. This section will give you more ideas, and lay out a specific plan for you to follow to increase your progress.

Remember, the opposite of nice is not being a jerk, it's being authentically you. More direct, more assertive, more expressive, and ultimately more alive. This allows you to then be more generous, kinder, and more loving with anyone you choose.

Also remember that intellectual insight and new understandings are extremely helpful, but only in so far as they help you take new action in your life. Repeated action over time — doing the uncomfortable thing again and again — is what's going to set you free.

Boldness Training Bootcamp, which is designed to help you shed excessive niceness and return you to your full personal power, is very much like going to the gym. I like to use this metaphor because everyone understands what it takes to get physically stronger. We all know that you need to go to the gym, or run, or swim, and do this activity again and again to get stronger.

If you went to the gym once per week and curled a five-pound weight a few times, and then left, would you be any stronger after a month? Sounds absurd, right? But somehow we don't use the same logic when it comes to changing patterns of behavior, communication, or thought. In those instances, we might say, "I kinda tried to speak up, by asking them a question, but they didn't listen to me, so I dropped it." If that's your attitude, this boldness training will never work!

Our mind says that simply because it's uncomfortable. The discomfort of lifting weights, or going for a run is somehow simpler, and often much easier to endure. We know it will end, and we often feel an immediate high after working out. We also know that if we keep doing it, we'll get stronger.

However, when it comes to Boldness Training, it can be less clear. After a "workout" where we said no directly, or made a choice that upset someone else, we can feel waves of self-doubt, self-criticism, or guilt. To make matters worse, we may have created relationships in our lives where we were constantly pleasing others and they've come to expect that. We may have trained everyone around us to demand we do their bidding, regardless of what we want.

As you become bolder, expressive, authentic, and powerful, you will overcome all of these challenges. You'll discover that some relationships evolve and grow as you do. There's more space for you to be you, and everything gets better. Other relationships turn out not to be much of a real relationship after all. It turns out the other person is enjoying having someone do what they want, and doesn't like the idea of that person having a will of their own.

In these cases, you'll be met with the "change back phenomenon." This term comes from family counseling, and describes the phenomenon of pressure one family member might feel when they try to make a positive change. Counselors discovered that other family members would often resist the change, even though it's for the better. They might confront the family member, or offer a more passive form of resistance through guilt-tripping or sarcastic comments. These indirect communications are unconsciously communicating: *I don't like change! Change back to the way you were right now, and everything will go back to normal and I'll be happy again. Change back!*

If you are met with a few change back behaviors, don't worry about it. It's a natural and normal part of the process. Some of your friendships and relationships will grow much deeper, and some will fall away. That's OK. You will then have space to attract more inspiring people in your life who love and support the authentic version of you.

As you do this, instead of others turning against you, and terrible things happening, you'll discover it's quite the opposite. Others become more interested in you, more attracted to you. People want to be your friend, date you, sleep with you, or marry you. They want to hire you, work with you, or work for you. They start to treat you with more authority and respect. Everything you want is just on the other side of your comfort zone.

So, are you ready to get uncomfortable in order to create the life you've always wanted? Are you pumped? I'm pumped. Let's do this.

THE PLAN

OK, here's the plan: For the next thirty days you are going to do one thing per day that challenges your nice-person programming. For example, today you are going to start a fight, and you are going to lose. No, I'm kidding. The challenges will be basic, fast, and easy to apply in your life. In fact, you might be surprised how little time this takes. Most of these exercises can be completed in several minutes. Some may require up to fifteen minutes. Time is not the obstacle here, discomfort is. And if you are willing to face discomfort in order to liberate yourself, then you are set for a life-changing month.

Remember, this is the three-step process for eliminating excessive niceness and becoming a more authentic, confident version of you:

1. Decide to be not nice.
2. Do the not nice stuff that makes you scared and uncomfortable.
3. Work through the internal backlash (guilt, anxiety, doubt, fear) afterwards.

The plan is simple. First, decide when you are going to begin. Unless you are going on a solo meditation retreat in the mountains next week, I suggest you begin today, or tomorrow. Not when you're less busy and it sounds easier, not when you finish that project at work, and not in thirteen years when your kids graduate high school and head off for college. Today. Now.

Ready?

Begin!

Week 1: Foundation

Day 1 – Clarity

Let's begin by getting clarity on two things. First, where you are now, and secondly why it's a must for you to break free to a higher level of boldness and authenticity.

Begin by taking the How Nice Are You Assessment on page 33. You may have taken it when you read that section of the book, but it's good to get a clear sense of where you are in this moment as you begin these thirty days.

Secondly, take a few minutes and get clear on why reaching the next level of growth and freedom is essential. In order to persist in the face of discomfort to achieve anything, we must have a strong internal motivation to help us make it through the hard times. The natural human tendency is to move away from discomfort over time, so in order to override this, write out your reasons.

Why is it essential for you to break free now? What has being too nice cost you in your life? What pain is it causing you? What pain is it causing others?

What will becoming more expressive, free, empowered, and loving bring to your life? What will your life be like on the other side?

Take as long as you'd like to reflect on these questions, and then write something down. Don't just answer these in your head. Get your thoughts down on paper or in your phone so you can read them later in this process, whenever you need a motivation boost.

Day 2 – I Don't Need Your Approval

Today is a fun one. Start by reviewing the 15 Common Signs of Approval Seeking on page 49. Pick one from the list that you'd like to reduce today. And then, starting right now, and frequently throughout the day, remind yourself of this powerful truth: I don't need your approval.

Say it silently in your mind right now. Repeat it before any social interaction. Repeat it while you're sitting in a meeting at work, or interacting with your boss or a customer. Repeat it as you check out at the supermarket. Repeat it before and during your date with that really attractive person you're nervous about seeing.

Repeat liberally. No need to force anything or make yourself feel a certain way. Simply let the words settle into your mind like seeds being scattered in a fertile field.

Day 3 – What Do I Want?

Open up a fresh sheet of paper or note file on your computer and ask yourself this question: What do I want?

Write freely, quickly, and without editing your thoughts. No one else is going to read this; it's just for you. If your mind judges what comes out, that's OK. That's what our minds are trained to do. Just keep writing, as quickly as you can.

I want...

I want...

I want...

And then, when you're done, ask yourself this question: What do I *really* want?

And write some more.

When you're done, take a few minutes to read over what you've written. Slow down and breathe. Notice how you feel. Find any discomfort in your body and bring your attention to it, meeting it with curiosity, acceptance, and love. No need to be alarmed. That discomfort is just a young part of you that is scared because it was taught that it was bad to want things. Just hold that part in your awareness with patience and love, and it'll calm down.

Then, throughout the day, ask yourself that question multiple times: *In this situation, what do I want?*

Notice what answers arise. If you can, and feel up for it, try acting on what you discover. For example, if you're talking with someone and not feeling satisfied with the conversation, ask yourself, *what do I want here?* Perhaps you discover that you want to end the conversation so you can talk with someone else. If you feel ready for it, simply tell the person at the next opportunity, "It's been great talking with you, Bob. I'm going to head over to the lounge area for a bit. I'll catch you later."

If acting on what you want seems too intense, or is too challenging right now, that's fine. We're only in Day 3! In that case, simply notice what you really want, without making it wrong or bad. Also notice how much fear there is around simply asking for or doing what you want. Let yourself be curious and fascinated by it all, trusting that you will be free before too long.

Day 4 – Your Bill of Rights

Remember this from Chapter 6? Did you make one? If not, go back to that section and create one now. It is a life-changing exercise.

Then, read your Bill of Rights this morning. Read it out loud. If you need privacy, do it on your way to work in your car. Pull off to the side of the road somewhere and belt them out. Strange? Sure. But liberating? You know it! So, let's get a little strange in order to be happy, free, and full of love. (You may even want to make a practice of reading your Bill of Rights once per day for the next few weeks.)

Then, throughout your day, notice how this changes your outlook and actions. Are you able to do something you normally wouldn't? Are you able to let something go and release guilt quickly and easily, when in the past you would have stewed about it for hours? Give yourself full permission to live from these rights. Embody them as much as you can today. Be brave.

No matter what, you are safe, you are worthy, and you are loved. It's OK to be you.

Day 5 – Strengthen Your Reality

Remember this exercise from page 176 where you wrote out the answer to some questions to strengthen your reality? If not, do it now! If so, read what you wrote out loud. Again, do so in the car, or in your room if you need the privacy.

Don't read it as if you're reading an operations manual. Read it as if you were sharing the most valuable thing in the world with your best friend, or spouse, or kids, and you knew it would change their lives if they heard it.

Here are the questions:

What do you love?
(What do you like, appreciate, and enjoy?)

What do you hate?
(*What do you dislike, what annoys you, bothers you, irritates you, or pisses you off?*)

What do you believe?
(*What do you believe in? Start each sentence with "I believe..."*)

What is great about you?
(*What are your strengths, positive qualities, quirks and endearing traits? What makes you, you?*)

What's your purpose?
(*Why are you here? What is the point? What are you going to do?*)

Let those words settle in, and live from that place today. Pay attention to your perception today, how you see things, and what you think and feel. Notice any tendency to dismiss it, or privilege others' perspectives more than your own. Own your reality today. Let it feel good.

Day 6 – I Am the Source

What if for all these years, you had it all wrong? What if the approval you were trying to get from others wasn't held by them at all? What if, unbeknownst to you, others were actually looking to you for *your* approval?

Does this sound far-fetched? Maybe not as you've grown during this challenge and from reading this book. Actually, it's a surprising truth that you only start to see when you open your eyes to it.

I'll never forget when I first discovered this could be a possibility — that others could want *my* approval. I was having a conversation with a sweet, intelligent, and beautiful woman in a supermarket of all places. I had exercised my boldness and had simply approached her to start a conversation. Within several minutes we were engaged in a fun and free-flowing conversation that extended into topics way outside the bounds of supermarket foods.

All of a sudden, I heard a slight quiver in her voice as she spoke. In an instant, I knew what was happening. She was nervous! I was completely blown away. For over a decade I thought I was the one who should get nervous because I was the one who needed the other person's approval. Now, I saw that she was nervous because she liked me and she wanted me to like her. The whole thing threw me for a loop and took me a few days to take in.

The question I have for you is, what if *you* were the source of approval?

For the rest of today, operate as if that were true. Imagine that each person you speak with, no matter how beautiful, powerful, successful, or intimidating, wants *your* approval. How would you act? How would you speak? How would you look at them?

Let this guide your behavior today, and perhaps every day for the rest of your life.

Day 7 – Own Your Shadow

You are not perfect. Or saintly. Nor do you need to be. Remember the discussion about your shadow in Chapter 8? There's actually many different parts inside of you. Our homeboy Freud just happened to name three of them: Id, Ego, and Superego.

The Id is about impulse, immediate desire, and is primarily self-focused. I want what I want, and I want it now. Sex, sweet foods, and pleasure. All fun, no work, no responsibility. The Superego is your internal school principal — trying to uphold order with a-hundred-and-one rules and commands for how you "should" be. And then there's Ego in the middle, trying to take these two wildly differing inputs and choose effective behaviors in the world.

So today, here's what you're going to do. Pay attention to your Id. That's it. Notice your impulses, your desires, and your reactions. Let yourself be more aware and curious about this part of you.

One moment you might notice you don't want to do some difficult task or chore. Maybe you feel a desire to forget all that and just go have fun. Later in the day, you might notice an overpowering rage when someone talks over you in a meeting. You feel a desire to smash them in the face. In the evening, you might notice a desire to do less around the house so your spouse has to pick up the slack and put the kids to bed.

What if you didn't suppress any of these thoughts or feelings? What if you didn't judge yourself for having them, or make yourself wrong?

Of course, you probably wouldn't want to leap across the table and attack Henry during the meeting, and maybe you would override your desire to shirk responsibility in the household. Paying attention to your Id doesn't mean doing whatever it says to do.

Instead, you can just be curious about this part of yourself. You can be amused at how wacky and outrageous some of those urges are. I remember I was doing this experiment many years ago when I worked at a psychological counseling clinic in a major university. We used to have to sit through these extremely slow, dry, boring meetings that would drag on way beyond any reasonable timeframe. They always seemed so unproductive, and often involved lots of venting and complaining with no real solutions or direct leadership.

On one particular meeting, I just started paying attention to my Id and what it wanted to do in there. And guess what? I had this image of me jumping up on the big board room table, unzipping my fly, and peeing right there, all over everyone's paper's and coffee cups. It was so utterly absurd, I had to smile. And then I carried the fantasy out in my mind. What would they do? How would Dana react? Would they scramble to get their scones out of the way, or would they stare in utter shock and disbelief? Needless the say, with my mind focused on such absurdities the meeting passed by very quickly and I was soon free to carry on with my day.

Pay attention to your shadow today. Be amused. Love her up.

You Rock!

Ok, that brings us to the end of Week 1. You are amazing.

Now that you're completing your foundation, it's time to get in the Forge phase. Here you will start diving in and facing more discomfort by taking specific action in the world. Remember that there can be discomfort after taking bold action. You may feel embarrassed, worried about what others think, or insecure. Your mind might make up dramatic stories about how everyone in the world noticed, and thinks you suck, and that terrible things will happen if you don't stop this challenge right now. That's just your safety police getting stirred up.

Remember to use the tools you learned earlier in this book, including the Peace Process, Energy Bubble, and Pattern Interrupts, among others. And above all else, stick with the plan. It's a good plan. If you really want to accelerate your progress, I recommend listening to the Peace Process guided audio once per day for the next seven days. It will greatly enhance your capacity to tolerate discomfort, thereby freeing you to do more of what you really want.

Week 2: Forge

Day 8 – Ice Showers

Remember those from Chapter 11? That wasn't an intellectual exercise. Cold showers can change your life. I'm serious. Doing them regularly strengthens your commitment, builds discipline and willpower, and can even reduce your body fat percentage.

Today when you get into the shower, take a minute to let yourself warm up, and then turn the water to as cold. Stay in the water for one minute. Be sure to lift your arms, get your chest and stomach, and let the water run over your head. You can count sixty seconds, or use a water-resistant watch. Once sixty seconds has passed, go back to warm for a minute or so, and then do one more sixty second blast of cold. Then enjoy your shower as usual, being sure to end with twenty to thirty seconds of cold water right at the end.

For maximum results, I suggest doing this in every shower you take, forever. But then again, I'm known for being extreme. At the very least, continue this practice for the remainder of your time in Boldness Training Bootcamp challenge.

Day 9 – Endure Disapproval

Today you are going to get some disapproval. *Ack! That's bad!* Fortunately, it will all be in your head. *Ooh, that's good.*

Find a quiet place to sit where you won't be disturbed for fifteen minutes. Then, think of someone you know and like. Someone who you want to like you. Close your eyes and imagine them disapproving of you for something you did or failed to do. Preferably pick something you actually want to do, not just some random offensive thing.

For example, let's say you get terrified about being late for meetings with your boss. Whenever you're late you have a mini panic attack and spend your commute freaking out about how bad it will be. In that case, imagine being late for a meeting and your boss disapproving of you for it.

Or, let's say you don't want to prepare all the meals in your household. If you were to tell your spouse that you want them to be responsible for half of the meals, you know they would object and get upset, telling you it's unfair because they already do X, Y, and Z. In that case, imagine making your request, and them being upset with you.

Do you have someone and something in mind? Good.

Simply imagine yourself going through with it, and let yourself see in your mind's eye their disapproval. Then, bring your attention to your body, right into the part that's most tense, tight, or constricted. It might be your chest, throat, stomach, or forehead. Maybe your shoulders hunch up and your jaw clenches. Wherever you feel tension, let your attention rest there.

Then breathe, notice, and feel. Stay out of your mind and in your body. You are simply increasing your capacity to tolerate this kind of discomfort. You don't need to make it go away, or solve anything. You are just hanging out for 15 minutes with these sensations. It's just a different kind of ice shower.

Day 10 – The Extended Order

Today involves going to a coffee shop or restaurant where you order at the counter. Make time for this in your schedule today.

When you get there, you are going to expose yourself to more disapproval by taking too long to order. When you get to the front of the line and it's your turn, take a long, slow look at the menu. Look pained by the number of choices. Rap your fingers against the counter. Ask lots of questions.

"Uuuuhhhhhhhmmmm… hmmmmm…" (long pause).

"What's the difference between Ginger Spice and Pumpkin Spice?"

Stay in it way longer than you want to. Yes, it's uncomfortable. Yes, someone might get upset with you. No, you're not hurting anyone. And that's exactly what you're showing yourself by doing this exercise. It might annoy someone, but you can handle it, and no one dies. In fact, that person who's all stressed out because you took an extra two minutes of their life could probably benefit from chilling their Type-A butt out anyway.

Day 11 – Disagreement Lite

Today you are going to pay close attention in your interactions with others and notice one thing: When you disagree. As you listen to someone speaking, ask yourself: *Do I agree with this?* Trust in your perspective and opinion.

When you notice when you disagree, simply take note of it. This is Disagreement Lite, so you don't actually have to say anything. We're just building your awareness about what you actually think, feel, and perceive.

Day 12 – Ask for Something For Free

Today is another fun one. Go somewhere, such as a food cart, sandwich shop, or other establishment and warmly ask for something for free.

"Excuse me, can I get have this bottle of water?"

"Can I get my Supreme Bowl for free?"

Notice your fear about asking before you ask. Notice their response. Notice your internal reactions to their response. Notice how you feel afterwards.

Any discomfort along the way? Good! That means you're growing. It means you are alive.

Day 13 – Ask for What You Want

Find an opportunity today to specifically ask for something you want. Not, "Will you pass the salt, please?"

Pick something that is edgy or uncomfortable and ask for it. Something that the nice version of you would never have asked for. Perhaps it's something that you judge as "too much" or maybe it inconveniences someone to give it to you. Stretch yourself here and lean into the edge of your comfort zone.

If your coworkers are going out to lunch, ask if one of them can bring you takeout from the restaurant when they come back. Better yet, ask if you can join them. Ask your spouse to listen as you share about something you're proud of or excited about. Ask your friend to give you back the item she borrowed.

Think about it for a minute and you'll know what the thing is. If it's a little (or a lot) uncomfortable to ask for, you know you're on the right track.

Day 14 – Share Something, Unsolicited

Today you are going to look for an opportunity to share something, without having been explicitly asked. This can be in any conversation, with colleagues, friends, or family. You're going to break the habit of only sharing when someone asks you to.

Instead of waiting for them to ask, just share something. When you see your colleague, tell them about the improv comedy class you joined. When you see your friend, tell them about the hilarious movie you watched a week ago. When you see your spouse, share something you found interesting from your day, without waiting for them to ask.

Take a page out of the book of Zaim, or your inner three-your-old, and just assume everyone is interested, simply because you're you. And you're awesome.

Day 15 – Disagreement for Reals

You know what's coming here. Today you are going to notice when you disagree with something that someone says, just like you did a few days ago. But today you are going to actually say something. If you'd like, you can review the many different ways to disagree, starting on page 277.

But trying too hard to get it right and make it perfect are often signs of trying to minimize discomfort. Instead, go for it. Let it be a little awkward, or messy. Also, pay close attention to how they react. You might be surprised to see how little they seem to notice.

Then, pay close attention to how your mind reacts over the following few minutes and hours. It could go down all kinds of catastrophe scenarios about death and ruin. Just smile at your safety police and love it up. The more you take bold action, the less power its words hold over you.

Day 16 – Disagreement Max

This one's awesome. Today you are going to disagree again, but this time you are going to casually throw the actual word "disagree" in there. You don't need to make a big deal about it, or bend the other person to your will or anything. You are simply using that word on purpose to show the scared, nice part of you that it's no big deal, and that you can handle anything.

If someone's sharing something and you disagree, you can simply say, "Interesting. I disagree. I think the most important thing to focus on would be blah blah blah."

Be sure to throw the actual word "disagree" in there. It might seem trivial, but it is a powerful liberating force for your subconscious mind.

Week 3: Freedom

Day 17 – I Am the Owner

Today you are going to see yourself as the owner of your life. Remind yourself throughout the day:

I am the owner of my life.
I create what happens to me.
I always have choice.

In addition, let yourself see everyone you meet as the owner of their life as well. Give them that gift and the dignity of seeing them as a powerful creator. They have power, freedom, and choice. Even if they seem stuck or helpless, remind yourself to see them as the owner of their life, the captain of their ship, and the master of their destiny.

Day 18 – Certainty Rant

Sometime today, perhaps on your car ride to work or in the morning, go on a two minute certainty rant. To review this technique, refer to page 252.

Put your heart and soul into it. Rant with gusto, power, and energy. *¡Con fuerte!*

Day 19 – Say No Today

The title says it all here. Find one opportunity to say "no" to someone today. Don't wait for the perfect moment, or figure out how to say it in the best possible way. Just do it. Remind yourself that the ability to say "no" is a muscle that grows stronger with frequent use. And that doing so gives you more freedom, power, and choice in your life, which increases your happiness and ability to freely and joyously love others.

Day 20 – Interrupt Someone

Find an opportunity today to casually interrupt someone. You can try using enthusiasm as you do it, as if something really fascinating just popped into your head. Again, it doesn't matter how you do it, or how smooth you are. Let it be clunky, or awkward, or messy. Just do it. Today.

Day 21 – Approach Authority

Actively move towards someone who you view as an authority. Likely targets can be your supervisor, boss, or boss's boss at work. In the past you may have had a bad habit of avoiding these kinds of people and turning the other way. Not today!

Today you are going to seek them out and initiate a brief conversation. It can be totally casual, as you ride the elevator together. You can knock on their office door, and ask them a quick question or two about an upcoming project. It doesn't matter what you say. The important thing is to approach them.

As you do so, remind yourself that they are just a person. Think of them using their first name, not their title. Remember, they were a kid once, and they have pains and fears and experience self-doubt too. Also remember that despite their status, you are the source of approval.

If you run your own business, are a stay at home parent, or don't work today, pick someone else. Who is an authority for you that you tend to avoid out of nervousness? Your dad? An attractive stranger? Someone who's well-dressed? Attorneys? Whoever it might be, find that person, call them, or reach out to them. Find a way to approach them today.

Day 22 – Say "No" Again

Today you are going to find another opportunity to say "no." Repetition is the mother of skill, and makes saying no easier and easier. This time, take it a little further and offer no with no explanation at all. Simply smile and say, "No, thanks." If the situation warrants an explanation, check your nice-person programming; it might not. That just might be a compulsive need to explain out of a fear of upsetting others. But if, upon further examination, you still would like to offer an explanation, keep it brief and with minimal details.

Day 23 – Have the Conversation You've Been Avoiding

Oh yeah. Now we're getting into the really good stuff! You know that conversation you've been avoiding? The one that makes you a little sweaty to even think about? The one that makes your stomach tense and you feel like you have to either throw up, use the bathroom, or run away? That one.

Maybe it's not that intense for you. Maybe it's just that tense conversation about parenting styles, or money, or sex that you've been wanting to have with your spouse. Maybe it's that conversation with a friend who's been talking too much about his ex, but you've just let him because he seemed so broken up about it. You're tired of hearing about it, and want to have time to talk about other things when you're together.

It could be with your mom or your dad. Your brother or your teenage son. It could be someone you work with, or work for (gulp).

Do you know who it is now? Most likely you do. It might be the one you initially thought of, and then dismissed because it seemed too awkward or uncomfortable.

Fortunately, we both know that discomfort tolerance is the secret super power for an incredible life of happiness, freedom, and fulfilling relationships.

So, let yourself discover who that person is, and what the conversation that you need to have is. Then go have that conversation today.

You got this, rock star.

I love you.

Week 4: Flight

Day 24 – Commit to Take Care Of Yourself

Decide today that you are going to take care of yourself. No, I don't mean relax in bed, binge watch TV shows, and go get a pedicure. I mean make a deep commitment that you are going to start taking care of yourself.

This means you are going to ask yourself what you want and need in different situations and really listen to the response. You honor what you desire, and value it deeply. If a situation is unpleasant or unhealthy, you take care of yourself by speaking up, or getting out of there.

One of my clients was a seventy-eight-year-old woman who had suffered a stroke. She had mostly recovered, but she had to monitor her blood pressure to make sure she wasn't getting stressed in her body, lest she have another stroke.

In spite of this potential consequence, she couldn't stop herself from pushing her limits, demanding that she cook all the meals, do all the dishes, manage all the household tasks, and manage the accounting for the family business. As we discussed these patterns, we came up with the name "Superwoman" for the part of her that demanded she do more, regardless of her health.

Through our work together, I slowly convinced her to change her top priority from getting more done, looking good to others, or keeping up with her sister, to just one focus. In fact, I suggested she write this down and repeat it multiple times per day.

Above all else, my top priority is to take care of myself.

She began to say this each day, and implement it in her life. She began slowing down when she was driving herself hard, and listening to another part of herself, which she called "Common Sense." This part told her to take breaks, to delegate responsibilities she didn't need to personally take care of, and to sometimes just go outside for a walk. This part also encouraged her not to schedule back to back meetings, as they tended to stress her out.

As she began to listen to this part and take care of herself, she changed dozens of things in her life. In that time, her life transformed. Her blood pressure went down, and her multi-decade pattern of frequent panic attacks vanished.

What might happen today, and for the rest of your life, if you were to decide to make taking care of yourself a top priority?

Day 25 – Hold Nothing Back

This morning, ask yourself this question: If I held nothing back today, what would I say? What would I do?

Let yourself reflect for a few minutes on whatever comes to mind. Then proceed with your normal day.

Notice how you show up in different situations. Notice where you might be holding back. Ask yourself in those instances: If I wasn't holding back right now, what would I say? What would I do?

This evening, before you go to sleep, reflect on these moments. Notice where you were bolder, more expressive, more you. How did it feel? Good? Exciting? Free? Was it a little unpredictable or scary?

Also, where did you hold back? What did you not say? What did you not do? How did that feel? Relieving? Predictable? Safe?

Notice whatever you notice, and draw whatever lessons you need from this day's experiment.

Day 26 – Ask for What You Really Want

Today you are going to ask for what you *really* want. Earlier in this program you may have asked someone for something you wanted. Maybe you got it, and maybe you didn't. Maybe it felt edgy or vulnerable to ask, and maybe it was simpler.

Regardless, it's time to ask for something else. This time, pick something that you want even more. Choose someone close to you — a dear friend, a family member, or your partner.

Approach them directly. Be authentic, and be vulnerable. If you are nervous about asking, reveal that as well. Put yourself out there and ask for what you really want, just as you want it.

If any guilt, fear, or other discomfort arises, embrace it. You are becoming a discomfort tolerance master.

Day 27 – 100% Me

This morning you are going to write out this sentence stem and complete it twenty times. Do it as quickly as possible and do not overthink what you write. Do not hesitate or slow down, just keep writing the sentence stem and completing it again and again until you reach twenty.

The sentence stem is:

If I were being 100% me today, I would…

Once you've done this, bring it forward into your day. Be that way as much as you can in as many situations as you can.

Enjoy.

Day 28 – Ehhh!

Today you are going to practicing applying one of my favorite techniques. I don't have a catchy name for it, so we'll just call it "Ehh!" and it goes something like this.

During the course of the day, you are going to do something that used to cause discomfort because you would take responsibility for other people's feelings. Maybe it's asking for something, saying no, putting yourself first, or anything else out of the *Not Nice* playbook.

When you notice that discomfort arising, and that old familiar feeling of guilt, you are simply going to wave your hand through the air, as if you're casually swatting at a fly. As you do this, say out loud, "Ehh! They'll be fine."

Imagine you are swatting away all the doubt, fear, obligation, and need to take care of others. In one simple wave of your hand, you release all of this, seeing them and yourself as creators and powerful adults.

It may take some practice, but once you've done enough of this kind of boldness training and internalized the messages in this book, you will be able to do it more and more. It's an amazing feeling to have something that would have caused you days of agony in the past float by in just several seconds.

Day 29 – "Hell Yes" or "Hell No" Challenge

Today you are going to experiment with only doing something if it is a "Hell yes!" for you. Anything less than a "hell yes" is a "hell no," so don't do it. Decline an invitation, don't complete some paperwork, or tell your coworker you can't get that task done for him today.

You may enjoy doing this, and it may feel liberating. Or, you may feel anxious, worried that your entire world will fall apart at the seams. Regardless, stick with it for the entire day. You're just flexing that discomfort muscle and getting it stronger, which will help you in all your relationships, and in all areas of your life.

If you enjoy it, you just might choose to do it again tomorrow.

Day 30 – See with The Eyes Of Love

Today you are going to practice seeing through all nice person messages, evaluations, expectations, and demands you place on yourself and others. Take twenty or thirty minutes and go to a busy place with lots of people, such as a food court, plaza, or mall. Then, just sit on a bench and look around you at all the people walking by. Find someone to focus on and let your attention settle on them. Breathe, relax in your body, and observe this person as they move through the world.

Can you get a gut sense of what they're like? Do they seem happy or sad? Excited or tired? Who are they with? Are they alone? Do they seem lonely or at peace? Are they with their parents, partner, friends, or kids? Do they seem open and loving, or closed and constricted? Let yourself wonder what their dreams are. Muse about what things they might fear in life. Are they too nice? Do they want others to like them? How have they criticized and judged themselves? What parts of themselves might they have hidden away or thought of as bad and wrong?

Don't answer these questions with your mind through rational analysis. Instead, just feel your breath and focus your attention on your heart. Let yourself feel these answers, sensing the essence of this person. Then, let yourself move on to someone else.

Do this for fifteen to twenty minutes. Afterwards, stand up and walk back to your car, or house, or office. What did you experience? What did you notice?

Is it possible that everyone else is wrapped up in their own fears, dreams, desires, and doubts? Are others terrified of being judged by their family, friends, peers, or even strangers? What was it like to see with the eyes of love?

Week 5+: Forever

As you know by now, this process doesn't end with Day 30. By now you have some solid momentum, and I encourage you to use it. Keep going! Each day, look for opportunities to practice being less nice.

Ask for what you want, say "no," speak up, share freely, disagree, share your perspective or opinion, interrupt, prevent someone from interrupting you, discover what you want, take care of yourself, and give yourself permission to be you.

Just like going to the gym, the longer you go, the stronger you get. The more social power and freedom you generate, which allows you to speak more freely, express yourself more boldly, and rise to higher levels of leadership in all areas of your life.

I want to thank you from the bottom of my heart for joining me on this epic journey, which never really ends. I am your brother on this same path, looking for opportunities each day to be more authentic, expressive, free, and truly loving with others on this planet.

I hope that we get a chance to meet one day, perhaps at one of my live events. I am amazed at the intelligence, heart, courage, and commitment of the people who attend those. I find that I grow just as much as everyone there, and there is a beautiful process of symbiotic healing for us all.

And who knows, perhaps we'll meet in a very different context. I just might happen to be in line at a coffee shop, waiting to place my order, and hear someone in front of me taking way too long to order, loudly saying, "Hmmm... What's the difference between a mint chip latte and a double mocha latte?"

I wish you all the best, my friend, on your path towards greater authenticity, freedom, happiness, and deeply fulfilling relationships.

With love and gratitude,
Aziz.

Oh, there's just one more thing I want to share with you. It's a selection of short stories from my own life of applying the pillars of *Not Nice* in my daily life. Enjoy.

EPILOGUE:

NOT NICE IN ACTION

By now you have a clear plan of exactly what you can do to start building your boldness and authenticity muscles. To further support you on this path, I wanted to share ten short stories of me being Not Nice in action.

In some instances, I am bold, direct, honest, and clear. In other instances, nice guy conditioning pops up and it is only afterwards that I see the automatic niceness that determined my behavior.

As you read these stories, notice your internal reactions. Are you amused, envious, uncomfortable, excited? These responses can give insight into your own level of social power and freedom.

I CAN, BUT I'D RATHER NOT

I wrote much of this book between the hours of 4:00 and 6:00a.m. Between being a dad to two small children, spending time with my wife Candace, working out, and running a business, that was the only time I found I could consistently carve out to make it happen. So I did. Level 5 Motivation, baby – whatever it takes.

On weekday mornings I would get up at 3:00 am, meditate for an hour, write from about 4:20 am to 5:00 am, then go to the gym. On weekends, I could write from 4:20 am to 5:30 or 6:00 am, until the kids woke up. Somewhere in the process, we ended daylight savings time, which meant our clocks rolled back an hour, and for a short period of time, sleeping schedules were wacky and my son Zaim was waking up at 4:30 am

Here is a text exchange between me and Candace on one of those mornings at 4:28 am:

CANDACE: Zaim's body is programmed to wake up at this time it seems.

AZIZ: Dang. Is he ready to get up? I leave for the gym in about 20, but I can be with him until then.

(pause)

AZIZ: (although I'd rather keep writing if he's still dozy)

CANDACE: Think I can get him back to sleep.

AZIZ: Ok. Thanks!

To some people, this might seem so minor, so insignificant that they wouldn't even think twice about it. But for a recovered Nice Person, this is a great sign of progress. My first response is me being authentic (by saying "dang"), then offering to support. In the past, I would have left it just at that. He's up, let me help.

As soon as I sent it, however, I noticed a feeling inside of me saying, "I don't want to stop writing right now. I'm just getting into it, and I have 20 minutes left!"

So, I sent the next text, expressing what I'd prefer. It wasn't a hard line. If he was up and wanting me, I certainly would have gone to get him. But notice the subtle power of the nice programming to eliminate even stating what you really want or don't want. Notice the subtle pull towards powerlessness, where I do what I think is needed, feeling I have no choice, and then deep down start to feel resentful.

Pay attention to those signals. And note how even if you start nice, or pleasing, or accommodating, you can always say more, or change your stance. You can always find a way to speak up for what you want. Always.

HALLOWEEN

Our son Zaim is almost three years old. He is very excited about trick-or-treaters coming to our house. He has an entire conversation planned out with these imaginary kids that goes something like this:

I say, "How old are you?"

They say, "Ten."

I say, "Whaaattt???"

As time passes, no trick-or-treaters arrive. He becomes sad and confused. Where are they? Are they not coming? Apparently not. This is our first Halloween in this house, and apparently our street sucks.

So we grab Zaim, his little baby brother, and the four of us hop into our car to drive to a street nearby that has tons of shops that give out candy to kids. We tell him we're going to find the trick-or-treaters and he can ask them how old they are. This excites and delights him.

It's worth mentioning at this point that Candace and I are pretty solid health nuts and eat a super clean diet with no processed foods or sugars. Candy consumption for kids seems inevitable, but our goal is to postpone Zaim's first highly concentrated chemical sugar-bomb experience until he's a bit older.

So there we are on Alberta Street in Portland, watching as kids and adults in costumes pass every which way. Zaim is enthralled and stares wide-eyed as ghosts, ninjas, a yeti, and Batman walk by. He begins carrying out his mission of asking other kids how old they are until he finds a ten-year-old.

The rain has stopped for the evening and the cool dusk air is rich with the smell of moisture, leaves, and fall. Our son is adorable as he slightly awkwardly approaches kids bombarding them with "how old are you?" as they attempted to walk past. It's a sweet, tender moment and life is good.

And then Iron Man shows up. A little boy in costume walks by us next to his mother. In response to Zaim's standard question, the little boy stops, turns and says he's four. Then his mother, who notices that Zaim has no bucket of candy and her son has a full bucket of candy says, "Honey, let's give him some candy."

Uh oh. We weren't prepared for this moment. "No, that's OK," I reply with a smile. It's fairly obvious that little Iron Man was in agreement with me on this point. His long pause conveyed his thoughts: *Yeah, what that guy said. No to giving out candy.* But his mom took my "no thanks" as some form of politeness and insisted. "Derek, give him a piece of candy. Just one."

In that moment, nice guy programming took over and I stood silently as Iron Man picked out a cherry lollipop to give to Zaim. We thanked them as they walked off. Zaim promptly unwrapped the sweet treat and marveled at the bright red color.

It was 6:20 pm, just 40 minutes before bedtime. The most sub-optimal time to introduce a sugar smash. So we had him smell it, which turned into rubbing it on his lips, which turned into "I want to eat this so bad it hurts." But we didn't let him. And he cried. And I held him as he asked me why he couldn't eat it.

It was humorously, heart wrenchingly tragic. Now, regardless of whether you agree with my stance on candy for almost-three-year-olds, this whole experience could have been avoided.

What stopped me from more firmly refusing the candy? Being too nice. Because in my mind, if I said in a clear and friendly tone, "No thanks, we're OK. We don't eat candy," then this woman would feel judged for letting her kid eat candy. I didn't want her to feel bad, or to judge me for being weird or uppity. So I said nothing.

Forget that. In my fantasy re-do, I simply tell her that we don't want it. If she has feelings about it, that's OK. It's quite likely she might not even think twice about it if we'd refused. I'll never know. But I do know that in the future I will be clearer about saying no, even if it's a little uncomfortable.

I GOTTA GO

I was standing outside at 11 pm in the humid air of Boca Raton, Florida. A man I just met earlier that day was telling me an in-depth story about his marriage, and how he was going to end it when he got home. I was tired, weak in my body, mildly feverish, and not engaged. How did I get here?

I was at a Tony Robbins' seminar called *Date With Destiny*. We were on day 5 of 6 and I had fallen hard with a cold, or flu, or whichever (I never really knew the difference). All I knew is I felt physically awful.

This seminar inspires people to examine their lives and make big decisions about who they want to be and the future they want to create for themselves. It's a powerful experience and helps me grow as a man, a husband and father, and makes me better able to serve my clients.

It also stirs up quite a bit in people, especially those who are living lives they know are not right for them, such as being in the wrong career, wrong relationship, or eating the wrong diet. It agitates you and inspires you to take action to make things better, or make drastic changes, instead of settling. All good stuff.

Except for this conversation with Antonio. We had done some sharing in a small group earlier that day, where I had first heard about his struggles in his relationship. As we were walking out of the seminar room for a quick break at a 11 pm, before we returned for the last segment that would likely go until 2 am, Antonio approached me and said, "So what do you think about my situation? Do you have any advice for me?"

If I were being 100% me, completely free to say and do whatever I wanted, able to fully take care of myself in that situation, I would have said, "Hey Antonio! I appreciate you asking me, man. At the moment I'm actually feeling pretty lousy and my energy is very low. I'm going to take a few minutes just to rest and reflect." Even now as I write, several months later, I feel a sense of retroactive relief. Ahhh. Freedom feels good.

But, that's not what I did. *What? Aren't you the guy writing the book on not being nice?* Ha, I appreciate the irony. But we teach what we need to reinforce most, and I am always learning and growing and pushing my own edge, just like you.

He had seemed somewhat lost when describing his situation earlier that day. I had also noticed a strong, pleasing, approval-seeking energy coming from him when interacting with me and others in the group, especially the women. So when he asked for my input, I decided to try to help him for several minutes, then take a few minutes to rest. Win, win.

What I didn't anticipate, however, was his level of need in that moment. It was less so for input, and more to simply share his experience. He wanted to have someone witness and see his struggle, the pain he was in, how he had been managing it, areas he felt guilty, why he was angry, and all the rest. It was a big deal. He was going to leave a marriage of seven years and they had one small child together. Of course, he's going to have lots of feelings he's going to need to explore, feel, share with others, and work through.

But I wasn't up for that on that particular night. So after about ten minutes of conversation (mostly me listening and giving him attention), I made my clear and decisive escape. "Antonio," I said, interrupting him to create a pause in his speaking, "I admire the courage it takes to do what you're doing. You are a thoughtful man and a good person. I know you'll get through this to the other side... but at the moment I need to take a few minutes to rest and take care of myself. I'll see you back in the room."

Immediately upon saying that, I initiated a good strong hug, and promptly moved away, eliminating the possibility of continuing the conversation. I walked through the warm night air for several minutes, breathing, feeling my body, noticing the wind blowing the palm trees above my head against the jet-black sky. I consciously let go of any energy of his I may have taken on. I also checked to see if there was any guilt about ending the conversation, about not doing whatever I could to help someone who was clearly wanting and hoping for my attention, support, and guidance. To my delight, there was none. I knew it was OK for me to do what I wanted and needed. And I knew if he wanted support there were other people there who would be excited to offer that.

This is yet another example of the subtle and simple power of being less nice and more you. As you read this story, you may think it's no big deal. You may have no problems interrupting, directing, or leaving conversations quickly and easily. Or, if you've found yourself stuck in conversations, giving when you'd rather not, unsure of how to break free, and then feeling impatient and irritable afterwards, this story might be the very thing that gives you permission and sets you free.

THE KEYCHAIN

It was late September and I was in Carmel, California, for the wedding of my best friend from childhood. I was outside with several of the grooms-men, who all happened to be guys I went to high school with. I loved each of them, and had so many fond memories of being together. My social anxiety was at its peak in high school and college, and the only place I felt relaxed and comfortable during those years was with my brother and these friends. They were like family to me and I love all of them.

As we're waiting around for the rehearsal, my friend Eddie approaches me and the groom's brother, Matt.

"Hey!" He says, enthusiastically. "I have something for you."

He reaches into his pocket and pulls out a small rectangular object and hands it to me. I take it in my fingers, unsure of what it is. Upon a closer look, I instantly recognize it. It's a key chain with an image inside. It was a keepsake from a punk show we went to in high school. There on the small, blown out image, underneath the scratched plastic of the key chain, you could see me, Eddie, Chris (the groom), and his brother JC, all wearing white t-shirts and strikingly similar sunglasses, smiling in the bright sun.

"Wow, haha!" I said. "I remember this. The *Warped Tour* in Santa Barbara. We saw *NOFX* there. It was awesome."

I paused for a moment, reminiscing about the sweet memory. Then handed the keychain back to Eddie.

"That's cool, thanks for showing that to me."

"No, it's for you," Eddie said. "You can keep it."

"No thanks," I replied without hesitation. My tone was warm and friendly.

Eddie took it back, paused for a minute, and then turned towards Matt. "You want this?" he asked.

"Sure!" Matt said, seemingly excited to get the nostalgic item.

I was telling this story a few days later to a client, who happened to have a huge fear of saying no to anyone, for any reason.

"Why didn't you just take it?" she asked. "You could always have just gotten rid of it later. That way you wouldn't have offended him."

"I'm not sure I actually offended him," I said. "He didn't seem too perturbed. Besides, my goal is to be authentic and say yes when I want to say yes, and no when I want to say no."

"Yes, but why didn't you want it?" she pressed.

"We had just moved earlier that year and I had a goal of getting rid of fifty percent of our belongings. I feel better owning fewer things and having more open space. I don't really keep drawers of items and keepsakes and such."

"Why didn't you tell him that?" she asked.

"I would have, if he had asked or seemed significantly hurt or upset. But often times saying no can just be a simple exchange of information and no one's feelings are hurt. Hence, no explanation is needed."

YOU TALK TOO MUCH

Yesterday morning I was at the gym, working out with a good friend of mine who's also my personal trainer. He's managing several clients while I'm there, so we get a few short conversations in when he comes to check on me.

This particular morning, I was lit up. I was feeling energized and excited about life. My body felt good, I had recently broken through yet another "injury" in my shoulder (which turned out just to be suppressed emotion). This last breakthrough further strengthened my confidence in my body, and in my ability to work out, get strong, and have the energy I wanted without pain or fear of pain. It was awesome.

I was also reading some fascinating books, learning and growing a ton, and just feeling on my game. As usual, we chatted a few times, he shared something he learned from a podcast, and I shared some recent insights I'd had. What was different about this morning is I talked more. I shared a couple extra stories. In one moment, when we both were about to say something at the same time, I kept going to share what I wanted.

In that very moment, I had the thought: *he didn't like that I kept talking. He wants to talk more and wants me to listen. I'm talking too much.* This is not a new thought, it's something that I've experienced for a long time. When I was younger, I would sometimes leave a friend's house, having had an amazing night of talking, laughing, drinking, and feeling really connected. But then when I got home that night, or the next morning, that thought about talking too much would creep back into my mind. I'd start to feel self-conscious and bad about myself. I would sometimes convince myself that my friends didn't really like me, because they were annoyed by how much I talked that night.

The crazy thing is I didn't even talk that much all the time. Just on days where I felt particularly jazzed up or excited. And yet, the programming to speak less, be quiet, and be nice is strong in me.

On this particular instance with Josh, I noticed the thought and simply dismissed it. No, I thought, *it's OK for me to be excited and talk more sometimes. He seemed very engaged, so he may have liked it. And if he didn't, that's OK. We have lots of time together and sometimes he may be a little annoyed.* How's that for boundaries, huh? Victory!

With this claiming of my value and refusing to turn on myself, I let it go and didn't give it any more thought that day. Then I got a text from Josh later that afternoon.

"Love seeing you all the time my man, and I love seeing you step up and play big. Proud of you, and stoked for all the things you are bringing forth!"

When I read it, I laughed out loud. The message was heartfelt and loving, which felt great. But what made me laugh was seeing how absolutely *dead wrong* that critic in our minds can be. The day I am the most energized, passionate, and talkative is the day my friend says he loves being around me.

This one is so powerful it's worth slowing down to really take in. Is it possible that when your mind tells you that you talk too much, that you're not interesting enough, that others don't like this or that about you, that it's completely, 100% the opposite? Is it possible that the more you freely let yourself out, with your energy, enthusiasm, passion for whatever lights you up, that others love being around you and want more?

PLAY DOCTOR WITH ME

Zaim, my three-year-old son, loves to play doctor with his daddy. The game has a set script that he wants to follow each time:

First, Teddy is the patient. He has been massively wounded by Scodger Digit, the giant pretend purple T-Rex who only hurts stuffed animals (not real animals, obviously, because he's pretend).

Teddy is transported to the doctor by another stuffed animal who has a car. Zaim has to ask the animal how many people he can hold in his car. If it's a lot, he exclaims, "Wow! That's a lot!"

When Teddy arrives to the doctor's office, Zaim says to Dr. T-Rex, "I have something to tell you…" pausing for dramatic effect. Then he exclaims, "Scodger Digit!!"

Upon hearing the name of his nemesis rival, Dr. T-Rex goes into a rage. He hates how Scodger Digit is giving T-Rex a bad reputation everywhere since he's a doctor trying to help people out (see how elaborate this game gets?).

In any case, it goes on from there, with a very specific sequence of healing the patient, poking him, operating on him while he's awake with no anesthesia, and then doing it again with another patient. Or it can just devolve into Teddy and T-Rex fighting each other with the medical tools.

Sounds sweet, doesn't it? It is. It's an adorable little game and a great way to bond with my little boy. And it has happened about 785 times so far.

The problem is not the game. It's that I felt that I had to say "yes" whenever he asked me. This pressure came from my internal desire to be a "good dad." I remember how much I longed for my dad to slow down and pay full attention to me when I was a boy. I remember how much I loved playing games with him, including chess and other strategy games.

I also read a story in a parenting book by Jon Kabat-Zinn, the well-known mindfulness teacher, which encouraged parents to be patient with the repetition that children crave. In his book, *Everyday Blessings*, he shares a story about reading *Jack and the Beanstalk* to his son over and over again. By shifting his focus and becoming even more present he was able to keep repeating the story and enjoy being with his son. It was inspiring and sweet. And for me it wasn't working so well.

Instead of feeling everyday-blessed I was feeling everyday-trapped. Remember the Resentment Formula from the "Be More Selfish" chapter? That's what was happening to me. I didn't want to play doctor, but I would say yes, and then I would feel irritated and unhappy. Then I would force myself to be in the moment and try to enjoy myself. Sometimes I would try to add new elements to change the script, but that was met with fierce resistance. So, I went through the same routine again and again. Miserable.

And then, I had an idea... I could just say "no."

What?! Crazy, I know. But how about that?

Instead of agreeing to play doctor when I didn't want to, I could simply say no. And since I still wanted to play with Zaim, I could simply offer to do something else. That evening, when I walked into the house after work and Zaim ran up to me shouting, "Daddeeeeee! Play doctor with me!" I simply said, "No... Hey, let's play the knock down game instead!"

"Ok!" he said, seemingly unfazed by the rejection of his request. He was into the knock-down game as well.

So simple. It may sound stupid-obvious from the outside. But all throughout the day there are little things we feel like we "have" to do for some reason. We don't want to disappoint, or upset, or hurt someone. We think saying no or asking for something makes us pushy, stubborn, unhelpful, or the old vague favorite: "bad."

Find the places in your life where you can make simple shifts just like this one. Pay attention to the resistance and resentment you feel; it's guiding you towards exactly what would serve you best. Then, you simply have to claim it.

IS THAT A NICE WAY OF SAYING NO?

As I've practiced being less nice and more real, my emails have become more direct and clear. Here is an example of me communicating with a colleague with whom I have an acquaintance-level relationship. I've interviewed her for my podcast and she provided me some assistance with one of my books. We have not spent time together socially, and don't know each other very well.

A few weeks back she sent me this email. I've shortened it to remove any identifying information.

```
Hi Aziz!

How are ya? I hope all is well--the last time we
emailed was about your book. How did it go!? I am
not sure if I told you, but my book is FINALLY done.

Since you just went through it I was wondering
if you had any insights into the best outlets /
tactics for selling books--any words of wisdom?

Anyways, I just figured you would have some
good ideas AND I don't think I had updated you
on everything = )

Cheers,
Captain Awesome
```

(Captain awesome is not how she signed her email. That's my own edit).

She seemed excited and I wanted to help her out. I know a little about book launches and promotions, but I have a friend who is a wizard at it. So I decided to offer a chance for the three of us to pow-wow on how to help her book crush it:

Hey Captain Awesome,

Congrats on completing your book! That must feel awesome

Checking out the book page on Amazon, I see it's 300+ pages. Beast. It looks really good and has a great cover.

As far as selling books, I have a few ideas. And, I happen to know a ninja master who is my Amazon (and other outlet) book selling guru.

His name is Patrick King - do you know him? He writes a ton about social dynamics, relationships, conversations, confidence, etc.

Here's my Brilliant Idea:

The three of us get on a conference call or zoom meeting and talk strategy for your new book. Some of your marketing plan is probably already set because you have a publisher. But I'm guessing there's still a lot on you as far as promotion. I have some ideas, and Patrick will have some (better) ideas.

I already ran it by him and he's into it. If this sounds good to you, let me know and we'll all figure out at time that works in our schedules.
You see? brilliant. That's why they call me Wile E. Coyote: Super Genius.

Best,
Aziz

These last two emails were just set up. This is where it gets really interesting. Here is how she responded to my invitation:

```
Hey Aziz!

Oh my goodness you are far too kind! I do
not want to take up that much of your time --
I was just pinging for any insights since you
had just gone through it. I also feel so bad
asking for free advice from consultants -- I
always then feel beholden to hire them (and I
just hired a book PR person!) As always, you
are so generous, any little tidbits would be
so appreciated, I don't want to make y'all get
on a call!

Cheers,
Captain Awesome
```

When I first read this, I could see that she was declining the invitation, which is fine. But then I started to wonder, does she think there's some obligation in the help I'm offering? Does she want the assistance, but is she being nice and not wanting to be "selfish"?

In the past, I'd probably leave it and just send a friendly email over with a few tips. In the past I would have been nice back. But instead I decided to be real:

```
Hey Captain Awesome,

Hmm, ok. Let me see if I can clarify a little.

I am not a marketing consultant and neither is
Patrick. He's a full-time author and I… well I do
all kinds of things : )
   In any case, my intention is to serve you and
build a relationship. No obligation, no expecta-
tion. I've found that building strong relation-
```

ships with other inspiring people in my field is rewarding and makes life more fun. You are one of those people.

I know Patrick feels similarly. In fact, we have casually discussed creating a Private Facebook group for people who are successfully running businesses in the confidence / communication / personal growth space. A way to learn from each other and continue to reach and serve more people.

So, if you'd like to meet via phone, I think you'd get a lot more info than some tips via email, and it could be fun and exciting.

I'm not sure if your response is not wanting to impose or perhaps a nice way of saying no? If it's the latter, that's ok to. I respect you being able to say no and decide what's right for you.

Let me know either way.

Best,
Aziz

P.S. If you're doing a promo tour for your book and want to do an interview for my podcast, we could promote it on there. We have about 30–35,000 downloads per month now.

Before sending the email, I re-read it to make sure it captured my authentic response. I wanted to clarify that it was a gift offered freely and point out that a phone meeting would provide much more value for her. That paragraph towards the end about her response being a nice way of saying no was something I was genuinely curious about. And it felt edgy for me to ask so directly.

I pressed send. There, I thought. *That's me being authentic and not being so nice. Great job, Aziz. Practicing what you preach.* So far so good, until... the creeping dread started to ooze its way under the door into my psyche. *Geez, that was awfully direct. You sound pissed off. She's going to think that you felt rejected and then got all huffy and pissed off about it. She's not going to want to speak with you after this. You totally ruined that connection. Way too direct.*

I reminded myself that **I want to live in a world where I am more bold than nice.** Where I express my authentic responses and ask real questions, even if it's uncomfortable. And then I moved on with my life.

Several days later I received this email:

```
Thanks Aziz! I am very grateful--I think real-
ly, really honestly it is because I dread phone
conversations. LOL. As a recovering awkward per-
son I LOVE my email [safe]. Anyways, I am about
to leave on a 2 week media tour so I do not want
to clog your inbox. If you think of anything ping
it my way!

Cheers,
Captain Awesome
```

Fair enough. So it was a nice way of saying no. As is almost always the case, my fears about the terrible reactions and the End Times that will come from me being more direct do not happen. Instead, she revealed more and there seemed to be no hard feelings. I sent her a few tips via email and that was that.

Each and every day we have dozens of opportunities to make a bold move and be more direct, more authentic, and a little less nice. Any time it's outside of your comfort zone, you may experience some internal freak-out after doing so, but remember, that's to be expected. It's a sign you are taking risks and being yourself, which only brings about good things in the long run.

490 PART IV: Action

MAN, I'M TOO NICE...

My dad and I finished our meal at a delicious Mexican restaurant called La Bonita in Portland. He was visiting for a few days and we decided to get some lunch together so we could catch up, since having extended conversations around the dinner table with two toddlers is a virtual impossibility. Winter was ending and it was the first warm, dry day in weeks. I had a fantastic time with my dad.

As we were getting up to leave, I brought our dishes over to the self-bussing area (it's a Portland thing). He went to go use the bathroom. Right outside the bathroom door, there was a young woman who was hunched over, fiddling with a key. The door was wide open and she was apparently trying to get the key out of the lock.

"Are you using the bathroom?" my dad asked as he approached her.

"I'm just trying to figure out how to get this key out," she replied.

Just as she said that, she apparently succeeded, as the small key attached to an oversized serving spoon came loose. At the same moment she was doing that, my dad walked into the bathroom and closed the door, assuming she was on her way out.

It all happened very quickly, and I wasn't too focused on the matter. But then I heard someone sitting nearby, who had witnessed the entire exchange, call out to the young woman, "There's another bathroom in the back!"

To which she replied, "Thanks. Man, I'm too nice."

Apparently, she had just struggled with the key and held the door wide open for my dad to use the bathroom. Instead of telling him when he asked, "Yes, I'm about to use this bathroom," she gave a vague response instead. Too nice indeed...

BUT HE'LL BE UPSET!

Remember back in the Say No chapter when I gave you five tips on how to say no? Well, one of those tips was to say no early.

When you know that you don't want to do something, if you stall or delay out of politeness, it just gets worse later on. That's exactly what I did.

A man who works as a coach reached out to me to interview me for his podcast. I get a lot of requests for this and sometimes I say yes, sometimes I say no, depending on my project schedule, and if I am drawn to the person and the work they're doing in the world.

With this particular request, I didn't really want to do it. I couldn't exactly say why, but I didn't fully trust my instincts, so I told my assistant to give him a nice-guy "no." Which was to say, "We're all booked up for the next four months, let's check back then."

Well, sure enough, four months later he emailed again. And I still didn't want to do it, but I already brushed him off once, so I had her send him my calendar link. We went back and forth with timing and rescheduling, and then finally he got something booked for a few weeks out.

Every time I looked at my calendar and saw that interview, I felt a sense of aversion. I didn't know why. I just didn't want to do it.

Meanwhile, I was writing this damn book about saying no, not being nice, and saying no to things that aren't a hell yes for you. *Lousy book, making me not be a hypocrite.* Actually, it was a beautiful blessing, and writing this only strengthens my commitment to take care of myself and not live life as a frightened nice guy.

So, I told my assistant in a morning meeting that I was going to cancel his appointment.

"What?" she exclaimed. "Oh, he's going to hate us."

"Possibly," I said. "But I really don't want to do it. And I have to honor that. There are many other people he can interview. I'll send him an email personally, being honest and vulnerable."

And so I did:

Hi XXXX,

I hope this email finds you well. I know Jenee
has been in touch with you regarding scheduling
an interview.

Part of me growing my business and reaching
more people has been to learn about managing my
time.

I have been realizing this last month that I
actually have a tendency to say yes to too many
things and over-commit myself, leaving less energy and time for clients, projects, taking care
of myself, and family.

As a result, I am scaling way back on the commitments I'm making to do interviews and other
things.

For this reason, I am going to cancel our upcoming interview. My apologies for the long delay. It's taking me some time to learn how to
properly manage my time.

I wish you all the best in your work, and know
you are doing great things to help people.

With love,
Aziz

There, I'd done it. I'd said no when I wanted to. Good for
me. I felt surprisingly relaxed and calm sending that. In the
past, I would have either just done the interview or said no
but felt absolutely freaked out and guilty afterwards. I was
giving myself a pat on the back later that day when I got this
provocative response.

```
Hi Aziz

Thanks for letting me know.

I can relate with scaling back as I too have
been taking on too much lately. Like you I am
giving more time to myself.

Here's the thing though. I am now left with
a big hole for this month's interview series.
Worse, I have told my readers, my list, my fami-
ly, nearly everyone I know I'm interviewing you.
They are going to think one of two things: I'm a
big fat liar or you're a complete asshole. Either
way, it doesn't look good for both of us.

So I'd like to suggest I email you 8-10 questions
and you email me back your responses.  I don't need
the answers until the 28th of this month so you have
plenty of time to fulfill your commitment.

I'll be in touch soon with the questions.

Regards

XXXX
```

That's when the feelings came in. My first response wasn't guilt, it was anger. I was responsible for his interview series? But he was the one who bounced it back and rescheduled it most recently. I made a commitment and he feels entitled that I answer 8-10 email questions? That will take way longer than the interview! Implying that I'm an asshole if I say no? Grrr!

So, I took a step back and just felt my breath. I tuned into my heart and found the fear and guilt underneath the anger.

I should do it. I said I would do it. I should just do it and make it short and get it over with.

But then I felt something deeper. A commitment to live life on my terms. To move towards what enlivens me and away from that which doesn't serve me, even if I can't rationally explain it, even if it makes others upset sometimes.

Once I reconnected to myself, I was less triggered. I was also clear that I would not participate, since I did not owe him anything. This was a free interview I was giving to help him grow his business and audience.

So, I responded with compassion and brevity. I've often found that less explanation is better.

```
Hi XXXX,

I'm flattered that you have shared with so many
people : )

Unfortunately, I will not be able to answer
those questions via email.

I'm sorry you feel concerned about how people
will respond. My sense is that if you tell them
the truth and are vulnerable, they will still
like, love, and appreciate you.

I wish you all the best,
Aziz
```

Maybe he'll dislike that response. Maybe he'll think I'm patronizing or condescending to him. Maybe he'll tell all his friends, family, and fans that I'm a complete asshole. That's OK. I feel at peace, and I feel respect and love for him. I want the best for him. And I am not responsible for how he sees me, and how he manages his feelings.

TOO SOON

A little while back I began working with an amazing tech team that helps people build complex online courses. I was creating my opus of a program, Confidence University, and I wanted it to be the most dynamic, engaging, and effective program it could possibly be.

To make this happen, I sought the guidance of a consultant who specialized in creating these kinds of courses. I purchased his online training program and found it very informative. I told him so, and we decided to work together on Confidence University, with his team managing all the back-end technology.

We had our first few meetings scheduled and I was buzzing with excitement. This program was going to be so powerful and was going to be able to reach so many people. Until then, I often had to turn people away who couldn't fly out to attend one of my live events or be in my ongoing Mastermind program. My other online training programs were not responsive or interactive at all, so it didn't capture the highly effective element of engagement and accountability that made coaching so effective.

But Confidence University was going to have all of that, and be accessible anywhere in the world. It was going to be a key step in me carrying out my mission to eradicate social anxiety and instill confidence all over the world.

Our first meeting went great, and he helped me make some key decisions about how to structure the program. I began laying out the material, eagerly anticipating our next meeting. Then I received this email:

```
Hi Aziz,

I'll be back in New York at the beginning of
the week. I am currently at infusion con and I'm
speaking at Memberuim on Friday.

I do have one favor to ask you. Would you mind
shooting a quick testimonial for me?

Actually let's push the limits lol
Can you shoot two short ones?

One about the course and one about the value
you've gotten from our strategic calls.
That would be amazing and thank you very much

Sincerely,
M
```

My initial reaction was one of surprise. A video testimonial? We had barely started working together. I enjoyed our initial meetings and had benefited from his course, but we had barely gotten started. The main project of Confidence University wasn't even underway, and I had no idea what it would be like to work with this tech team. It was a clear no for me.

But then... Enter the voice of the approval seeker: *What if I say no and he gets upset with me? What if it manifests as him not giving me his knowledge, or secretly sabotaging our project together? What if he's mad at me?*

"Feh!" I said, waving my hand through the air. Enough of that nonsense. I opened up my computer and sent this email:

```
Hey Mike,

I like the bold ask. A bit too soon.

I appreciate the beginning of working together
here, but don't feel ready to offer official feed-
back yet.

I'll finish putting together the course plan,
then we'll get together and figure out the scope
of work and discuss moving forward.

If all goes well, and I love our work together,
I will be more than happy to shoot some testimo-
nials.

Thanks,
Aziz
```

ABOUT THE AUTHOR

Dr. Aziz is a psychologist, author, and coach who is internationally known as the world's leading expert on confidence. Through his coaching, books, videos, and online media, he has helped thousands of people break through shyness, social anxiety, and self-doubt to create richer, happier, more confident lives.

What is most remarkable about Dr. Aziz is his own personal struggle with self-doubt and social anxiety. After reaching a low point in his own life, he made a powerful decision to do whatever it would take to get the confidence he always wanted. This lead to a passionate pursuit of studying confidence from every source, including books, audio programs, seminars, and a doctorate degree in clinical psychology from Stanford and Palo Alto Universities.

Dr. Aziz is the author of the best-selling books, *The Solution To Social Anxiety* and *The Art of Extraordinary Confidence*, as well as over a dozen e-books, including *5 Steps To Unleash Your Inner Confidence*. He is the host of the podcast *Shrink for The Shy Guy* and the *YouTube* show, "The Art of Extraordinary Confidence." Dr. Aziz is most passionate about his direct work with individuals and groups in coaching programs and weekend seminars. To find out more about all of the resources Dr. Aziz offers, go to SocialConfidenceCenter.com.

Dr. Aziz lives in Portland, Oregon with his wife and two boys. To find out more about his personal story and inspiring journey to confidence, visit the "About" section of the website listed above.

ADDITIONAL RESOURCES

BOOKS:

5 Steps to Unleash Your Inner Confidence

This e-book contains powerful and proven techniques used by the world's top psychologists and coaches to help you overcome your fears and self-doubts. Whatever area your lack of confidence is impacting, this e-book can help you. It gives you the basic tools and strategies you need to start mastering your confidence today.

To download your free copy today,

go to http://SocialConfidenceCenter.com

The Solution to Social Anxiety

In this inspiring, breakthrough book, Dr. Aziz guides you on the path out of social anxiety into lasting confidence. You will discover why you feel anxious around others, and the exact steps you need to take to develop social confidence in all areas of your life.

To get your copy today, visit http://SocialAnxietySolution.com

The Art of Extraordinary Confidence

This book playfully and ruthlessly sheds through the stories, excuses, and self-doubt that holds you back, showing you the core reason you aren't taking bold action in life: fear. Dr. Aziz expertly guides you through any fear that is in your path so that you can live with more boldness, power, confidence, and freedom.

To learn more about this book, visit: http://SocialConfidenceCenter.com

CONFIDENCE TRAINING PROGRAMS:

The Confidence Unleashed System

In Dr. Aziz's complete confidence system you will discover the world's most powerful tools for overcoming fear and anxiety, eliminating self-doubt, and taking bold action in the world. Discover how to boldly speak up at work, confidently approach attractive strangers, and be the most powerful and confident version of yourself in dating, business, and your social life.

To learn more,
visit http://ConfidenceUnleashedNow.com

The Confidence Code

In this program, you will discover exactly how to unlock your social skills and conversation mastery. Learn how to feel relaxed talking with anyone, always know what to say next, create engaging and memorable conversations, and join group conversations. The more you master conversations, the more successful you can become.

To learn more, visit http://YourConfidenceCode.com

30 Days to Dating Mastery

This step-by-step program will help you take you from feeling stuck and shy with women to a place of bold confidence and freedom. Through daily Strategy Sessions you will discover how to see yourself as attractive, overcome approach anxiety, confidently ask women out and get dates, and really enjoy dating and connecting with women. Each day you have a specific mission which helps you take action and rapidly build confidence so you can start getting dates and find attract the woman you've always wanted.

To learn more,
visit http://30DaysToDatingMastery.com

COACHING PROGRAMS AND LIVE SEMINARS:

Unstoppable Confidence Mastermind Program

This is an exclusive 1-year program that is limited to a small number of people. It includes weekly group coaching calls with Dr. Aziz, Mastermind retreats, access to Dr. Aziz's Confidence Library, and VIP passes to all his live seminars.

To learn more, visit
http://ConfidenceUnleashedNow.com/mastermind

Supremely Confident Conversation Master Weekend Intensive

In this 3-day event you will master your ability to comfortably and confidently talk with anyone. You will discover how to easily start conversations with anyone in a completely relaxed way, always know what to say next to keep the conversation going, and become more dynamic, charismatic, and engaging. Most importantly, you will learn how to comfortably be your authentic self so you can enjoy connecting with others at work, in dating, relationships, and life.

To learn more, visit http://SocialConfidenceCenter.com/Events

Unlimited Dating & Relationship Confidence

In this 3-day immersion event, join with Dr. Aziz to radically increase your confidence in your love life. Through exercises, coaching, and taking action in the world, you will discover how to let go of any fears that block you from approaching those you find attractive, initiating relationships, and deeply connecting with others. You will also learn how to create fun, exciting, and deeply fulfilling relationships by being your most authentic self.

To learn more, visit http://SocialConfidenceCenter.com/Events

The Ultimate Confidence Breakthrough Weekend Intensive

Join Dr. Aziz in a life-changing 3-day LIVE event where you will discover how to instantly activate feelings of power and confidence so you can handle any situation in your life. You will also learn how to rapidly eliminate fear, social anxiety, and self-doubt so you feel comfortable in your own skin no matter what, and finally stop worrying about what others think of you once and for all. People leave this event feeling more bold, free, and powerful than ever before.

To learn more, visit http://SocialConfidenceCenter.com/Events